C000062879

Borderland
Castles and Peles

BORDERLAND CASTLES and PELES

A concise guide to the Strongholds of the
Anglo-Scottish Border, compiled for the use of
Motorists, Cyclists, Walkers and others interested in
these picturesque survivals of Medieval Times

*Copiously illustrated with
Original Photographs specially taken by the Author,
Wash-Drawings and Plans.*

Complete with Glossary and Bibliography

BY
ROBERT HUGILL

**SANDHILL
PRESS**

First published in 1939 by Ed. J. Burrow & Co. Ltd., 125 Strand, London W.C.2 and Imperial House, Cheltenham.

Reprinted in 1996 by Sandhill Press Ltd., 17 Castle Street, Warkworth, Morpeth, Northumberland, NE65 0UW.

ISBN 0 946098 41 7

All rights reserved. No part of this publication may be reproduced, stored in a retrieval system, or transmitted in any form, or by any means, electronic, photocopying or otherwise, without prior permission of the publishers.

Cover illustration: *Warkworth Castle* :
an original watercolour by Fred Stott.

Printed in Great Britain by Martins the Printers, Berwick upon Tweed.

CONTENTS

ILLUSTRATIONS

(Reproduced from the original edition with additional enlargement of The Barbican, Alnwick Castle.)

LIST OF ILLUSTRATIONS - *continued*

PLANS

MAP I

SCOTLAND (ANCIENT)
before the Union of the Crowns in 1603

★ Kershopefoot on the Border marked
the limit of the West Marches. The
Middle Marches stretched from
Kershopefoot to The Hanging Stone.

MAP II

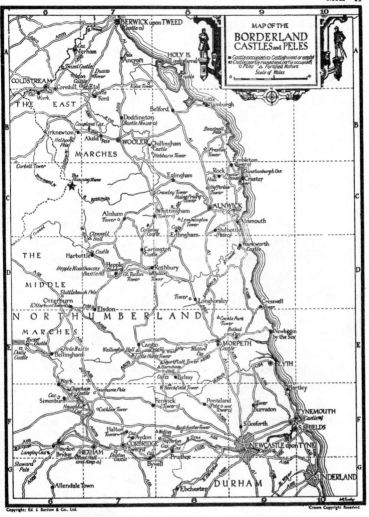

MAP OF THE
**BORDERLAND
CASTLES and PELES**

■ Castle (occupied) ■ Castle (ruined or empty)
▥ Castle (partly ruined and partly occupied)
⊙ Peles △ Fortified Manors

Scale of Miles

Copyright: Ed. J. Burrow & Co., Ltd.
Crown Copyright Reserved.

THE STUART SOVEREIGNS
after the Union of the Crowns in 1603

★ The Hanging Stone on the Border
marked the division between the
Middle and the East Marches.

FOREWORD

By The Right Hon. Viscount Ridley, C.B.E., J.P.

THERE can be no county in England richer in historical architecture than Northumberland, an architecture that tells a tale of the ceaseless, bitter strife of border wars. We find, in travelling through this county, no evidence of the elegant flowering of the sixteenth- and seventeenth-century masons, no setting for a peaceful and domestic life.

Until the accession of James I of England in 1603, few mansions were built, or farmhouses and quiet villages, such as were scattered in the " tame and sneaking South of England," but the fortified manors, the crenellated farmhouses, or pele towers, that denote a hardy and belligerent past.

The number of castles and pele towers now standing in ruins is, to my mind, a hopeful symbol for the future. For who, of those that lived on the Border three hundred years ago, would have believed that a permanent and unthreatened peace could ever hold between the two countries, any more than we in 1939 can look forward with confidence to an era when Europe will find a permanent solution of her interminable frontier problems.

There are so many of these pele towers still standing in Northumberland, that the tourist who ventures into this beautiful and comparatively unknown countryside will find much to interest and enthrall him, besides the beauties of its coast, its river valleys and vast stretches of moorland.

Mr. Hugill has written a most useful guide for sightseers. He gives us the most helpful details as to how and where to find a stronghold, and its history, sufficiently brief to be read on the spot and fascinating in its compilation of historical incident. I feel sure that this book will fill a much-needed want, in supplying the information we require without having to dig into more lengthy and ponderous volumes, and to make known to a wider circle the treasures that abound in our romantic county " stained in the very stone with History."

Ridley

AUTHOR'S PREFACE

THE area covered by this book lies between the Tyne and the Tweed (with its tributary, the Teviot) on the east, and on the west is bounded approximately by the Liddel and Esk Waters down to Carlisle. Thus, it is chiefly the English Borderland which is represented, yet enough of Scottish territory has been included to illustrate the Scottish side of Border warfare, and to cover the activities of the Armstrong clan who played such an important part in Border affairs.

Well over a hundred strongholds, ranging from magnificent piles to ruined bastle-houses, are described, with some attention to the more picturesque incidents in their history and to their outstanding architectural features. The writer has endeavoured, too, to throw some light on the domestic side of life in medieval times. The *military* aspect of Border strongholds which was, of course, paramount has received special attention in the Introduction which follows.

The great majority of castles and peles in the area chosen have been included. In deciding what few to omit, the writer has generally been guided by two considerations—what there is to be seen ; and whether the structure is a relic of former times. Some modern mansions, while standing on the sites of ancient towers, retain no essential part of them ; and other large and picturesque residences called castles cannot claim even this slender connection with Border history. As regards the first consideration just mentioned, it refers both to quality and quantity. Many pele-houses, for instance, are externally and internally unremarkable ; and other places are so fragmentary as to be sites rather than "sights." But exceptions have been made where history or legend appears to justify them.

Then there is the question of accessibility. "Can we see the place?" is, after all, a natural question. The answer will usually be found favourable. Where the house is a private residence, an intrusion may not be justifiable, even when the excuse is a good one, yet the writer has pleasant recollections of meeting with the utmost kindness on such occasions, and he willingly takes this opportunity of expressing his deep appreciation of them.

SETON

"This castle or fortresse we doe thincke to be a strong place and metely for the defence of all that country against Invasion and Incourses in time of war as well as for the chastising of evil disposed people when they offend."
—*Border Report.*

Publishers Note to 1996 edition

This comprehensive guide to over one hundred strongholds of the Anglo-Scottish border was first published in 1939 by Robert Hugill. Born on 21st April 1892 in Gateshead, Robert Hugill was a dedicated and scholarly writer as evidenced by the painstaking detail of this work which became a model for subsequent writings on the subject. An article which appeared in the Evening Chronicle in 1984 gives a tantalisingly brief insight into his life and work:

Veteran Tyneside author Robert Hugill has died, aged 92.

At least 12 of his books were published - and he was still writing right up to the day he became seriously ill.

He never married and lived alone in the house he designed himself in Cochrane Park, Newcastle.

His first book - an on-the-road guide to Northumberland and the Borders came out in 1931.

His other books included the histories of local castles and a travel book on Spain, which won the Newcastle Writers' Club award in 1967.

His last book was a thriller called 'Said the Spider to the Fly', published in 1979.

Born in Gateshead, he took a maths degree at Durham University and then fought in the trenches in the First World War.

And his memories and the notes in his own diary were the basis for his last, unfinished work - 'Return to Picardy'.

He worked on and off as a teacher, but turned to writing full time when he was 46 years old.

His niece, Mrs. Ann Coatsworth, 74, of Castle Close, Prudhoe, said: "He was a marvellous man, a real character.

"He disciplined himself to writing so much every day right up until he fell ill."

Robert Hugill died in Newcastle upon Tyne on 19th April 1984 at the age of 92.

INTRODUCTION

IN the area covered by this book—as already outlined—there are over a hundred castles and peles more or less extant. They vary in type from simple bastle-houses which served the bare necessities of protection to complicated structures of magnificent extent; and illustrate every phase of military and defensive architecture through six hundred years.

A CONJECTURAL SKETCH OF A
MOTTE-AND-BAILEY CASTLE

It has been truly remarked that the story of the past is written not only in history books but in stone.

As the title of the book suggests, the Border fortresses group themselves into two main categories. The two types have a good deal in common, and occasionally they merge, but broadly the distinction holds. Of the two, the castle was the first to make its appearance. Before William of Normandy came to this country Edward the Confessor had enlisted the help of Norman knights to defend Herefordshire against the Welsh, and these knights introduced a type of fortress that was primitive compared with the Norman castles of a century later. A wooden tower of three or four storeys' height was built on an artificial mound or *motte* of earth, the edge of which was palisaded, and its base encircled with a protective ditch known as the "hedgehog" because it was edged with thorns and brambles—the barbed wire entanglements of those early times. Sometimes the defences of such "castles" were extended by means of a second ditch, flanked with ramparts and enclosing an oval space known as the Bailey. The Bayeux Tapestry, traditionally the work of William the Conqueror's Queen

I

(a copy of it appears on the walls of the Black Gate Museum, Newcastle) shows fairly accurately, if naively, the form of these strongholds. The Keep is shown as being gained by a steep gangway across the inner ditch. This was the forerunner of the later drawbridge. Such early Norman fortresses bore a strong resemblance to the already existing Anglo-Saxon *burhs*, which in some cases (as at Bamburgh) they supplanted. The castle, however, was the military headquarters of a feudal lord dominating a district, whereas the *burh* was a village or communal settlement.

Little stone was used in the first castles, and even in the reigns of William the Conqueror and his son, Rufus, very few stone castles were built, a notable exception being the White Tower of the Tower of London. With tower and palisades constructed mainly of wood, fire was a great danger. Besiegers shot arrows tipped with burning tow, or slung bales of " Greek fire " from catapults. " Greek fire," an invention of the Byzantine Greeks, was a highly-inflammable mixture of sulphur, pitch, naphtha, etc., and burned so fiercely that it could only be extinguished with vinegar, wine or sand. Raw hides, too, were used to put fires out ; or roofs were covered with them when danger threatened.

It was partly to minimise such a danger, partly for permanence, and partly for strength that stone came into general use, and the palisade round the top of the *motte* evolved into a high, thick wall enclosing a small court, and protecting wooden buildings against its inner side. The central wooden tower disappeared, and it was not till a good deal later that its usefulness was recognised in the form of the Great Tower or Keep, which was the central feature of many later castles. This Great Tower was also known as the Dungeon or " Donjon," a word that was to come to mean a prison, generally on the ground floor or beneath it, while the Elizabethan word " Keep " took its place to designate the complete tower.

The type just described, with a central enclosed space, is known as the Shell-Keep. It is exemplified at Alnwick Castle, though with considerable modifications, the buildings within it being stone structures forming the chief residential part of the castle, and the wall being guarded by half-round towers. The development of the round tower from the square was due to the experiences of the Crusaders, who had found to their cost in attacking the Byzantine castles of the East that round towers presented no vulnerable angles to mines and rams. Another military improvement brought back from the Crusades was that of the flanking tower projecting from the walls to enfilade them. This, too, is well shown at Alnwick. The transitional stage was the polygonal tower, of which there are many examples in the North.

2

INTRODUCTION

The building of the Great Keep of Norman and Plan-tagenet castles followed generally accepted lines. In constructing the walls, inner and outer shells close to each other were first erected, then the space between was filled with rubble grouted with liquid mortar or hot lime, which bound the whole into one formidable mass. Any mural passages or rooms were

ST. LEONARD'S TOWER, MALLING
built by Gundulph, Bishop of Rochester, *circa* 1070

provided for before filling. The result was a very lasting structure, as modern workmen with modern tools have discovered. A contractor engaged in installing a central-heating system at Naworth told the writer of the great difficulty he had found in making apertures for pipes ; the owner of Clennel Tower, built in later times but in a similar manner, gave up the task of piercing a wall. A few years ago it took six weeks to make a doorway in a wall in the Tower of London.

The massive Norman Keep of Rochester Castle has likewise come down to us owing to the fact that the contractor to whom it was sold by the local authorities in the nineteenth century for demolition found it an uncommercial proposition and abandoned the task !

Where transport was difficult, the stones were small, since they had to be carried by pack-horse. This is the case at Bamburgh, the stone for the Keep having been brought from North Sunderland. The builders did not fail to avail themselves of any convenient supply of worked stone. Carlisle Castle contains stone from the neighbouring Roman station of Stanwix, and from the Cathedral; and the later strongholds of Staward and Thirlwall and Halton are built largely of Roman-worked stones.

To raise the bases of the walls out of reach of mines or rams, the base of the Keep was often a solid block of masonry; and where this was not done the walls were planted on massive boulders on, or barely below, the ground, such as is well seen at Langley, at Proctor Steads (near Dunstanburgh) and at Askerton. This is why underground rooms and " oubliettes " are a rare feature of Norman castles and, indeed, of Border strongholds in general, and why subterranean passages exist more frequently in the popular imagination than in reality.

The lowest room of the Keep was either vaulted on supporting pillars, or roofed with great oak beams. It was generally believed in early times that a single arch of more than twenty feet would collapse with its own weight, but the basement of Carlisle Keep was originally bridged with a single vault, and it is thirty-two feet wide. In the Keep basement stores were kept, the entrance to it usually being from the floor above by a hatchway and a ladder. Only a few narrow loopholes pierced the thick walls of the basement, producing a gloom that nowadays inevitably suggests a prison, but it was not till later times that the basement was put to this use. On the first floor the walls did not need to be so thick and the loopholes could be made wider. The main entrance here was gained in early times by a sloping gangway which could be drawn up, or from the rampart walk. Later Keeps usually had an external flight of stone steps. On the second floor were the Governor's quarters, and the top floor was occupied by the women. The windows in these upper rooms could with safety be made larger, but not too large since they were not glazed. Shutters kept the weather out when necessary. Generally speaking, the Keep was not intended as living quarters, but for defence, which was conducted not so much from the lower storeys as from the roof, whence the foot of the walls, their most vulnerable part, could be guarded. To make this easier, wooden platforms or brattices were built out from the parapets on projecting beams, and through openings in the floors arrows were fired or molten lead, burning pitch and the like dropped on the heads of attackers. Over gateways and doorways and other weak points these galleries were sometimes made permanent in stone, resting on stone corbels with openings between them which went by the name of machicolations.

4

INTRODUCTION

It has been said that the Keep was not intended as living quarters. These were more often supplied by buildings in the Bailey, where there were other premises such as stables, laundries, breweries and workshops, usually of wood, against the curtain wall, together with a Great Hall, which was the private apartment of the Castle Governor in ordinary times. The Oratory or Chapel, an essential part of every Norman castle, was nearly always so arranged that there were no living quarters above it, in order to preserve the sacred nature of the building.

The defences of the walls included a Gate-House, which in its turn was sometimes defended by an outer defensive structure known as the Barbican. Any intruders who forced the Barbican Gate found themselves between two parapeted walls linking it with the Gate-House. Other obstacles were drawbridges, portcullises and massive gates. These last were generally of oak, reinforced with iron, and with two leaves which were tongued and grooved at their edges, and when closed were secured with great oak drop-bars that swung down into holes in the stonework of the jambs. Iron lattice-gates were also common; and at Naworth, Bywell and Corbridge Vicarage Pele there are fine specimens of such grilles, the spaces between the bars being filled with oak planks.

By the construction of strongholds of this description the Norman and Plantagenet kings strengthened their hold on the country. But the weakest link of the feudal system lay in the barons, who took every opportunity of increasing their powers and possessions. Thus, during the struggle between Matilda and Stephen for the throne, at least a thousand " adulterine " castles sprang surreptitiously into existence, and many of their builders proceeded to exercise " gangster " rule over their less powerful neighbours. " Every shire," records the contemporary Anglo-Saxon Chronicle, " is full of castles, and every castle is filled with evil men." When Henry II ascended the throne, one of his first steps was to take control of all such castles. Those that were not destroyed were enlarged or strengthened as royal fortresses, and in the North some new strongholds were built to back up Henry's resumption of the Earldom of Northumberland, a county which had been under Scottish rule. Carlisle, Bamburgh and Newcastle-upon-Tyne were given back by Malcolm of Scotland; a royal castle was built at Harbottle in Coquetdale; Wark-on-Tweed was restored to strength; the great Keep at Newcastle was built; and the king encouraged the erection of Belsay, Bothal, Mitford, Prudhoe and others. Some of these new castles were doomed to be burnt by King John when he wreaked vengeance on the traitorous barons of Northumberland. Morpeth and Alnwick Castles were of earlier date, as was Norham, which was the work of Prince

5

Bishops of Durham to protect the " northern home " of the see from the Scots. Carlisle Castle, begun by William Rufus and strengthened by Henry II some sixty years later, was used by Edward I as a base for those extensive campaigns north of the Border which earned for him the name that appears on his tomb in Westminster Abbey—*Malleus Scotorum*. But the Scots had their turn—the overwhelming victory at Bannockburn in the next reign exposed the English Border counties to their ravages, and the result was renewed activity in castle-building ; Dunstanburgh, with its great Gate-House which also served as Keep, being a stronghold that went up at this time. But the English marches were not made even comparatively safe till the third Edward encouraged his Border knights and squires to crenellate their houses for their own protection. Ford, Etal, Chillingham, Blenkinsopp, Crawley, Widdrington, Langley, Chipchase and Naworth are some for which a licence was granted at this period. Richard II's reign was another disastrous one for the English Borderland, but it was redeemed by the glorious fray of Otterburn. During the Wars of the Roses the Northumbrian castles played their part. Dunstanburgh was taken and retaken five times and left ruinous ; Bamburgh was battered into subjection, Alnwick surrendered for want of provisions ; Bywell and Langley were also taken. The rebellion of Perkin Warbeck against Henry VII drew James IV of Scotland across the Border in support of the Pretender ; and prior to the battle of Flodden, James of the Iron Belt again swept down on North Northumberland. Norham fell before the huge ammunition hurled by Mons Meg, while Etal, Ford and Chillingham were others taken and destroyed. But Flodden reversed the tide of invasion, and it became the turn of the Scottish Borders to be devastated with fire and sword in the two terrible expeditions of 1523 and 1544. The rout of Solway Moss, which broke the heart of James V, was a further blow to the Scots at this period.

The lawless North Tynedale clans did not fail to take advantage of the general disturbance to do a little raiding of their own—they plundered the country to within eight miles of Newcastle and burnt Tarset Castle. The vigilance of Henry Percy, the sixth Earl of Northumberland, as Warden General of the Marches brought them to heel ; but again, during the Pilgrimage of Grace, a rising intended to restore the Catholic religion and the monasteries, they were troublesome, and on one occasion allied themselves with the thieves of Liddesdale to storm Haughton Castle.

In 1541 Sir Robert Bowes and Sir Ralph Ellerker made a survey of Border fortresses for Henry VIII. It reveals many of them to be in great decay, and when, a few years later, the Sieur d'Essé with a large French force entered Northumberland, he met with few obstacles, a state of affairs also due partly to the Northumbrian landowners, many of whom preferred hunting to commanding their garrisons, and stayed away from the musters, or came badly armed. The treaty of 1551 brought peace again, and the following year the Western Debatable Land, for long a haunt of outlaws, was cleared of them and divided by the Scots Dike. But the improvement was only temporary— when Elizabeth came to the throne the state of the English Borders was pitiable. Glendale was repeatedly being raided by the Kers of Cessford : a Scottish force had come to Morpeth and driven the cattle back as from a fair ; country farmers were blackmailed by freebooters ; the gaol at Morpeth was crammed with Redesdale prisoners ; and Scottish raids were so incessant that it was seriously proposed to build a wall along the Border Line after the style of the Roman Wall, with " ensconces " or forts at every mile.

So came 1603 and peace. Thereafter there were only three major occasions when Scottish armies once more marched through the English Borders—during the Civil War, and during the Jacobite Risings of 1715 and 1745.

* * * * *

Turning to the pele-tower, we find that its evolution was on rather different lines from that of the castle, though the origin of the word " pele " (the Celtic *pill*—hill-fort) indicates that both began in a similar way. But eventually the term, " pele," became more significant of the tower than its accompanying defences, such as a surrounding wall, or barmkin, or a moat. This tower had certain characteristics in common with the Norman Keep, the basement being usually vaulted and loopholed, and the first floor gained by an external ladder or stair. In emergencies the basement was used as a stable for horses, the cattle and sheep of the vicinity were driven inside the barmkin, while women and children took refuge in the upper storeys of the tower, and the able-bodied men mustered to repel the attackers. Even though the average pele was practically fire-proof, with a roof of stone slabs pinned with sheepshank bones, flagged floors and stone stairs, the inmates were sometimes driven to surrender by being smoked out. As the old ballad has it :

> " Nae bastles or peles
>   Are safe frae thae deils,
> Gin the collies be oot or the laird's awae—
>   The bit bairnies an' wives
>   Gang i' dreid o' their lives,
> For they scumfish them oot wi' the smoutherin' strae."

The autumn was the season of the year when raids were most dreaded. In former days cattle could not be fed in any great numbers throughout the winter months, and towards the end of November any spare sheep or cattle were killed and salted. Cattle which could not be driven were naturally of no great use to the raiders, so they used to pay their visits not much later than October, and generally on such nights as those of the Harvest and Hunter's Moons, when there was light to show their way back over the difficult tracks of the Border wastes. To counter these visits, " watch and ward " were maintained by the Borderers, who took turns at manning carefully chosen posts at places like fords and well-known " thieves' rodes "; and to ensure that these sentries did their duty, gentlemen of some standing, known as " setters and searchers," were appointed to visit the posts. Thus in Upper Coquetdale, " Fulbere, Cleughfoot, Whytelawleche, and Sandforth above Barrow " were to be watched by the " Inhabitors of Barrow, Harbottill, the Peylles and the Holystone, the Woodhouses and Yerdop, with six Men nightly: Setters and Searchers, Percevall Fenwyke and Ser John Hall." Any watcher not found at his post was liable to a fine of six and eightpence.

It was not only raiders from over the Border who were feared. Redesdale men frequently stocked their larders with Coquetdale beeves; and Coquetdale men were noted for the skill with which they could twist a cow's horn or disguise a horse so that their owners would not recognise them; the Charltons and Robsons of North Tynedale and the Grahams of the Debatable Land on the Western Marches were as often in league with the Scots as not; the Armstrongs of Liddesdale made themselves so notorious on their own side of the Border that their own king made a special campaign to exterminate them; and clans living as close to each other as the Featherstonehaughs and Ridleys of South Tynedale were sometimes at loggerheads. In all these disturbances the pele and its humbler relative, the bastle-house, proved invaluable.

As to what exactly is a pele and what a bastle-house, there is a good deal of confusion, due partly to the wide variety of names by which they are known locally. Tower, castle, pele, pele-tower, pele-house, bastle and bastle-house—one meets with them all. Of these, pele (or pele-tower) and bastle-house seem to the writer to be the best: the first as applied to carefully-planned defensive structures three or four storeys high; the second as descriptive of those strong dwelling-houses unremarkable externally except for the massive construction of their walls and the smallness of their windows. A few in this latter class that have distinctive features are described in these pages, and a few more may be mentioned here. At Falstone a farmhouse near the church has a vaulted basement used as a sitting-room, and so has Little Ryle Farm in the Vale of Whittingham. Other bastle-houses are Ridgend near Falstone,

INTRODUCTION

Peel o' Hill a little to the north of Bewcastle, Kirkwhelpington Vicarage, and one in the main street of Thropton. There are, of course, very many more than these. Formerly nearly every stone house built in the Borders was intended for defence, and the church, too, was useful though its sanctuary was often violated. The tower of Ancroft Church, described in the book, is a fine example of one specifically intended as a refuge, and others that appear to have been used for this purpose will be found at Kirkwhelpington, Stamfordham, Edlingham, Eglingham, Ingram, Long Houghton, Bywell St. Peter's, and Burgh by Sands near Carlisle.

The organisation of Border defences was closely connected with the disposition of castles and peles. Both the English and Scottish Borders were divided into three Marches. On the English side the Eastern Marches included northern Northumberland and ended on the Border Line at the Hanging Stone, a rocky outcrop a little to the south of the present Line, near Auchope Cairn. Berwick, Wark and Norham were the castles that bore the brunt of the defence of this section. The great pile of Alnwick Castle was near the eastern edge of the Middle Marches, which included the rest of Northumberland; while Cumberland and Westmorland formed the Western Marches. The long line of castles and peles in Coquetdale from Harbottle to Warkworth was an important one; and the castles of Carlisle and Naworth commanded strategic points on the west, especially Carlisle, since it stood at the end of the Border Line and was also the residence of the Warden of the Western Marches. The Warden of the Middle Marches usually resided at Alnwick Abbey, or at Harbottle; and the Eastern Warden at Berwick, which was well supplied with artillery in later years.

A Warden's position was no sinecure. He had to keep law and order in his territory, to suggest advisable reforms, to hold all necessary Courts and Sessions, to keep the monthly days of truce for the apprehension of murderers, burners of houses and those " thrice fyled " (i.e. testified against), to punish those who had Scottish servants or had taken Scottish spouses (the punishment for the latter offence was death), to seize the goods and flocks of any Scot found using English pastures—these were only a few of his duties; and in addition he had to find time to supervise the arrangement of watches and beacons, see that castles were kept in good repair, tour his territory from time to time, and even conduct a system of espionage. Out of his salary, which would be worth today from £4,000 to £5,000, he had to pay those of two Deputy Wardens and two Land-Sergeants, and there were many other demands on his purse. The Scottish Wardens were paid on a beggarly scale, sometimes not at all! Generally speaking the office of Warden was unpopular, and it was difficult to get the right sort of man to hold it.

The days of truce referred to above were arranged by mutual agreement between the Wardens on both sides of the Marches, and were held for the general airing of grievances, chiefly connected with stolen cattle, sheep or goods, and for the apprehension of " wanted " men. The truce generally lasted from " sonne to sonne." It was such a day that saw the illegal arrest of Kinmont Willie, whose subsequent rescue from Carlisle Castle raised such a storm on the Border. Certain places were favoured for the meetings—on the Eastern Marches at Foulden Rigg, Norham West Ford, near Wark Castle, Carham, and the Riding Burn near Carham ; on the Middle Marches at Cocklaw, Gammelspath, Stawford and the Reidswire ; on the Western Marches at Kershopefoot (where Kinmont Willie was taken), Rockcliffe and Gretna Church. Those attending such meetings had to come " in peaceable wise, without harness, axe, bill, spear or bow," and with no other weapon but a sword or a knife. The numbers on each side were usually limited to a thousand. A curious oath administered to men who professed to be innocent of cattle-lifting was as follows : " You shall sweare by heaven above you, hell beneath you, by your part of paradice, by all that God maide in six daies and seaven nights, and by God himself yee are whart out sackless [i.e. entirely innocent] of art, part, way, witting, ridd, kenning, having, taking or recetting of any of the goods and cattels named in this bill, so help yow, God, etc." Though called Monthly Truces, these meetings were often neglected by busy Wardens, and sometimes a year or more would elapse without one. The Wardens were supposed to take leave of each other " in all kindlie sort," but the day did not always end so peaceably. The Raid of the Reidswire was a notable example of a truce that flared up ; and another that ended in tragedy ten years later was the meeting on Windygyle, where Lord Francis Russell was slain. Frequently, however, there were officially recognised combats to decide the ownership of disputed cattle. The claimants could hire professional champions to fight their causes. A celebrated champion was Robert Snowdon of Hepple who when only sixteen fought and slew John Grieves, an experienced Scottish champion, in a pitched battle with small swords. A man accused of cattle-stealing could acquit himself of the chaige without combat by driving an animal into the Tweed or Esk where they formed the boundary line. If the animal crossed safely, the man was assumed to be the rightful owner, but if it were drowned before gaining mid-stream he was liable to pay its value to the plaintiff. Another curious old law was that of the Hot-Trod, which permitted the owners of stolen cattle, within six days of the theft, to penetrate the enemy's territory in pursuit of them, without let or hindrance. To signify their mission, one of the pursuers had to carry a smouldering turf on a spear, and the party were expected to advertise their progress with hue and cry, bugle and horn. Bloodhounds, or "sleuth-dogs," were often used in the tracking of cattle-stealers.

It will be gathered that it was rough justice which was dealt out in such fashion. But it served well enough for the rough and ready men concerned. With the Union of the two countries there came, of course, a big change in Border affairs, though for some years raiding still went on between rival clans and by individuals who refused to recognise the new order of things.

The change affected as well the castles and peles of the Border. The increasing use of artillery had already seriously impaired their effectiveness—after the Union they were either neglected and allowed to fall into ruin, or were adapted and extended in accordance with the demands for greater comfort. It is interesting to note that today only two castles—Carlisle and Tynemouth—continue to serve the military purpose for which they were intended. Of the remaining fifty-two, more than half are ruinous or empty. Alnwick and Naworth are far and away the finest of the Border strongholds still occupied, and it is remarkable that the same families should still be holding them as in pre-Union days. Bamburgh remains magnificent despite drastic restoration. Newcastle Keep, also injudiciously repaired, is an early stronghold of notable interest. Warkworth, though ruined, ranks high among Border castles for its marvellous Keep, which is the best specimen of late medieval building in the North Country. Norham is a gloriously romantic ruin, and a testimony to the building powers of the Bishops of Durham; Prudhoe retains the outlines of the perfect Border hold, though sadly decayed. Hermitage is unique, both in its majestic construction and its setting. Dunstanburgh on its spume-sprayed rock is unforgettable. Among smaller strongholds, there are the perfect towers of Langley and Belsay, and the perfectly-preserved manor-house of Aydon; and for sheer picturesqueness, Featherstone, Ferniehirst, Haughton, Chipchase, Scaleby, Askerton, Holy Island, Bothal Bywell, Cartington, Etal, Ford and Chillingham deserve to rank with those already mentioned.

In many cases it was the *size* of a castle that led to its desertion and subsequent decay. The pele-tower, since its tendency was to expand, made a better bid for survival. Though only a very small number exist as detached habitations today, many continue their existence as part of houses built to adjoin them in later times. Among these are Welton, Halton, Whitton, Embleton, Alnham, Elsdon, Proctor Steads,

Lemmington, Shilbottle, Little Harle, Rock, Drawdykes, Laner-cost, Beechfield and Clennel. In only one of these cases—at Welton—has the pele been allowed to fall into decay, but where the pele has remained isolated it has usually become ruinous, though the stout basement is often found more or less intact after the rest of the tower has gone.

Among the changes made to peles to fit them for modern habitation were the facing of interior walls with plaster, the insertion of larger windows, the replacing of flagged floors with boarded ones and wheel-stairs with easier flights, the substitution of slates for tiles fastened with sheepshank bones, and the conversion of the basement stable into a living-room—a process admirably carried out at Elsdon where the vaulted ceiling is groined and decorated in plaster and the walls are adorned with coats of arms.

What of the future of Border castles and peles? Some of them, it is inevitable, will continue their gradual process of decay. Others, like Chillingham, Belsay and Langley, will be deserted as, for various reasons, their occupation becomes undesirable. But thanks to the care of private owners and of the Government, which has arrested the decay of many northern castles, there will continue to exist for generations to come a goodly number of these noble and characteristic examples of Border architecture.

THE PERCY BADGE
(The Crescent and Manacles)

PERCY

§ ALNWICK CASTLE

(Map II, C8.)

The most magnificent of the many strongholds of the Border is, fortunately, accessible to the public, thanks to the Duke of Northumberland whose principal seat it is. During the summer, from the Tuesday after Easter Sunday to about September, the interior of the Keep is shown on Tuesday and Saturday afternoons, parties being conducted at 2.30, 3.15 and 4 p.m. Tickets, obtainable at the porter's lodge in the Gate-House, cost 1/-, and visitors are first shown the baileys, walls and towers, then handed over to the guidance of the housekeeper for the interior tour. For photography, permission is necessary.

The gardens, beyond the Lion or Warder's Tower, are not shown unless by special arrangement; but permits for Hulne Park can readily be obtained free of charge at the Estate Office at the Clock Tower. For the ascent of Brizlee Tower in the park a separate permit is required. The Duke's recent change of residence to Lesbury House a few miles away has not affected these arrangements.

In these days when what is outworn is liable to be neglected or swept away in the march of progress, it is interesting to recall that only by a series of most fortunate accidents—miracles, almost—is Alnwick Castle today so superb a specimen of medieval grandeur, and the finest and most complete of any in the North Country. Incredible as it may seem now, there was a time when the castle was so ruinous that it was nearly abandoned in favour of Warkworth as the seat of the Dukes of Northumberland. Even when the selection fell upon Alnwick, the subsequent restoration was disastrously out of keeping with the character of the ancient fortress, and had it not been for the taste and determination of a later Duke (the fourth—Duke Algernon) the appearance of the castle today would have been sadly incongruous.

NOTE :—Castles and peles accessible to the public are shown as follows:

* Under the care of H.M. Office of Works or of the local authority.

† Other unoccupied strongholds, some ruinous.

§ Permission to inspect the interior necessary, but usually granted.

Another point of particular interest is that Alnwick Castle is not the result of a number of accretions, as many a castle is that has started perhaps as a manor-house and been enlarged and fortified as the exigencies of the times and the extent of the owner's fortune decided. Alnwick Castle occupies now the same area as when it was built, and its walls in many places show the original masonry. Nine hundred years ago, it was a *munitissimum castellum* presenting substantially the same imposing exterior as it does today.

As early as Saxon times there may have been a stronghold here, since the position is a fairly strong one. Indeed, Mallory mentioned Alnwick in his *Morte d'Arthur* as having been perhaps the Joyous Garde of Lancelot, one of the Knights of the Round Table, but that romantic distinction is more likely to belong to Bamburgh not many miles away. The history of Alnwick as a castle begins about the middle of the 12th century, when Eustace-fitz-John, who had married Beatrix de Vesci, the heiress of Alnwick, built himself a stronghold and surrounded it with a wall of stone, following a fashion then coming into vogue. Most Norman fortresses before this time were defended by a wooden, palisaded wall.

The stone wall was often needed in the next two hundred years, when Northumberland was almost as often in Scottish hands as in English, and there was no Border Line between the countries—only a Debatable or No Man's Land whose boundaries were rarely the same for two decades running.

In the year 1309 a new era in the history of the castle began with its purchase by Henry de Percy. The word "purchase," however, hardly fits the odd transaction, which would appear decidedly shady by modern standards. The estate had been left in trust to Bishop Bek, the powerful prince-prelate of Durham (a great builder of castles himself, by the way) but, his code of ethics not being in accord with his priestly office, he deliberately picked a quarrel with the heir, a natural son of William de Vesci, and made the recriminations that followed an excuse to sell the estate and castle, and to pocket the proceeds. It gives one more confidence in human nature to learn that the purchaser not only treated the rightful heir with kindness but became his protector, thereby partially making amends.

Henry de Percy, who thus became Lord of Alnwick, was a Yorkshire baron descended from the heiress of the doughty De Percies who came to England some few years after 1066. The name of the family came from that of a Norman hamlet, the word *percee* meaning a clearing or glade—in other words the site of a settlement in a forest—and indicates a family of very ancient lineage.

ALNWICK CASTLE

Henry de Percy acquired Alnwick Castle at the beginning of the most critical period of its history. In a few years' time Bannockburn was to be fought and lost by Edward II, and as a sequel Northumberland was to be overrun by Scottish warriors filled with a new national pride and burning to avenge the terrible humiliations inflicted on them by Edward II's father, the mighty " Hammer of the Scots." For fifteen years after Bannockburn the humble folk of the county, peasants, shepherds, even the communities of monks and nuns, went in fear of their lives. The only comparatively safe habitations were in the vicinity of some castle or pele, or within the walls of towns like Alnwick, Berwick and Newcastle. Even when the struggle became more evenly balanced it took the best part of a century and crushing defeats like Halidon and Homildon to convince the pertinacious Scots that England could hold her own on the Northern frontier.

Through all this harassing time of wars and rumours of wars Alnwick Castle, garrisoned by three thousand men-at-arms and a body of light horse, proved literally a tower of strength. It was like a great granite cliff, round the base of which the waves surge time after time only to fall back again, broken or baffled.

To meet these attacks, the fortifications of the castle were strengthened. As Warden of the Eastern Marches (like most of his descendants), the first Lord Percy built the great Barbican or entrance gateway, and it is his motto " Esperaunce," which appears on its front. In his time, too, the walls were partially rebuilt, the fine Constable Tower being his work ; and his son added the two lofty towers that guard the entrance to the Inner Courtyard.

Just as this century, the fourteenth, was a notable one in the history of the castle, so it saw the emergence of the most picturesque figure of the Percy Line—the gallant Hotspur whose fame the corroding centuries have barely dimmed. He it was who led the English in that fray at Otterburn, under a summer moon, that inspired more than one ballad and was the subject of Froissart's admiring pen, his account of it reading like a piece of the rarest romantic fiction. Hotspur had a prominent *rôle*, too, at Homildon Hill near Wooler, where the swift struggle ended in an overwhelming defeat of the invaders. In his *Henry IV*, Shakespeare gives a vivid and affectionate picture of Harry Hotspur's impetuous gallantry and puts into Prince Hal's mouth a humorous eulogy of the warrior who kills " some six or seven dozen of Scots at a breakfast, washes his hands and says to his wife : ' Fie upon this quiet life ! I want work.'

" ' O my sweet Harry,' says she, ' how many hast thou kill'd today ? '

15

" ' Give my roan horse a drench,' says he ; and answers, ' Some fourteen,' an hour after, ' a trifle. a trifle.' "

Hotspur, alas ! did not live to inherit the title of Earl, which had been bestowed on his father, the Marshal of England at the coronation of Richard II. He died at Shrewsbury, pierced through the brain by an arrow, and his body, as that of a traitor to his king, was afterwards drawn and quartered. The estates, after the death of Hotspur's father in revolt at Bramham Moor, became forfeited to the crown, but were restored by Henry V, who by this royal clemency secured the devotion of the Percies to the house of Lancaster. In the Wars of the Roses the new Earl and four of his sons sacrificed their lives in fighting for Henry's son.

A later Earl was betrothed to Anne Boleyn, but when Henry VIII became enamoured of that gay lady their engagement was broken off, and Anne as queen went on to her fate, a sad end for that lovely, slender neck of hers.

Another Henry Percy concerned in the Gunpowder Plot was committed to the Tower for fifteen years, and there became friendly with Sir Walter Raleigh.

With the eleventh Earl the male line of the Percies came to an end, and thereafter the vast estates through various marriages of the heiresses of the line passed to a Yorkshire baronet, Sir Hugh Smithson, who became Lieutenant-General of Ireland in 1763 and in 1766 was created Duke of Northumberland and Earl Percy. It will be seen that neither the present duke, nor any earl, of Northumberland has descended from the male line of the De Percy of William I's court.

With this brief history of the Percies, so inseparable from the story of their stronghold, let us turn our attention to the Castle.

The formidable Barbican which now fronts an open space agreeably shaded with lime trees was formerly guarded by a moat and an iron gate. Attackers that broke through these defences were still exposed to assault from the parapeted galleries overhead from which blazing pitch, ropes of burning flax, molten lead, stones or arrows could be showered down upon them ; while ahead was a stout portcullis and another tower !

The Percy Lion ramps fiercely above the gloomy archway ; and on the battlements stone figures of men-at-arms strike aggressive attitudes. These figures have aroused some controversy. The usual story is that their purpose was to give the enemy an exaggerated impression of the strength of the garrison, but it seems that it was the custom in medieval times to add such figures for decorative effect. The truth is probably a compound of the two. One writer protests that the enemy would have to be very simple-minded to be taken in by such " motionless and diminutive soldiers." They are, however,

16

almost life-size; and when living figures were also manning the walls the effect in the heat of the attack would be in favour of the defenders. This was borne out during the restoration of the walls in 1854 when, in the dusk, it was sometimes difficult to distinguish between workmen and figures.

Passing right through to the Bailey we find the door of the porter's lodge, where tickets are obtained, on the left. As likely as not a chaffinch or two will fly out from the doorway at our approach, for the present porter is a great lover of birds and has won their entire confidence.

The open space confronting us constitutes the Outer Bailey. Ahead is the tall Keep, with the still taller Prudhoe Tower rising to a height of ninety-eight feet on the side facing us. To the right of the Keep an archway leads to the Inner Bailey. The walls enclose an area of about five acres.

On the curtain wall to the immediate left of the Gate-House (i.e. the Porter's Lodge) is a small stone sentry-box called the West Garret (from the French, *guérite*, meaning a tower); and in the corner rises the Abbot's Tower, where the Abbot of Alnwick Abbey used to lodge when his presence was needed at the castle. Notice hereabouts the masonry of the lower part of the curtain wall. Its lines are wavy, the stones are rather small, and the joints of the cement are wide. These are signs of the original Norman work of the De Vesci castle. The next tower is a modern one replacing two old structures, removed to open out the view from the Keep. Below it is a terrace which we shall visit later; and in the distance the sweetly flowing Aln bounds the spacious " Pastures."

On the other side of the Gate-House, the Clock Tower is prominent. It is there that applications are made (and readily granted) for permits to Hulne Park, and for the ascent of Brizlee Tower.

Between the Clock Tower and the Gate-House is the Garner or Avener's Tower; and to the left of the Clock Tower is the Auditor's Tower. None of these towers in the Outer Bailey is visited by conducted parties, though the Stables opening from the courtyard adjoining the Clock Tower are generally shown. Here is preserved, with others, the magnificent state-coach of the third Duke. An unusually large laburnum tree behind the Clock Tower, presenting a lovely spectacle when in full bloom, is also sometimes shown.

Passing through the Middle Gate-House archway we come into the Inner Bailey, and immediately on the left see the entrance to the Inner Courtyard of the Keep, through a gloomy arched way. Ahead, the large space is enclosed by an imposing stretch of curtain wall with towers at intervals.

The tower in the far corner is the Record Tower, and from it a sentry walk leads to the left past Hotspur's Chair to the fine old Constable's Tower, recognisable by its gabled roof, and especially interesting because it has stood unaltered these six hundred years. To the left of it the stepped wall descends towards the Postern Tower, from the vaulted basement of which the Sallyport, a narrow gate, communicates with the grounds outside the walls. Through this gate on critical occasions during a siege a messenger could slip out unobserved; or a small force, acting on the principle that the best means of offence is to attack, could sally out to make some sudden disconcerting movement against the enemy.

A little to the right of Hotspur's Chair the wall bears traces of having been extensively rebuilt. The place is known by the grim name of Bloody Gap, the tradition being that a party of Scots who broke through here were slain to a man. This may have happened in 1327 when a Scottish army passed through Alnwick on its way to Newcastle. Sir Walter Scott, describing his stay at the castle as the guest of the third Duke, mentions that " he had the honour to sit in Hotspur's Seat and see the Bloody Gap."

Taking our bearings again from the Record Tower in the corner, to the right of it another sentry walk passes through the East Garret, below which will be seen a large area of Norman masonry, to the Warder's or Lion Tower, a massive structure protecting another entrance into the Bailey from outside the walls.

All this can be seen at a glance, but later an opportunity should be taken to mount to the battlements and, perhaps from Hotspur's Chair, look northward towards Scotland whence in those dread years after Bannockburn the enemy so often came. Standing there, it does not take much effort of imagination to roll back the years.

A descent can be made, too, to the Terrace below the Keep, where some old cannon preserve a semblance of defence. At the end of the terrace, in the wall of a tower, is carved a large representation of a Victoria Cross, commemorative of Henry Hugh Manvers Percy who gained that decoration " for valour " at Inkermann during the Crimean War.

Down the slope from the castle will be seen the Lion Bridge taking the Great North Road across the Aln. On its parapet is the Percy Lion, its tail as stiff as a poker as it glares menacingly towards the Border. Oliver Wendell Holmes, the American essayist, in his delightful *Autocrat of the Breakfast Table*, makes a reference to this poker-like tail as an instance of how trivial things may remain in the memory when more important things are forgotten : " I remember the Percy Lion on the bridge over the little river at Alnwick—the leaden lion—with

NEWCASTLE—BLACK GATE,
WITH KEEP BEYOND

Plate I

WARKWORTH CASTLE FROM THE RIVER

Plate II

ALNWICK CASTLE FROM THE PASTURES

Plate III

THE BARBICAN, ALNWICK CASTLE;
ETAL CASTLE—GATE-HOUSE AND KEEP;
EXTERIOR OF COUPLAND CASTLE

his tail stretched out straight like a pump handle—and why? Because of the story of the village boy who would fain bestride the leaden tail, standing out over the water—which breaking, he dropped into the stream far below, and was taken out an idiot for the rest of his life."

There seem to be one or two slips in this account. The tail, for instance, does not stand out over the water, and probably never has done.

It is time to return to the Keep entrance. Formerly we should have had to pass over a drawbridge spanning a moat, but even without these obstacles it would be difficult and dangerous to force a way through to the Inner Courtyard if the flanking towers bristled with spearmen and archers. On the battlements of these two towers are more stone figures, and below them are the shields of various families connected with the Percies—De Vesci, Plantagenet (one of the Percies married the sister of John of Gaunt), Arundel, Umfraville, etc., the central shield bearing the arms of Edward III.

Beyond the first archway fitted with two massive oak doors, a passage on the right leads to a guard-room, beneath the floor of which is a bottle-necked dungeon, the only entrance being an opening in the floor of the guard-room. No window, no light, no fresh air, no chance of escape! It is a grim reminder of days when pity for one's enemy was accounted womanish. Notice the doorway of the guard-room—it has had *double* doors, strongly barred, and in the walls are iron staples for the securing of prisoners. It would seem that the guard-room was occasionally used as a prison, too. Here will be seen some heads from figures on the battlements, and their fine workmanship and rendering of detail will doubtless arouse astonishment. They have, of course, escaped a good deal of the weathering that has obliterated the finer lines of the figures still in position.

Just beyond the guard-room is the indispensable castle well, fitted with an elaborate wooden windlass, and surmounted by the figure of St. James, the patron saint of wells, in the act of blessing the waters.

If we turn now and look back, we shall see that the inner face of the archway we have just come through is richly ornamented with a chevron pattern and semi-circular in shape. It is, indeed, part of the old Norman castle; and beneath its old stones have passed some famous personages in history—King John, Henry III, the first four Edwards and, not the least splendid of them, Princess Margaret Tudor, daughter of Henry VII, when on her triumphal progress into Scotland to marry James IV.

It is related by the ancient chronicler that this princess was met by the earl and brought through the park " where sche kyld a buk with her bow. After which sche was conveyde to

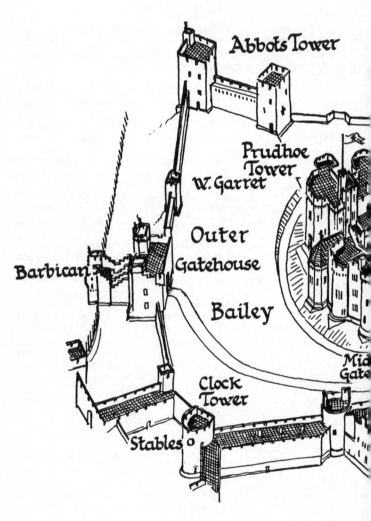

Abbots Tower

Prudhoe
Tower

W. Garret

Outer
Gatehouse

Barbican

Bailey

Mid
Gate

Clock
Tower

Stables

AERIAL VIEW

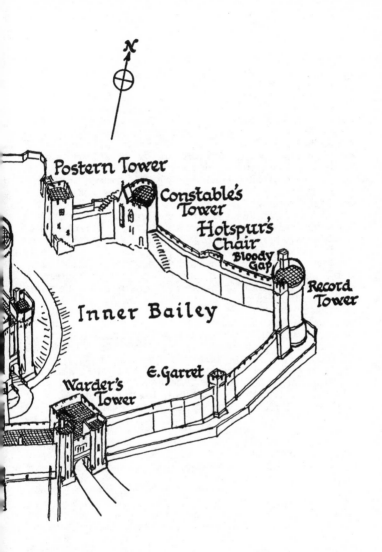

Postern Tower

Constable's Tower

Hotspur's Chair

Bloody Gap

Record Tower

Inner Bailey

E. Garret

Warder's Tower

√ICK CASTLE

21

the said castell, where sche and hyr company was welcomed by the said lorde, the wich maid hyr varey good chere." The "said lorde" was the fifth Earl of Northumberland, perhaps the most magnificent of the Percies, and his attire on this occasion surpassed itself, "being goldsmith's work garnished with pearls and stones." Yet on the evidence of his own Household Book this princely gentleman possessed no sheets for his beds, and had only eight tablecloths. He was wont to dine from mutton-bones and salted fish, and what little furniture he possessed he carried from castle to castle in seventeen carts and a waggon. His mode of living, however, was probably little different from that of most English noblemen of the sixteenth century.

Crossing the Inner Courtyard we enter the Keep itself beneath a finely groined and arcaded portico. Here the porter hands us over to the guidance of the housekeeper, who shows us the following apartments in the order described. A little time is allowed in each room, but perhaps not enough to leave anything but rather confused impressions without some such account as the following, which can be referred to afterwards to refresh the memory :

In the ENTRANCE HALL the arms hung on the walls were used by the Percy Tenantry Corps, a local body of volunteers in existence about a century ago, and brought into being by the fear of a French invasion. Sir Walter Scott thought the weapons were " in indifferent order," though one odd-looking specimen caught his collector's eye. Old powder-horns line the beams of the ceiling very effectively.

A broad STAIRWAY of Rothbury freestone leads up to the Vestibule. Each stair, twelve feet wide, is a single stone ; and so, too, is the landing, twelve feet square ! It can be imagined that its transport over twelve miles presented not a few problems. The use of stone here and in the Entrance Hall was a deliberate device in the scheme of the restoration of the castle to enhance, by contrast, the richness of the grand staircase and the state apartments.

The intention of the fourth Duke who effected the restoration was to remodel the interior in the style of an Italian palace of the Renaissance period, and to this end he enlisted the services of many of the finest Italian artists and craftsmen of the day. The ceilings, for instance, were carved by the celebrated Signor Bulletti, with a staff of twenty-five English and Scottish craftsmen. Some of the marble work, the chimney-pieces and certain medallions, were executed in Rome, and the friezes were painted by Signor Mantovani, who came specially from Rome for the purpose. The general scheme was under the guidance of Signor Montiroli and the great Italian antiquary and architect, Commendatore Canina. The restoration, begun in 1854, cost nearly a quarter of a million sterling, took ten years to complete, and gave work to three hundred artizans.

The first note of richness is struck in the VESTIBULE, the floor of which is an exquisite mosaic, and the panelled ceiling is of delicately-tinted stucco. Among the pictures are those of the present Duchess and the late Duke, both by De Lazlo. That of the Duke is so strikingly lifelike that the housekeeper is occasionally startled on coming upon it unexpectedly. The portrait of the fourth Duke, Algernon, the creator of most of these splendours, also hangs here and will, of course, be regarded with special interest.

We go on into the LIBRARY, lined with 16,000 volumes. The woodwork here is of oak lined with maple. An interesting object is the Sherborne Missal, a fourteenth-century manuscript book penned by John Whas, a Benedictine monk. It is richly illuminated, and the detail is amazing, as the reading-glass provided will reveal. The book was bought in 1800 for £215! More than once of recent years American collectors have offered many times that sum for it. Exhibited in various cabinets are various Cromwellian relics (his night-cap is one!); a pair of gloves and a work-bag of Queen Elizabeth's, which will interest the ladies; as will a cap made from the hair of Mary Queen of Scots, and a clever needlework picture of Charles I.

The MUSIC SALOON is entered by double doors of walnut carved deeply in intricate floral designs. The shutters of the windows are similar in motif. Each of these shutters took one carver a year to complete. The ceiling is exquisitely decorated with recessed panels, moulded and coloured to harmonise with the wall-covering of richly decorated yellow damask. The fireplace supported by graceful figures is entirely of marble. The pictures include many old masters, among them a fresco by Piombo, said to incorporate some of Michael Angelo's work.

The DRAWING ROOM, which we enter next, offered a problem to the restorers because of its peculiar shape, only one wall being straight; but this obstacle has been triumphantly overcome in the disposition of the ceiling panels. This room remains exactly as restored in 1854. Some Louis XIV buhl cabinets here are perfect pieces of their kind. Among the valuable old pictures are a Giorgione, and a head of Christ (" Ecce Homo ") by Carlo Dolce, a work of haunting beauty and sadness.

Two large inlaid cabinets here have a unique history. During the French Revolution they were looted from the Tuileries, and subsequently acquired by the third Duke who contrived to convey them intact to England. The white hand of Marie Antoinette herself—who knows?—may have opened these exquisitely inlaid doors.

The DINING ROOM contains several of the family portraits, including the great treasure of the castle collection—a portrait of the tenth Earl Percy by Vandyck. Over a fireplace of Sicilian marble, supported by a faun and a bacchante, hang portraits of the first Duke and Duchess. And here, too, is another De Lazlo of the present Duchess which is accounted the most striking portrait of the three in the castle by the artist of this very lovely lady. The ceiling is of natural wood—yellow pine on a background of American cedar.

The walls of the narrow CORRIDOR that leads us back to the Vestibule are hung with paintings, among them three by Canaletto whose work is remarkable for its striking effects of shadow without loss of detail ; and others by Wilkie, Richardson, Landseer, Carmichael, etc. Some letters patent granted to various Dukes display huge royal seals.

The CHAPEL is surveyed from the balcony at the back of it ; whence the groined roof, the mosaic work of the walls designed by Montiroli, and two lovely old Mortlake tapestries, one on each side, are all well seen. Prayers are held every morning at nine o'clock when the family is in residence.

The Duchess's Boudoir is not usually shown ; though a peep can sometimes be contrived.

There is one other attraction that deserves mention— a collection of British, Roman, Anglo-Saxon and Medieval antiquities kept in the Postern Tower. This can be seen on application to the porter.

To complete one's impression of the castle it should be viewed in the distance, as a whole ; and an admirable way of doing this is to go down to the Lion Bridge, then turn along the Pastures beside the river, by a public footpath. From the bridge the part played by the Prudhoe Tower in enhancing the outline of the Keep becomes emphasised—it seems to soar above the rest of the structure with a rare effect of " pride of height." It is this view, with the bridge included, that is the subject of Turner's picture of the castle by moonlight.

From the Pastures the outline is different, yet equally illuminating, for the whole length of the castle is revealed, and we realise its imposing scale as the eye travels from the Record Tower past Hotspur's Chair and the gabled Constable Tower, up to the clustered round towers of the Keep, to fall again towards the square-topped masses of the Abbot's Tower and the dark Barbican. Truly a noble picture !

REPUTED ARMS OF HENRY II
into whose possession the barony of Bowes passed
in the latter half of the 12th century

§ AKELD PELE
(Map II, B7.)

The hamlet of Akeld, two miles west of Wooler and consisting now of a farm and a few cottages, was formerly a more considerable place, as the foundations of many houses show. Since it was also on the very verge of the Cheviots, in those days a waste given over almost entirely to moss-troopers and outlaws, it must have suffered severely from raids, and the worthy inhabitants must often have been glad of the protection afforded by that "lytle fortelett castle-house without a barmekyn" which Sir Robert Bowes included in his list of Border holds for the information of his sovereign, King Harry.

The word "castle-house" conjures up an imposing picture, and it is with a feeling of disappointment that one comes upon the reality, a barn-like building of only two storeys and with a double stairway at one end giving it more the appearance of a bastle-house than a pele. The explanation is that the stronghold has undergone drastic alterations, in order to convert it into a building of use to a farmer.

Enough remains, however, to indicate the original size and strength of the place. The vaulted basement, very strongly built of huge stones, is unusually long—nearly sixty feet—providing ample accommodation for cattle and horses. One reason, doubtless, why Akeld was selected as a unit in a scheme of Border defence planned by Thomas Lord Dacre, Warden of the Marches, in the years after Flodden. Ten men, ready to ride, were to be provided by Akeld, thirty by Newton, twenty by Etal, ten by Ford, ten by Cornhill, ten by Wooler, etc. The owner of Akeld at this time was John Wallace, a member of the family that built Coupland Castle ninety years later.

Akeld Tower stands close to historic ground. The old salters' road past the pele climbs the slopes where, on Holyrood Day, 1402, was fought out to its bitter end the battle of Homildon Hill, that ended in a crushing defeat for the Scots. The contest, which raged beyond the present highway and past the village of Akeld, left so many Scottish dead on the field as to give it the appearance of a hedgehog, the spines of which were arrows in the bodies of the slain.

ALNHAM TOWER
(Map II, C7.)

Alnham lies at the very foot of the Cheviots, and as its name implies is in the valley of the Aln, hereabouts called the Vale of Whittingham. Locally the village is known as " Yeldom." It is easily reached through very pleasant country, either from Alwinton, Whittingham or Rothbury. The tower will be found beside the church. For centuries it has been used as the vicarage, and today, modernised and added to, forms a comfortable and picturesque residence.

The position of Alnham on the edge of the hills, which rise bare and steep behind it, was of course very precarious in former days, and one is not surprised to learn that it was the object of repeated attacks. From these Alnham Castle, a fortlet belonging to the Earl of Northumberland, suffered most, and today it is entirely gone, though the turf-covered foundations of its tower and barmkin are locatable on a green knoll opposite the church. This was the " Turris de Alneham " mentioned in a list of Border fortresses in 1415. The vicarage pele was built later. Among the frequent references in past records to inroads by the Scots is one dated October 22nd, 1532, in which the Earl of Northumberland complains that " the Scottes of Tyvydail [Teviotdale], with the nombre of 300 personages and above, Launce Carr beyng theyre governer, which is a deputye of the Marchyes, hathe not only brunte a towne of myne called Alenam on Thursday, beying ye 10th day of this instant monthe of Octobre, with all the corne, hay, and householde stuf in the said towne, and also a woman." The afterthought is odd, to say the least of it.

The present pele was built at least four hundred years ago, for in the Border Survey of 1541 it is described as " the mansion of the vycaredge." A hundred years later it was described as ruinous and fallen, and, since it was uninhabitable, for some years the living was held by the rector of Ilderton.

Today the old tower forms a picturesque part of the house. Its modern battlements are finished in a similar manner to those of Whitton Tower. Tall trees shut out the cold winds from the north, and the situation is as peaceful and pleasant as one could wish to find anywhere.

† ANCROFT CHURCH TOWER
(Map II, A7.)

In a district so restless and unsafe as the Border was for many centuries, the motto appears to have been, " Any port in a storm " ; and in some cases the port took the form of the church tower. It was not often, however, that a pele was built specially on to the end of the church, but this is what happened at Ancroft, a hamlet five miles due south of Berwick, and five miles, too, from the nearest part of the Border Line.

The church that the monks of Holy Island built about eight hundred years ago for the thriving community (perhaps larger then than now) had only a chancel and a nave. It was not till some two hundred years afterwards that "the lytle fortresse nere unto the church" was built. The only entrance then was from within the church, but now there is a door in the south wall. On this side of the church, too, will be seen a stout buttress, designed to strengthen the wall of the chancel. Above the groined basement of the tower there are three storeys, and access to the leads is by a winding stone stairway. The odd little bell-cote on top contains a bell from John Wesley's Chapel in London.

The tower is a roomy one, and during a certain period in its history was, like the pele in Corbridge churchyard, used as the vicarage. In 1734 the incumbent was called William Beauly. He probably found his flock deficient in numbers, for not very many years previously the dread plague had visited the "cloggers" of Ancroft and left a tragic trail. The last time the writer was in the village he was shown the field of the "broomie-huts," to which the plague-victims were carried by the panic-stricken villagers, and left under rustic shelters of broom. If they made a recovery, well and good; if not, as more usually happened, body and shelter were burnt. A crude method of isolation that was not so heartless as it appears since the sick would, at least, have the inestimable boon of fresh air, the value of which was not recognised till much later in medical practice.

LOUVAIN
(later quartered with Percy)

GILSLAND

ASKERTON CASTLE

(Map I, F3.)

This remote castle, a delightful private residence since its restoration in 1922, stands on high ground to the north of the King Water on that lonely road that skirts the south-western flank of the Cheviots between Gilsland and Bewcastle. It appears to have been built when Triermain Castle, further south, fell into decay and was no longer capable of protecting the barony of Gilsland from the inroads of the Liddesdale Elliots and Armstrongs. From this advanced post news could be sent to Naworth or Carlisle of any invasion that promised to be serious. Affairs of a less urgent nature were dealt with by the Land-Sergeant who was resident here with a small garrison.

The castle was built with a view to easy defence—it forms three sides of a quadrangle, and the fourth side is enclosed by a stout curtain wall (now partly modernised), where the entrance is through a massive gateway. Some of the windows are still protected by iron grilles. The masonry of the walls is massive, especially in the lower courses, which are of huge natural boulders. There are towers at the south-west and south-east angles, and the initials T.D. on one of them are those of the builder, Thomas, second Baron Dacre of Gilsland. The date of the castle is thus fixed to the beginning of the sixteenth century. The well on the edge of the lawn is a very ancient one. For a hundred years its position was lost sight of, then ten years ago it was revealed by the employment, it is said, of a water-divining rod in the hands of Mr. Herbert Stanton. At the north-west angle of the courtyard is part of a large hall with a fine timbered roof. An old-fashioned fireplace in the present dining-room is surmounted by a ten-foot lintel inscribed in raised letters with the name of a later owner—THOMAS CARLETON 1576. The drawing-room, ceiled with great oak beams, was once the private chapel. Here a wheel-stair commences. The turret where it emerges is carved with the names and initials of many visitors, some of them of considerable interest. The view is far-reaching, and one realises how well this Tudor castle is placed for its purpose as an outpost.

BLACKETT

AYDON CASTLE

(Map II, F7.)

Aydon Castle, still a private residence after nearly seven hundred years, lies about two miles to the north-east of Corbridge. It can be gained by road from Aydon; or by footpath from Corbridge, the latter approach giving a fine first impression of this ancient stronghold high up above the Cor Burn, flowing here in a wooded ravine.

In early times the manor was held by the Aydon family, till the heiress, Emma de Aydon, a royal ward, was given in marriage by Edward I to Peter de Vaux (or Vallibus); then soon passed to Robert de Raymes of Bolam, who in 1303 extended and fortified the manor-house here, at the same time as he crenellated his other house at Bolam, now known as Shortflatt Tower. More like a small castle than a manor-house, Aydon is one of the most interesting fortified dwellings in the county. Later owners were the Carnabys (who also owned Halton), the Carrs, the Collinsons and the Blacketts of Matfen.

The defences of Aydon are still wonderfully complete. A strong outer wall, defended by loopholes and turrets, encloses three courtyards, in the inner of which is the main building. The entrance is on the west side by a wide arch leading into the outer courtyard. To the left of this gateway there is a garde-robe on the outside of the wall; and the second of two towers has a strong vaulted basement that may have been used as a lock-up. Beyond an inner battlemented wall furnished with a rampart walk there is a small courtyard, in which a flight of stone steps leads up to the entrance. A fine piece of corbelling supports a parapet protecting the stair landing, and the approach has at one time, as the line on the wall indicates, been covered over. The door, set well back in a pointed arch, has had a stout fall-bar to strengthen it. In the main part of the building is the Great Hall, with two fine windows of the type for which Aydon is noteworthy—lancet windows separated by a decorated shaft and enclosed within a pointed arch, and formerly iron-barred and shuttered. The room overlooks the dene; and a ladder leads up to the roof, from which there are finer views still. Here we have some conception of the feat of the Scottish moss-trooper who is reputed to have saved his life by leaping to a rock on the verge of the chasm. He and his companions, captured in a raid by Sir Robert Clavering, had been condemned to be hurled into the ravine, and he was the only one to escape. Hence the name given to the spot—" Jock's Leap."

There are four of the original fireplaces remaining. One bearing the arms of the Carnabys (two bars and three " roundels " —really the arms of the Haltons) is in a room which appears to have been a kitchen, judging by a stone sink or spout projecting through the wall above the dene. Another fireplace in the east wing has six corbels curiously carved to represent human heads. The chimney of the room below the Great Hall is provided with a conical stone cowl with outlets at the side, very similar to those on the Gate-House of Dunstanburgh Castle. This chimney, with a series of stone spouts draining the battlemented roof and a great buttress supporting the end of the east wing, are features that add to the picturesque appearance of the south front. Interesting, too, are the pivot-holes in the sides of the embrasures of the roof, since they show they have once been fitted with swing-shutters, as at Bothal Gate-House.

In the basement of the west wing, entered by a shouldered doorway from the yard, are the stables, the stone roofs of which are barrel-vaulted. The mangers, too, are of stone, the best insurance against a blaze in the days when " sparks " were often flying, and fire was the dreaded ally of the ruthless Scots.

CARNABY

ARMS OF RICHARD II

§ BAMBURGH CASTLE
(Map II, B8.)

Bamburgh Castle has, without doubt, the most strikingly spectacular situation in the North Country. The high basalt boss of rock that it crowns so triumphantly is washed by the sea ; and from miles around its high square mass arrests the eye.

Bamburgh can be easily reached from the Great North Road from several points between Belford and Alnwick, or can be approached by the coast road. The castle grounds are open to visitors (charge 3d.) every Thursday from 2.30 to 4.30 between Whitsuntide and the end of September. The interior of the Keep is not generally shown since it now consists of a number of suites of rooms which are occupied throughout the summer.

Bamburgh Castle must be one of the oldest in the country. Its history is long and vivid. According to Malory, the Joyous Garde of Sir Lancelot du Lake, one of King Arthur's knights, stood here. That is conjectural, but it is certain that Ida, King of Bernicia, and his son, the terrible "Flamebearer," made Bamburgh their capital. It was known then as Dinguardi. The palisaded structure he built on the rock formed later the nucleus of a redoubtable stronghold against Penda the Heathen and his invading hordes. It is related that he instructed his men to pile the wood of the destroyed village dwellings against the wall of the castle to fire it. From one of the Farne Islands Aidan the missionary saw the smoke rising and cried out, "See Lord, what ill Penda does ! " and as if in answer to his prayer the wind changed direction, driving smoke and flames in the attackers' faces.

It was as the capital of Northumbria that Bamburgh got its present name, after Bebba, the Queen of King Ethelfrid.

The castle as it stands today did not begin to come into being until after the Norman Conquest when, in the reign of Henry I, the Keep was built. That was over eight hundred years ago, when the stronghold had already been in existence six hundred years ! So old is Bamburgh. During the Wars of the Roses the castle was sadly battered and must have remained in this condition for a long period. On the death of Lord Crewe, Bishop of Durham, who owned the castle at the beginning of the eighteenth century, he left a princely sum to be devoted to charities, and in pursuance of the administration of the fund Dr. John Sharpe, Archdeacon of Northumberland, the chief of the trustees, restored the castle at his own expense.

31

A considerable part of the work done under the Bamburgh Trust is " for those in peril on the sea." On stormy occasions a look-out is kept from the castle, the coast is patrolled for eight miles, and a lifeboat and life-saving apparatus are maintained ready, while sailors shipwrecked on the coast are provided with food and clothing and shelter, and the means of returning to their homes. A happy contrast with former days when Bamburgh men had a sinister reputation as wreckers, looking to the sea for their " winter harvest."

A further and very complete restoration was carried out by the first Lord Armstrong when he acquired the castle near the end of last century. The result, while it does not meet with the unanimous approval of antiquaries, is a majestic outline that arouses one's admiration from whatever quarter the castle is regarded.

The entrance to the castle is from the south-east, by a modern bridge leading to a gateway guarded by flanking towers. Beyond, a passage is cut through rock to the Inner Bailey. In the eighth century a chronicler, writing of " Bebba," mentioned " an entrance hollowed out of the rock." But this was probably on the north-west side. On the way we pass under the Constable Tower, the base of which is obviously very old.

The walls enclose eight acres. In the south-east corner once stood the chapel of St. Peter. At the north end is a windmill, where barley, oats and peas were formerly ground for the poor of the district. In the Inner Bailey stands the great Keep, its walls from nine to eleven feet thick. The stones are small in size. They were quarried some distance away—at North Sunderland—and were probably made smaller than usual for easy portage. The curiously-shouldered, nail-studded door stands beneath a fine Norman arch. The basement, arched and vaulted, is appropriately gloomy. Here hang " Ida's watch-chains," as they are jocularly called, used in Dr. Sharpe's time to assist in salving vessels which had run aground. The chains were passed under the keel and buoyed at each end. In one room of the basement is the well, sunk through basalt for seventy-five feet, then through sandstone as far again. The well is older than the keep, for it is mentioned by the eighth-century writer already quoted. The chief rooms in the upper storeys are the Court-Room, the Library and the Armoury. Among the portraits in the Court-Room are those of the two Dorothy Forsters—one of them Lord Crewe's beautiful wife, the other of her niece, the heroine of Besant's romantic tale of the Fifteen Rebellion, *Dorothy Forster*. A stairway goes higher in the thickness of the wall to a peculiar passage running round three sides of the keep and also in the wall, and so narrow that alcoves have been provided to allow two persons to pass. It was here that Lord Armstrong's former chauffeur saw the

ghost of the "Pink Lady," the pathetic wraith that haunts
these quarters. Hearing footsteps approach he stepped into
an alcove to make way and, happening to look down, caught a
brief glimpse of buckled shoes and an old-fashioned dress. On
inquiry he found that there was no one but himself in that part
of the keep at the time! The bedroom of the Pink Lady

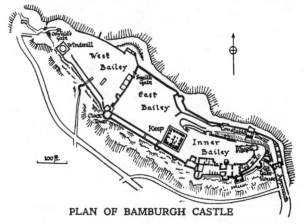

PLAN OF BAMBURGH CASTLE

remains. It is curiously shaped and holds strange shadows,
even in the day-time.

From the summit of the Keep, or from the ramparts
soaring up from their rocky foundations there are magnificent
views all round ; and it is not difficult to let one's imagination
dwell on some of the more stirring events that have made history
about this great rock and its fortress. Danes swarming from
their beaked boats to burn and pillage. . . . William Rufus
building his "malvoisin" tower or Bad Neighbour outside the
walls to subdue the Earl of Northumberland besieged here,
and later the earl's young bride faced with the choice of
surrendering the castle or of seeing her lord's eyes put out....
David I's Scottish warriors goaded by the jeers of the garrison
into breaking through the new walls on the north side....
Edward II after Bannockburn landing from a small boat beneath
the walls. . . . Bamburgh capitulating to the Earl of Warwick
on Christmas Eve, 1462, the garrison having eaten all their
horses. . . . The bombardment two years later by the King's
great guns, "Newcastle" and "London," "Dijon," "Edward"
and "Richard," each shot from which was to cost a head on
the block. . . .

Such scenes in the moving film of Bamburgh's story are
not the least part of its fascination.

HUTTON

§ BEADNELL PELE
(Map II, B8–9.)

Beadnell, locally known as " Beadlen," is a fair-sized fishing village on the Northumbrian coast a little to the south of Seahouses. In the centre of it, where the road turns sharply near the church, is the three-storeyed pele, nowadays an inn called, " The Craster Arms."

A pele of the small type, it is in excellent preservation, and retains some of the characteristic features in spite of a much-altered interior. The basement, for instance, is vaulted, and on the left of the side entrance within is a curved projection denoting the position of the newel stairway that once went up to the next floor, but is now blocked except for a part near the bottom, used for storage. The walls are six and eight feet thick. Part of the wainscoting on the ground floor conceals an ancient fireplace.

The outside of the pele is adorned with a fine coat of arms, that of the Crasters, with a raven as crest and the optimistic motto, " Dum vivo spero "—" While there's life there's hope," all done very effectively with an addition of flowing laurel wreaths. The raven or crow is a pun upon the family name, which was formerly spelt " Crawster." This punning device was a common one in former days, a familiar example being that of the Armstrongs (the Liddesdale clan), which was a bent arm. The Crasters are an old Northumbrian family still living in their ancestral home, Craster Tower, six miles to the south.

Also to be seen on the side of the tower is the lead sign of one of the early insurance companies, dating from the time when the fire brigades were subsidised by them. A former tenant told the writer that more than one collector had made him a tempting offer for this plaque. The three castles show it to have been a Newcastle company, and it bears the number, 7058.

We have several peles in the county that as vicarages lend themselves to spiritual service. Here is one that caters for bodily needs.

TREVELYAN

BELLISTER CASTLE
(Map I, F4.)

The road south-westward from Haltwhistle to Featherstone (it begins by crossing the South Tyne) passes close to Bellister Castle on the summit of its long, low mound. The moat that surrounded it has dried up, its contours almost lost, and the old fortress has also fallen on evil days. It is a mere roofless shell, yet its broken walls neighboured by a modern, castellated mansion form a very attractive group as seen across the little park.

The Blenkinsopps came to Bellister in the sixteenth century when Blenkinsopp Castle fell into decay, but the tower had already been in existence for some time. In the Border Survey of 1541 it is described as being a bastle-house, a term which seems to indicate that, at the most, it was a pele, and that the present name of " castle " is hardly justified. At the same time, it must be admitted that the size of the mound suggests a place of more considerable extent, and it is quite possible that the present house occupies the site of a bailey surrounded by a barmkin.

On the south side of the tower an aged tree spreads its great limbs, one of them running horizontally out in such a way as to suggest a gallows ; and the local tradition is that such was its use in former times, when as many as seven bold moss-troopers were strung up at once. But seven is a favourite number with weavers of such tales !

The legend of Bellister concerns the haunting of the ruin by the fretful spirit of the " Grey Man," who was once hurried out of this world in the following gruesome circumstances. A wandering minstrel called at the tower and was given food and the promise of a night's rest in accordance with the custom of the times. But before long the lord of Bellister began to be suspicious of the stranger, fearing him to be a spy or an assassin sent by a neighbouring enemy ; and showed his apprehensions so menacingly that the visitor deemed it wiser to slip out of the tower instead of retiring to his room. That only confirmed the baron in his suspicions. Calling for his bloodhounds, he set them on the track of the old man. The scent was so strong that they outstripped the party of pursuers and, overtaking the fugitive on the bank of the river, tore him to pieces before they could be called off. For the rest of his uneasy life the baron was kept in a constant state of fear by the visits of the minstrel's ghost, pointing an accusing finger and affirming its innocence; while the peasants told with bated breath how they'd heard in the woods beside the Tyne the ghostly baying of hounds and the anguished shrieks of the Grey Man of Bellister.

FITZ JOHN

MIDDLETON

BELSAY CASTLE
(Map II, E8.)

There are two Belsay Castles, the old and the new, within a bowshot of each other just outside the village of Belsay which is about fifteen miles north-west of Newcastle. Unfortunately neither of the buildings is visible from a public road, and special permission is needed to visit the old tower.

The modern Castle, or rather Hall, is an imposing mansion in pure Greek style, with columns and a Doric entablature, surrounded by beautiful gardens and a well-wooded park. The tower to the north-west of it is the old home of the Middletons, a family still more ancient, for they were settled here in Norman times, and have given their name to at least four places in the county. The great Edward I was once an honoured guest of the Middletons while on his way to Scotland ; but in the next reign, during the lawless years following Bannockburn, Sir Gilbert de Middleton was a rebel against royal authority, and raising a large force of Border raiders he ravaged the county, Norham, Bamburgh and Alnwick being the only castles that held out against him. One of his most daring exploits, which led to his undoing, was the kidnapping of the sacred person of the Bishop-elect of Durham, together with his brother. Middleton held his prisoners to ransom in Morpeth and Mitford Castles, and when the money was forthcoming directed that it should be paid at Mitford. By a ruse, however, the castle was surprised and Middleton taken, the sequels being his execution and the forfeiture of his estate. A later Middleton regained the family possessions by his marriage with the heiress of Sir John Striveling, to whom they had been granted ; and it was probably this Middleton, too, who built the castle, which is today one of the most perfect and imposing of its kind in Northumberland.

Built on almost a square plan and over sixty feet high, Belsay Castle like Chipchase is noteworthy for its great corner bartizans, which overhang the corners on corbels. One of the turrets is square and contains the newel-stair, the darkness of which is made visible by small loopholes. The basement is vaulted in the usual style ; and the principal room is lighted by finely-proportioned windows, one of which is traceried. Both turrets and battlements are embrasured, and on the flat sides the latter are carried at least two feet out from the walls by corbels, between which are machicolations for the delivery of missiles on the heads of attackers. Formerly the walls were adorned, like those of Bothal, with shields carved with coats of arms; and as at Bothal may also have been surmounted by stone figures, two fragments built into a wall in the park looking as if they might have been part of some such mock defenders. A wing added to the tower in 1614 bears that date and the inscription, " Thomas Middleton and Dorothy his wife builded this house " ; and below are the arms of Middleton with those of Striveling, denoting the alliance between the two families.

Some fine old trees stand near this magnificently rugged tower, which has seen six hundred years pass and looks stout enough for as many more.

BOLBECK

PLANTAGENET
(Royal Arms of England from A.D. 1340 to about 1405)

† BERWICK CASTLE
(Map II, A7.)

There is little left of what was in its day one of the most famous castles on the Border. Almost exactly a hundred years ago the last of the ancient structures that had withstood siege and counter-siege, been occupied in turn by Scots and English, was razed to make room for a railway station !

But part of the walls and towers still remain a little above the Royal Border Bridge, and are approachable by the riverside path.

As the lowest bridge town on the Tweed, that northern Rubicon among rivers, it was inevitable that so wealthy a town as Berwick should have its castle to command the river crossing ; but it was by the orders of Henry II, great-grandson of William the Conqueror, that the stronghold was brought to its full magnificence, and for three hundred years after that it continued to be garrisoned—not always by English forces, it goes without saying. Thus, Robert Bruce held the castle for fifteen years, defying the utmost efforts of Edward II to dislodge him. Edward III, however, was a more formidable enemy. He blockaded the town most thoroughly for three months and when the inhabitants in spite of great hardships continued to resist, he tried to force the issue by a device that showed the worst side of his character. Word was conveyed to Sir Alexander Seton, deputy governor of Berwick, that unless the keys of the town were delivered up, his two sons would be hanged on a gallows within sight of the castle walls. The father made the hard choice, notwithstanding the entreaties of his wife, who would have saved her sons at any cost, and next morning

> " The trumpets sounded out oure the Tweed
>   Wi' a blast o' deadly sound ;
> Auld Seton and wyfe gaed up on the wa's,
>   For theyre sonnes to death were bound."

The site of the gallows in Tweedmouth is still known as " Hangie Dyke Neuk."

In 1377 there was a stirring chapter in the history of the castle. One night (they say) it was surprised and taken by eight desperate Borderers, who slew the governor, Sir Robert Boyton and, joined by forty confederates, for eight days held out against 7,000 English archers and 3,000 cavalry. Then the castle was retaken and the audacious band put to the sword.

It was at Berwick Castle where a curious punishment was meted out to the Countess of Buchan for the " crime " of having crowned Robert Bruce at Scone. By the order of Edward I (his favoured candidate for the Scottish throne was Balliol), she was exposed in an iron cage on the castle walls, and there for four years was an object of public curiosity and mockery.

After the union of the two countries, the castle was allowed to fall into decay. Some of the stones had already been used for the new town walls, and later the parish church was built out of material from the ruins. The construction of the railway completed the destruction, and of the Great Hall where Edward I presided over a distinguished assembly to choose a Scottish king, and later received the homage of the Scottish nobility—of that historic building not a trace remains. Such is the price of progress.

The ruins near the river comprise the " White Wall " with a flight of steps near it, known locally as the Breakneck Stairs, leading down to the Water Tower, from which formerly a strong chain or boom crossed to the other bank to prevent the passage of hostile craft.

Most of the Castle has gone, but the bastions, mounds and flankers of the Elizabethan Walls into which it was metamorphosed provide a superb promenade circuit of the old town. Meg's Mound commands the river and its three bridges, symbolic of three ages in the history of the ancient town. Brass Mount on the seaward side is an equally good point of vantage. A little to the south of it the walls are pierced by the Cow Port, the most ancient gate in Berwick. Its massive iron-studded doors remain and are worth inspection. The Sally Port whose echoing arch leads out to the Quay not far from the Old Bridge should also be ferretted out by the artist or photographer or, indeed, by anyone who enjoys finding himself transported, for a while at least, to another age than this.

CROMWELL

† BEWCASTLE CASTLE

(Map I, F3.)

The name should really be Bew Castle or Bueth's Castle ; for this remote spot on the very fringe of the western Cheviots and " miles from everywhere " was part of the lands of that Saxon earl, Gilles, Son of Bueth, " who was slain in truce by Robert de Vaux at Feterlana, now Lanercost." His Norman slayer built Lanercost in expiation of the deed ; and this castle, too, may have been his work. " Bueth's Castle," if there was one, must have been an earlier wooden structure on the same site, which is, as at Tynemouth and Newcastle and Crawley, a place the Romans selected for a station, in this case beyond the Wall. The ancient ramparts are very plain, and doubtless were usefully combined with the exterior defences of the later fortress. The Maiden Way, the Roman road from Birdoswald, is now only a green track, but formerly it was the chief route through what the old chronicler called " a mountainous waste." This explains the importance of the castle— it barred one of the chief roads into England from Liddesdale, the lair of the lawless Armstrongs and other notorious raiders. Not that the men on the south side of the Border had much better reputations—Kershope Bridge on the way to Liddesdale is referred to in one old document as " a common passage well known to the thieves of Tynedale, Bewcastle and Gilsland as to the thieves of Liddesdale." In Scot's *Guy Mannering*, it will be remembered, the stout Dandie Dinmont riding his nag Dumple over Bewcastle Waste was attacked by footpads ; and even as late as 1632, if we are to believe the information given in a list of vicars in the church, one incumbent of Bewcastle called William Patrick was a notorious freebooter, and his curate was his right-hand man !

The huge keep, built partly of Roman stones from the station it stands on, is so badly broken down that its architectural details are almost lost ; but there are indications that it was rebuilt in Tudor times, when it was a royal fortress. But thanks to the Scots it was soon in decay again, and just after the peace between the two countries was reported to be in such

41

a condition that there was no room in it " wherein a man maye sytt drye." Nevertheless a garrison of a hundred men was maintained there for some time longer before being withdrawn to Carlisle, and the castle dismantled. During the Civil War the last shattering blows were delivered against the already battered hold, and a spot called " Cannon Holes " on the bank of the stream is pointed out as the site of Cromwell's cannon during the attack.

Bewcastle has figured so much in Border wars that, as Lang writes, " the very word Bewcastle seems to re-echo the trumpets of the Wardens' Raids " ; but today it is as if the gaunt ghost of a castle had reared itself above the peaceful moorland hamlet, and it is hard to imagine there ever were such picturesque and hard-riding ruffians as the Elliots and the Armstrongs, the Fosters, the Grahams and the Musgraves.

FORSTER (OR FOSTER)

BLENKINSOPP

BLENKINSOPP CASTLE

(Map I, F3.)

The road westward from Haltwhistle passes close to Blenkinsopp Castle, which can be reached from a by-road on the left a mile before reaching Greenhead.

There is little left of the old castle of the Blenkans, who chose this knoll above the Tipalt Burn for their manor-house. Restored by the Coulsons (who were succeeded by the Joiceys) the place today is less like a Border hold than a mansion, with its handsome modern doorway and modernised windows, and clematis, virginia-creeper and ivy adorning its walls.

In very early times the place was known as Blenkan's Hope, the word " hope " meaning a valley, but was later corrupted, like the family name. The Blenkinsopps retained their estate after the Norman Conquest, and became known on the Border for their fighting qualities. One of them was Governor of Roxburgh Castle in the fourteenth century. His effigy is to be seen in Haltwhistle Church, and there are other gravestones bearing the Blenkinsopp arms—a band between three cornsheaves. It was this same Thomas de Blenkinsopp who got a licence from his sovereign to fortify his house, and the result was a square tower with a vaulted basement and walls more than seven feet in thickness. A deep ditch on the north and west, a stream on the south, and a steep fall of land on the remaining side completed the defences. We do not hear much of the castle in Border history, but it must have taken a good part in turbulent affairs for it was reported to be very ruinous in Elizabethan times. Like Thirlwall, not far away, Blenkinsopp was built of stones from the Roman Wall, and during its restoration about sixty years ago many carved and Latin-inscribed stones were found. At the same time the beginning of a subterranean passage was unearthed at the north-west corner, and this may be the legendary passage connecting with Thirlwall. A mile and a half, however, is a long way to travel underground ; and few legends of this nature have been substantiated. The builders of such castles rarely thought of going below ground, even for their foundations, which were often planted

43

barely below the surface, and even underground dungeons were the exception.

The restoration has left parts of the old walls, in one of which remain what appear to be original windows, the sills of which are adorned with a twisted moulding, and the garden wall to the left of the entrance has many carved fragments built into it. Fine lawns and gardens complete the charm of this dignified mansion.

Blenkinsopp has its ghost—that of the lovely " White Lady " who from time to time wanders disconsolately about the castle, trying to tell someone of the vault where she hid a chest of treasure belonging to her lord, young Bryan de Blenkinsopp, and by doing so estranged his love for ever.

CONYERS

DARCY

BOTHAL CASTLE
(Map II, E9.)

Striking eastward from the Great North Road at Morpeth
you will, probably not without some difficulty, come upon
Bothal Castle two and a half miles further down the valley,
where the Wansbeck flows in a deep and wooded hollow The
name (*bottel*—house or village) indicates that this sheltered
spot was a settlement in Saxon times, when the knoll on which
the castle stands was in all likelihood fenced in to make some
sort of stronghold. It was not till the fourteenth century
that the castle was built, or rather, the manor-house of the
Bertrams was turned into a fortress by royal licence.

The builder, Sir Robert Bertram, was one of Edward III's
staunchest knights—at the battle of Neville's Cross, he was
one of the twelve knights who were warmly commended by
the king. It was not long before the castle passed into Ogle
hands by the marriage of an heiress. A son of the marriage
who took his mother's name of Bertram had to fight for his
inheritance against his own brother who, thinking that the
castle should have passed to him, attacked the place with two-
hundred archers and men-at-arms. After four days, Bertram
surrendered, but sought official aid ; with the result in due
course that a Sheriff's proclamation was read out at the castle
gates to the effect that " Sir Robert Ogle and all the other
people abiding therein should be put out without delay upon
pain of forfeiture of life and members."

The castle is the scene of Robert White's delightful ballad
of *Lady Jean*. The daughter of the house, she is expected
to marry Lord Dacre, whom she dislikes ; but her true love,
Umfreville of Otterburne, arrives just in time. A bugle note,
" not loud but clear," announces his arrival in response to her
urgent message, and she rushes out " amang the apple-trees
an' up the walk " to reach his side and fly with him to Otterburne, leaving Lord Dacre "dowf and blunkit" (whatever that
may mean) when he discovers her absence, while her father
stamps with rage and her mother mourns the breaking off of
a very good match.

The chief remaining part of the castle is the Gate-House,
which has always been its most important feature, the castle

being similar to Dunstanburgh and Bywell in this respect. The figures on the battlements, partly decorative and partly intended to deceive, remind one of Alnwick Castle. Flanking the entrance are two projecting turrets, which do not, oddly enough, match each other in size. The fine traceried window above the archway is of the period, but the upper mullioned windows are of later Elizabethan date. An interesting feature of the architecture is the number of shields on the battlements and the walls just below bearing the arms of the Black Prince, Edward III, Percy, Bertram, Darcy, Conyers, Felton, etc. Those of Edward III on the centre merlon of the three over the archway, showing the leopards of England taking precedence over the lilies of France, are very rare in this form. Still more rare, probably unique, are those, to the left, of the Black Prince, with a border of coins, or " bezants " taken from the arms of Cornwall, of which he was the first Duke.

The entrance was formerly guarded by a portcullis, and its groove remains. There were also two gates, at the inner and outer archways ; while three meurtrieres (now blocked) in the vaulted passage had also to be reckoned with by any attackers. In the ordinary way, these openings could be used for taking in stores, thus avoiding the narrow spiral stair to the first floor.

In 1576 a survey of Bothal Castle mentioned a prison in the Gate-House, but it is not easy to locate, since the likely rooms all have bolts and bars on the inside, facilities, as Bates remarks, for keeping their gaolers out with which prisoners were not usually provided !

The Great Chamber of the tower is on the first floor. It has some fine windows, one of them brought from Cockle Park Tower some ninety years ago when the tower was converted into a residence for the Duke of Portland's agent. The two original windows (one above the archway as described) stand in vaulted recesses and have stone seats. What with the portcullis coming up before one of the windows, and the aforementioned meurtrieres in the flagged floor, this room cannot originally have been very comfortable, and was probably not intended for residence. The wheel-stair between the first and second floors shows mason-marks similar to those on the Barbican of Prudhoe Castle, indicating that the same workmen were engaged on each. The battlements exhibit an interesting feature seldom seen. At the sides of the merlons are pivotholes for swing-shutters to guard the crenelles, allowing an archer to shoot then let the shutter fall back into place before the enemy could return fire.

The Bailey, stretching as far as the peaceful Wansbeck, shows few traces of the Great Chamber, the parlour, the seven bedrooms, the gallery, the buttery, the pantry, the larder, the kitchen, the bakehouse, the stable, the nursery, the chapel or the " pastrie " which once stood in it against the curtain walls. But the " gardinge " remains where there flourished, four hundred years ago, all kinds of " herbes and floures, and fine applies, plumbes of all kynde, peers, damsellis, nuttes, wardens, cherries to the black and reede, wallnuttes, and also licores verie fine." It is still a fertile and lovely place.

ANDERSON

†§ BURRADON TOWER
(Map II, F9.)

Halfway between Newcastle and Blyth, and in sight of the sea, stands the ruined pele of Burradon. Though its stark simplicity suggests an early structure, the tower is probably not the old one mentioned in the Border Survey of 1415, but seems to have been built by Bertram Anderson who acquired the manor in 1548. The weatherworn walls are complete as far as the parapet, and even part of this, supported on corbels, remains on the north and east sides, together with some projecting stone spouts. The original doorway on the east side is protected by machicolations projecting on three sets of corbels, through the openings of which unwary intruders could be surprised. The vaulted basement is very complete. It has had a loophole at each end in a splayed recess, but one has been converted into a door. Close to the old entrance a stair begins in the thickness of the wall and continues as a turret-stair in the adjoining corner, but the foot of it has been built up. On the south side two of the original windows remain. A painting of the tower by T. M. Richardson a hundred years ago shows buildings adjoining two sides, and traces of these remain. The place was habitable then—at least the two lower apartments were. On the first floor the fireplace bears the initials L.O. (for Lancelot Ogle) and the date 1633 on its decorated lintel. Formerly there must have been a barmkin. It is certainly suggested by the present enclosure, filled with tall trees that cast their shadows over the dark and broken walls.

BALLIOL

†§ BYWELL CASTLE
(Map II, FG7.)

From Bywell Bridge over the Tyne the eye, roaming over the lovely prospect of glancing stream and banked woods, is caught by the turrets of Bywell Castle rising from the trees on the northern bank.

This is the chief part, and almost the only part remaining, of the unfinished castle built by the 2nd Earl of Westmorland in the fourteenth century. The Neville family held the barony from the days of Edward III up till the time of the Rising of the North, an attempt to restore the Roman Catholic religion in the reign of Elizabeth. The rebellion failed and the earl, being attainted, forfeited his estates. In earlier times the barony was possessed by the De Balliols, one of whom was the founder of Balliol College, Oxford.

In 1570 the tower was declared to be a good defence for the town (Bywell was a much bigger place formerly), but the sturdy, self-reliant inhabitants seem to have preferred to trust more to their own defences. Each night, winter and summer, they brought their cattle and sheep into the main street, and posted a sentry at a gate at either end. Sometimes the massive tower of St. Peter's Church was used as a pele. Their worst enemies were " the thieves of Tynedale," who knew of their prosperity as expert workers in iron and in the making of bits, buckles and straps for harness.

After the Battle of Hexham, during the Wars of the Roses, the ill-fated Henry VI fled to Bywell for safety, but my Lord Montagu was hot on his track ; and " How or whither the King escaped," says the chronicler, " God only knows, in whose hands are the hearts of kings." But escape he did, to go on to Bamburgh, where again he was harried.

Judging from the weakness of the site, which neither commands the position of the old bridge nor has the advantage of height, the castle cannot have been intended for any great defensive purpose, apart from the great Gate-House, which has been carefully and nobly planned. Here, more so even than at Dunstanburgh or Bothal, the Gate-House *is* the Castle. Part of the unfinished curtain-wall remains, linking the Gate-House with a modern house built on the site of the castle Gun-House, the vaulted basement of which is used as a cellar. The key of the castle can be obtained at this house on payment of a small sum (for charity).

The Gate-House faces the Tyne, and its archway on that side was formerly guarded by a portcullis, and by an oaken door, which still remains, and is in two leaves with a wicket in one half. High overhead, protruding from the battlements on corbels are machicolations, through the openings of which attackers could be assailed while trying to force an entrance. On each side of the passage-way there are doors into vaulted basements and, towards the inner arch (nearer the highway), the ancient iron gate of the stair to the first floor. This gate is worth examining closely for the fine construction of its grille. The horizontal bars are riveted and clasped alternately to the uprights, and the spaces between have been filled with oaken planks, some of which remain. At the beginning of the stair-way, an intruder could be attacked from overhead, through a meurtriere which communicates with the room above. This room has large windows, and a garderobe in one corner. A very narrow wheel-stair goes up to the battlements (the flat roof has gone), which are higher on two sides to afford protection for the stairs, and to the octagonal corner turrets, with flat roofs and meurtrieres on three sides. Needless to say, the view is a very charming one.

PLANTAGENET
(Royal Arms of England from
about A.D. 1405 to 1603)

CLAVERING

CALLALEY CASTLE

(Map II, C7.)

Close to Whittingham and in one of the most secluded parts of the lovely Vale of Aln, the fine mansion of Callaley Castle encloses the ancient tower of the Claverings, where they lived for nearly five hundred years.

The family came here after the De Callaleys who in Norman times held the estate by a tenure that included the curious duty of sending a cart to Bamburgh with the trunk of a tree for the King's hearth every other day between Whitsuntide and Lammas. Of distinguished descent, the Claverings had some equally distinguished descendants—among those of Eva, Baroness of Clavering, who was married no fewer than four times, were a king of England, a queen of England, a Duchess of York, a Duchess of Clarence, a Duke of Bedford, a Marquis of Montacute, an Earl of Westmorland, an Earl of Northumberland, an Earl of Salisbury, an Earl of Kent, *the* Earl of Warwick, a Lord Latimer, a Lord Abergavenny, an archbishop of York, and an Earl Marshal of England !

The will of Robert Clavering, who died in 1582, in the reign of Queen Elizabeth, makes interesting reading. Included in the inventory of his goods are : one black cloak faced with taffeta, valued at 40s. ; a long furred gown, 46s. 8d. ; plaids, 41s. 8d. ; a stone and a half of English iron at 16d. a stone ; two firkins of soap . . . and " fyve swermes of bees in the garding " !

The old tower is mentioned in the records of Border fortresses as far back as 1415 ; and concerning its erection in the valley instead of some more commanding and secure spot, there hangs a very interesting tale, really the story of how a lady got her own way, a process as familiar to the fair sex seven hundred years ago as it is today ! Apparently the lord of Callaley began to build on the Castle Hill, a conical height that is part of the range of hills to the south, but as fast as the work progressed it was demolished again at night ; and watchers posted to solve the mystery were horrified at the stroke of midnight to see a

Plate IV

EXTERIORS OF BYWELL, BOTHAL
AND CHILLINGHAM CASTLES

Plate V

BAMBURGH CASTLE FROM THE SOUTH

Plate VI

CARLISLE CASTLE—GATE-HOUSE AND KEEP

Plate VII

NORHAM CASTLE—MARMION'S ARCH AND KEEP:
EXTERIOR OF EDLINGHAM AND
DILSTON CASTLES

huge boar appear and overthrow the new walls, then cry out loudly :

> " Callaley Castle, built on the height,
> Up in the day and down in the night ;
> Builded down in the Shepherd's Shaw,
> It shall stand for aye, and never fa'."

The boar, however, was merely a personal servant of the lady of Callaley, who disguised himself each night to perform his " supernatural " work, and, it is hardly necessary to add, the Shepherd's Shaw or meadow was the site favoured by the lady.

The medieval tower forms part of the west wing of the present mansion, on the front of which there is, together with a profusion of rich carving, an interesting old sundial with the reminder, UT HORA SIC VITA, " Life is but an hour," and a handsome escutcheon showing the arms of the Claverings combined with those of allied families. A new wing in harmony with the rest of the mansion was added by Alexander Browne in 1890, and the old private chapel of the Claverings was restored. This was a Catholic oratory, the family having been staunch adherents of that faith, and Callaley a centre of Catholicism in the Vale of Whittingham. A priest appears to have been in continuous residence at Callaley, and after the Reformation no doubt a hiding-place, or " priest's hole," was devised somewhere in the old building ; while the sacred chalices, too, were specially designed so that they could be taken to pieces and concealed in a small space. The old Border tower sheltered not only its occupants, but their faith as well.

FELTON

BERTRAM

§ CAMBO PELE

(Map II, E7.)

The beautiful village of Cambo lies on high ground to the north of the Newcastle–Otterburn road near where it is crossed by the Rothbury–Hexham road. Wallington Hall, the seat of the Trevelyans is near. The village was formerly a station on the old coach road from Newcastle to Jedburgh, which came this way from Belsay, then passed over the wastes of Ottercops Moss past Winter's Gibbet to Otterburn. Wild country such as the moss-troopers favoured stretches to the north and west, and a pele would emphatically be a necessity in the days before the Union.

The pele, or rather the lowest storey of it, is now used as the village post-office, but the tall, three-storeyed building retains externally many characteristic features. It is very massively built, some of the lower corner stones being enormous, the walls are four feet thick, and the roof is stone tiled. In the gable is the outline of a small window that has been blocked. It is referred to in the Cambo Women's Institute Book, *In the Troublesome Times*, where Mr. George Handyside, then a tenant of the tower, is quoted as saying ,'' My father and grandfather had this shop before me, and before them it was kept by a warlock [i.e. a wizard], and people daursn't owe him anything ! There was a woman lived where our kitchen is now, and she kept a cow, and when she churned she used to lock the door for fear the warlock cast an evil eye on the milk and turned it sour. His shop was upstairs, that's his window that's walled up.''

That was in 1814 or thereabouts. In 1818, as the date above the shop window records, the pele was considerably altered to render it more habitable, and has undergone few changes since. At the time of the " warlock " it appears that the ground floor was used as a " hemmel " or cattle-shed, while an outside flight of stairs led to the first floor, which was guarded by an iron door. There is no trace now of these extra safeguards. You can buy stamps in what was once the stable, and drop your card into a post-box let into the stout gable, while ivy is the worst enemy of the rugged front that looks pleasantly to the south as if glad to forget a danger that once threatened from another quarter.

52

THE BLACK PRINCE

*CARLISLE CASTLE
(Map I, G₂.)

As one of the main gateways into England, the Merry City of Carlisle, like Berwick at the other end of the Border, was in need of extra defence ; and the castle which supplied it first came into existence with William Rufus who, having forced Malcolm of Scotland to submit to him, resumed possession of Cumberland and built the fortress to support his claim. This first castle was almost certainly a wooden tower on a mound surrounded by a ditch. It was probably not till sixty or seventy years later that a castle of stone rose on the bank of the Eden opposite the ford. It naturally became an object of special attention by the Scots; but their attentions were vain—the castle was so strong that for five and a half centuries it remained invincible, and only then fell to a Scottish force fighting for the English Parliament, a record paralleled only by Prudhoe and Alnwick. The mighty Edward I made Carlisle his base for his hammering of the Scots at the close of the thirteenth century, and it was here, in the Great Hall or Palace of the Castle, that he held a parliament with magnificent ceremonial that lived as a tradition ; and that his son the same year was proclaimed king and received the homage of his nobles. The building which saw all this pageantry was pulled down by the government about a hundred years ago, the excuse being that it would cost too much to repair ! As Lang comments, " Vandalism in those days was a vice which affected not alone the private individual."

The most determined attempt to take the castle was by Robert Bruce. Using every engine of war then known— ladders, malvoisins, " sows " and the like—he battered and assaulted the Norman walls, but the garrison held firm, losing only two men, and all the Scots could do was to trample down the cornfields in the neighbourhood and drive off all the cattle. By Elizabethan times the castle had got into bad repair. " Three sides of the strongest tower [i.e. the Keep] were in a state of decay ; the walls were sadly dismantled ; the artillery dismounted ; the powder reduced to two barrels, and nearly all the stores valueless." The Queen, however, ordered the fortress to be reconditioned.

To Carlisle Castle, in 1568, Mary Queen of Scots was brought from Cockermouth, and began that unhappy period of imprisonment and plotting which ended so tragically nineteen years later at Fotheringhay. Only eight years later the castle was the setting for what is perhaps the most fantastic and stirring episode in Border history — the rescue of Kinmont Willie by the Duke of Buccleuch. The freebooter, a prominent and notorious figure on the Western Marches, had been taken treacherously at a Wardens' Meeting, which was always a day of truce "when all persones whatsoever that come to these meitings sould be saife fra any proceiding or present occasioun, from the tyme of Meiting of the Wardens, or their Deputies, till the next day at the sun rysing." His release was the work of a small force of Scots who at night forded the swollen Eden, forced the Sallyport, then pushed on towards his cell, making a tremendous din to give the impression of greater numbers. The doors of the dungeon were forced, and Kinmont Willie, chained as he was, was carried bodily away. Lord Scrope did not pursue. Perhaps he was secretly glad to see the prisoner go. But it was otherwise with his queen—furious at the news, Elizabeth demanded the surrender of Buccleuch. This was eventually done, and when he appeared before her, the queen demanded how he dared to carry out such a raid. He replied, " Madam, what would a man not dare to do? " a retort that filled Elizabeth with admiration. " By God! " she cried, " With ten thousand such men our brother of Scotland might shake the firmest throne in Europe."

In his *Rogue Herries*, Hugh Walpole has given a vivid picture of Carlisle at the time of the '45 Jacobite Rising. General Wade could not reach Carlisle in time owing to the badness of the roads, and Prince Charles took city and castle with ease. A skirmish at Clifton followed, then Prince Charles and his Highlanders marched northward, leaving a small garrison to delay pursuit. Nine days later they surrendered to "Butcher" Cumberland, who went on towards Scotland—and Culloden!

The castle is of a usual Norman type, with Gate-House, Inner and Outer Baileys, and a massive Keep. It is under the care of H.M. Office of Works, but is still used as the head-quarters of the Border Regiment, who have established an interesting military museum in the Keep.

Across the outer moat of the Castle, a stone bridge now takes the place of the drawbridge that formerly could be hinged up against the Barbican entrance, as at Warkworth Castle. To the left of the entrance, where some corbels show, was a flanking turret; and other defences included loopholes in the parapets of the Barbican, a portcullis, an oak folding-gate and an inner door. Similar defences are repeated at the Captain's Gateway leading to the Inner Bailey, with the addition of three meurtriere openings in the roof of the passage, so that intruders could be assaulted from above. In Henry VIII's reign a half-moon battery for artillery was placed in the inner moat before the Gateway, and was approached by a breastwork from a drawbridge on the right. The Outer Bailey then contained only a few wooden buildings. In the west wall is the famous Sallyport by which the bold Buccleuch broke into the castle

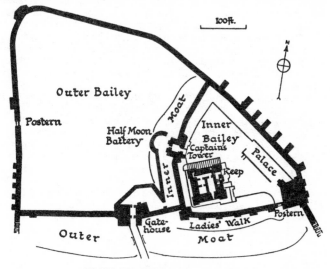

PLAN OF CARLISLE CASTLE

that dark, wet and misty night in April nearly three hundred and fifty years ago. The inner side of the Captain's Gateway is beautifully decorated with a trefoil device, and armorial shields. The heavy, flattish arch here was added to provide a passage for artillery along the walls, which were widened at the same time.

The twelfth-century Keep is a typical Norman structure, with walls eight to fourteen feet thick, many mural passages and chambers in its upper storeys, and characteristic angle buttresses running from ground to parapet. The basement was formerly one single vaulted room, and the other floors have been partitioned and otherwise altered. The original entrance was on the first floor, as at Newcastle. Later a ground floor entrance, with a portcullis, was made. In one angle is a newel-stair, mounting from the basement. The second floor is interesting for the cells in the thickness of its wall, and their carvings executed by prisoners. Many of them are of animals, suggesting the work of poachers awaiting sentence of death for " misfeasance of vert and venison "; and others are attributed to Major Macdonald of Keppoch, a prisoner after Culloden, who was kept here for three years and nine months before his execution. His tools are said to have been tenpenny nails! Another curiosity, in the inner basement dungeon, is the " Weeping Stone," which owing to its composition attracts moisture from the air, and was used by prisoners to allay their thirst. Their tongues have worn a deep hollow in it.

Besides the Keep in the Inner Bailey there are the remains of an Elizabethan building, on the wall of which is preserved a unique stone panel, the only one of its kind on the outside wall of any castle in the country. It shows the arms of Elizabeth quartered with those of France, " the lion trampling the fair lilies down," and records that the Queen constructed this work at her own expense while Lord Scrope was Warden of the Western Marches. In the corner beyond the Keep stands a finely-traceried stair-tower, the only part remaining of the fourteenth-century tower where the Scottish Queen was lodged. A little postern gate beside it led out to the Ladies' Walk beneath the walls, where she used to take the air. A good way of getting a general impression of the castle is to walk the ramparts. The contrast between the grey and the red stone will be noticed. The former usually denotes the older work, but some of it was supplied by the demolition of part of the Cathedral, when General Leslie repaired the fortress after he had taken it for Cromwell during the Civil War. As might be expected with the Roman station of Stanwix so near, many of the stones are of Roman workmanship. The views from the walls are very fine.

AYLMER

CARTINGTON

† CARTINGTON CASTLE
(Map II, D7.)

Two miles to the north-north-west of Rothbury as the crow flies, and nearly twice as far by road, lies Cartington Castle, that ruin so fascinating to the artist and puzzling to the antiquary.

It is easily accessible. From the highway a lane goes past a row of cottages to a gate, from which we cross two fields. Two tall gateposts in the shadow of some fine old trees mark the entrance in the surrounding barmkin, and from it steps lead down to a sunken courtyard beneath the ruined walls. Cartington can be reached by a footpath from Rothbury which climbs the hillside behind the town and passes the " Ship Stone," but the way is not easy to find.

The history of Cartington Castle goes back to ancient times. Parts of the structure have been standing for nearly six hundred years, but there have been many alterations and additions to the original castle built by the Cartingtons. By the marriage of an heiress the manor passed to the Radcliffes about 1494, and later in a similar manner to the Widdrington family ; and it was a bold member of this staunch Royalist family, one Roger Widdrington, who as deputy warden of the Middle Marches " did the Queen [i.e. Elizabeth] and the country much good." A later Roger Widdrington, " an old blade, well-versed in these parts," threw in his lot with King Charles during the Civil War, and as a result he was banished, his wife was fined £400 (a much more considerable sum then), and his castle, worth £8,000, was pulled down. Later, however, it was rebuilt. A subsequent owner, a Talbot, apparently lost his estate through taking part in the '15 Jacobite Rising.

A great occasion in the domestic history of the castle was when it was visited by Princess Margaret, the sister of Henry VIII, then the wife of the Earl of Angus. A few weeks before, at Harbottle Castle, she had given birth to a daughter (through whom King James of Scotland later claimed the English throne), and was still so ill when moved that she could not bear horses in the litter, which had to be carried by Lord

57

Dacre's servants. From Cartington she was taken to Brinkburn Priory, then on to Morpeth.

As already mentioned, the ruins present something of a puzzle (albeit an attractive one), the restoration carried out in 1887 by Mr. C. C. Hodges for the late Lord Armstrong having to a certain extent made " confusion worse confounded." Thus, the beautiful traceried windows looking down on the courtyard have no relation to any particular floors within; and a flight of steps beside the main door appear to lead nowhere at all. Originally the castle was of two towers adjoining each other. The sunken courtyard may or may not be a later addition. The wall surrounding it can hardly have kept anyone out, though at one corner there is a stout little pele-like tower with a vaulted basement and an upper room equipped with a garde-robe.

After the Restoration of Charles II, when Sir Edward Widdrington rebuilt his ancestral home, a new doorway was inserted at first-floor level, but it has disappeared, though the steps to it unaccountably remain. The present gateway, flanked by two great pillars, was also built then. But how did the carriages reach the new entrance? That is one of the puzzles of Cartington. Probably the courtyard was partly levelled up with earth at that time. Among the interesting features of the ruins are the vaulted basements, which form a perfect warren, with various stairs, one of them in the thickness of the wall going down to them from the first floor. In the north-east corner is a remarkable well with steps down to it. The dungeon, with a manhole in the roof, the only entrance, was in the southern part of the same wing. On the north side are the remains of a small courtyard and buildings, and a unique flying buttress supports the wall of the north-west turret. The newel-stair has been restored in the tall look-out turret on the south side, and from the top there is a fine view of Border country, the hills to the east looming up impressively across a little valley. Shrubs and climbing plants on the grey walls and broken façades lend their kindly disguise alike to the havoc wrought by time and the " improvements " of the restorer.

KER

† CESSFORD CASTLE

(Map I, C4.)

The ancient stronghold of the Kers, more a Border tower than a castle in the usually accepted sense of the word, has an imposing position on the northern fringe of the Cheviots, about midway between Morebattle and Crailing. The site is a strong one, and the outlook is wide, especially towards the north and east. Not far away are two old roads formerly well travelled by those who were foolish or determined enough to cross the dreaded Debatable Land. One of these ways goes up Bowmont Water and over Cocklaw ; the other is the Roman Dere Street, the green road by which the Scots, carrying the body of the dead Douglas on a bier of birch and hazel, returned from the battle-field of Otterburn.

There were Kers on the Scottish Border as early as the fourteenth century. Their reputation appears to have been no better than it should have been ; but from them are descended the present ducal house of Roxburghe and that of the Marquesses of Lothian. An Andrew Ker was given the barony of Cessford by Earl Douglas in 1446 ; and a later member of the family, Robert, was Warden of the Middle Marches. He appears to have carried out his duties with some ruthlessness, for he was set upon and slain by three Englishmen, but only one of these escaped to boast that he had pulled the Scottish lion's tail. The Kers were unpopular, too, on their own side of the Border. They had, for instance, a bitter feud with the Scotts of Buccleuch, and in pursuit of this, " anything went." On one occasion we find Ker of Cessford joining forces with the English Lord Grey to make a foray on Buccleuch's lands, and after raiding Hawick and ravaging the countryside as far west as Ettrick and Yarrow they set fire to Catslake Tower, the home of the dowager Lady Buccleuch, who perished in the flames. A year or two later a distinguished member of the Buccleuchs, Sir Walter Scott, Warden of the Middle Marches, was stabbed to death in Edinburgh High Street by a gang of Kers and their friends.

In revenge, the murdered knight's widow obtained the outlawry of the whole of the Ker clan, and though the severity of this sentence was somewhat relaxed, it was many years before the actual criminals dared return to their native haunts. Eventually this age-old feud was ended in a charmingly romantic way. As final penance for the murder of Sir Walter, the Buccleuchs demanded that Ker of Cessford should visit St. Giles' Church in Edinburgh, and on his knees in public humbly ask pardon for the crime, and that the rest of the clan should agree to bury the hatchet. Ker of Ferniehirst demurred at these requirements until Janet Scott, Buccleuch's sister, tried her persuasive powers. Where threats and arguments had failed, the charms of this lady succeeded. The two fell in love, and their marriage put a seal to the peace between the clans.

Cessford Castle is a comparatively small tower—it measures about sixty feet by seventy—but it had a formidable reputation in former days. The Earl of Surrey, no mean judge of castles, accounted it stronger than any in the Borders save perhaps Bothwell's castle of Dunbar and Fast Castle. But the thick walls that defied many an English attack are surrendering to the assaults of wind and weather, the west wall being the most ruinous. It will be seen that the lowest storey, approached through an arched passage, is barrel-vaulted in the usual fashion. On the first floor there has been a large room with a vaulted roof, probably the main living room. It has a large open fireplace and, at one end, a spacious window with seats. On the west side of the tower rises a turret, enclosing a newel stair, and the dungeon is below ground here. There has been an outer curtain-wall, and a deep moat. Ninety years ago a workman digging near the north wall of the tower unearthed a sword and a dagger. The sword, richly chased and embossed with silver, was basket-hilted and measured forty inches in length. The blade bore on one side the Scottish crown, and on the other the date, 1511. The dagger, about twenty-six inches long, was decorated on its blade with the Scottish thistle and a crown. Vivid reminders of " days long gone of not-returning time."

GREY

CHILLINGHAM CASTLE
(Map II, B7.)

" That part of the English Border in which stands Chillingham Castle," says one writer, " is the most romantic spot in the British Islands." Such pronouncements are difficult to substantiate, but few discriminating people will disagree that this vicinity is exquisitely beautiful in its contours and verdure. Backed by the great hill of Roscastle, from its lovely park the many-towered stronghold looks out across the Till Valley to the Cheviots.

It is easy to reach Chillingham since it stands on the main road from Alnwick to Chatton ; or can be approached from the Great North Road by the road crossing Belford Moor.

Chillingham Castle has fallen upon evil days. Untenanted, emptied of its treasures, most of its interest nowadays is in its picturesque exterior. The castle and grounds are not usually shown. Those visitors particularly wishing to inspect them, or sketch, or take photographs, should apply personally to Lord Tankerville at his residence in the village. Permission is usually readily granted.

The wild white cattle,* for which Chillingham is widely known, are, however, still shown every weekday from 10—5, and on Sundays from 2—5. The charge is 1/-, and application should be made at the Park-keeper's cottage a short distance beyond the church.

The foundation of the castle goes back to early Norman times, but it was not till the reign of Edward III that licence was given to crenellate it. As one of the principal towers on the Border it naturally had to meet many attacks. At the time of Flodden, for instance, it was taken by James's army and dismantled. In the seventeenth century, after the necessity for defence had passed, the famous architect Inigo Jones was engaged to re-design the castle to give better accommodation and greater comfort, and the result was largely as we see it today.

---

* To save this famous herd from extinction, a Chillingham Wild Cattle Association has been formed, the annual subscription of one guinea enabling members to visit the herd free of charge, and to certain other privileges. Non-members pay as above.

Four ancient towers are connected by the later buildings, enclosing a courtyard, on one side of which are cloisters and a fine stairway leading to a balustraded portico. The dank and dimly-lit baronial prison, used in the stern times of the Greys of Heton and Wark, still exists at the north-east corner of the pile. In the floor of it a trapdoor leads to a deeper dungeon, an *oubliette* (dread word !) of the type to be seen at Alnwick and Warkworth, where a man could only too conveniently be " forgotten."

The grounds are neglected—but enough remains of the Italian garden on the west side, where the old jousting-ground was, to show how charming it must have been in its prime. From it broad stone steps lead up to the spacious lawn, built high above the level of the old moat ; and here we see at a glance the dignified front, looking rather blank with its bare windows.

The wild cattle are generally supposed to be descended from the aboriginal herds that roamed in the great Caledonian forests in prehistoric times. Centuries of inbreeding have decreased their size and rendered them liable to certain complaints, but the herd remains one of the major curiosities in this country. The cattle show many of the traits of wild animals. When the cows calve, they hide their calves in some thicket, generally in " Robin Hood's Bog," and only visit them in order to feed them. If the calves at this stage are surprised, they " freeze " like a hare, lying with heads close to the ground. The cattle feed at night, and bask or sleep through the day and, though fierce if pressed, will generally move off on the appearance of a human being. In the winter they are more docile and friendly, in the manner of most wild animals when food is scarce. They are gracefully shaped in spite of having short legs, the back is straight, the horns finely curved, the skin so thin as to appear cream, and their cry is that of creatures of the wild.

In 1872, the King of the Herd had the distinction of being shot by Edward VII when he was Prince of Wales, and much fun was subsequently poked at the manner of the killing. One local poem ran as follows :

" He's a warrior, ye knaa, and the papers are full
Iv a tarrible encoonter he had wiv a bull !
He slowtered the bull, but his critics will say
That the Prince was cuncealed in a bundle iv hay ;
An' thit it was ne feat at a' te lie hid
An' slowter the bull in the way that he did ;
But some folks are selfish, an' winna hear tell
Iv ony greet feats unless dune be thorsel."

There is so much of intense interest at Chillingham, so many reminders of a virile, if rough-and-ready, period in our history, that one hopes it will long be preserved intact.

HERON

CHIPCHASE CASTLE
(Map I, F5.)

Backed by dense trees and looking southward across one of the most beautiful stretches of the North Tyne Valley, Chipchase Castle lies a mile and a half to the south-east of Wark. It can be well seen in passing, since the main road on the east side of the river adjoins the park. Chipchase is a private residence and so is not usually shown to visitors.

The castle really comprises two buildings—the old thirteenth-century pele and, built on to it, a Jacobean mansion—and both are admirable specimens of their kind ; so that the spot is of particular interest to any one interested in the development of architecture.

The history of Chipchase goes back to the reign of Henry II, when it was a hunting-ground or chase owned by the Lords of Prudhoe, the mighty Umfravilles. It was they who erected a small fort to defend the village that existed then, and later built the tower that now forms so striking a part of the building. The more modern portion was added by Cuthbert Heron in 1621, and is perhaps the finest example of Jacobean work in the county.

The Herons took a prominent part in Border affairs. Sometimes too prominent a part. For instance, Sir George Heron, Keeper of Tynedale and High Sheriff of Northumberland, was slain in one of the last of the Border frays—the Raid of the Reidswire, fought twenty-eight years before the union of the two countries. When, to save complications, the Scots returned their prisoners, they gave them each a falcon, with the grim pleasantry that live *hawks* for one dead *heron* was no mean compensation ! Of such a nature was the humour of our forefathers. The emblem of the Herons was a bird of that ilk, and tradition had it that so long as the heronry in the park existed the fortunes of the family would not fade. Be that as it may, the castle passed out of the ownership of the Herons about the end of the seventeenth century.

Short of getting permission to enter the grounds, the best point from which to see the castle is from the byroad that runs along the south side of the park towards the Tyne, since it is from this side that the older tower on the west front is seen. It is noticeably massive and lofty, and its appearance is enhanced by the elaborate corbelling on which the battlements overhang the walls, and by the great round bartizans at the corners. The interior of the tower, too, is wonderfully complete. Part of the original oak portcullis that guarded the entrance actually still remains in its slot. The room above from which it is worked is less than a yard wide. The basement is vaulted, and the room on the first floor appears to have been used as a kitchen or guard-room. Above it is the Hall, with fine windows in recesses, from one of which a passage leads to a little oratory in the thickness of the wall. There is another little mural room in the south-east corner; and a wall-passage to a garde-robe. The roof of this room is vaulted, which is unusual on the second floor, and the plastered wall is painted with a foliage pattern, a scheme of wall decoration dating from Tudor times. From the basement of the tower an underground passage has been traced for some distance towards the south—towards, that is, where the now-vanished village stood, the " cheap " (market) in the " chase," which gave its name to the castle. Such an emergency exit must have proved useful on not a few occasions.

Above the entrance to the beautiful manor-house is the Heron shield showing three herons, and crested by a heron under an oak tree. An odd feature of the front of the house is the number of representations of bears supporting various coats of arms, among them Musgrave and Carnaby.

Of Chipchase is told the thriller called " The Long Pack," though Lee Hall, near Bellingham, also claims the gruesome distinction. The story is fairly widely known since it was broadcast. The castle, left in the charge of a maid-servant, a man and a youth, was visited late one night by a pedlar who got permission to leave his big pack in the cellar till next morning. When the man had gone, the girl's curiosity led her to approach the pack, and to her horror she saw it move. Realising that a plot to rob the house was afoot, she called the old man, who fired an old military gun into the pack; and later when the man's confederates approached the house in expectation of an easy entrance, they were greeted with a volley that slew four of them. Near the east end of Bellingham church is an odd tombstone known as " The Long Pack " that is supposed to mark the grave of the central figure of this story.

Distant views of the castle can be got from the roads on the opposite side of the valley, the best of these being from the lane past Park End, when the Tyne is seen curving below and broad meadows slope up to the shapely pile outlined against its dark trees.

CLENNEL

CLENNEL HALL
(Map I, D5.)

It is remarkable that a tower so near the Border (it stands close to Alwinton) should have continued to exist till the Union, especially as it is on the line of one of the oldest of the roads across the Border, the ancient Clennel Street, one of the most frequented of the notorious " Thieves' Rodes."

But its defences appear to have been strong. In 1541 it is reported in the Border Survey as being " a lytle toure of thinherytaunce of one P'cyvall Clennel, gent, newly reparelled and brattyshed by the same P'cyvall." The owner was also engaged in making a barmkin round his tower. The bratticing alluded to would be a wooden staging with loopholes in its floor and constructed so as to protrude over the parapets and command the foot of the walls. A much-worn date above the original entrance to the tower is usually said to read, 1365, but the fortress was not mentioned in records till the Survey quoted. There were, however, Clennels here as early as the reign of Henry III, and a Clennel was Constable of Harbottle Castle in 1434. One member of the family offended Edward I by allying himself with the Scots (probably a wise move for one so liable to their attacks) and was imprisoned in a castle on the bank of the Wye for three years, during which his bill for his keep and other expenses averaged three pence a day ! In the eighteenth century the estate passed by the marriage of an heiress to the Wilkinsons, another old family, in whose possession it remains.

The old tower now forms part of a large and picturesque mansion, close under the Cheviots but sheltered from their blasts by a grove of ancient sycamore and ash. The interior of the pele has been modernised, in one place a bath-room having been made partly in the wall, five feet thick. From the vaulted cellar, which has a loophole, a stair goes up in the wall. On the first floor is to be seen over a window a unique feature, described by Bates as the most interesting bit of ancient work he had ever seen in Northumberland. It is part of a plaster frieze in bas-relief showing a scene supposed to represent

Chevy Chase. According to one authority the costumes are no earlier than sixteenth-century. The tower formerly had another storey, and the gabled roof is modern. The ivy that covered the walls has been removed, disclosing pointing as clean as when it was done, a tribute to the excellence of ancient materials and craftsmanship.

ERRINGTON

† COCKLAW TOWER
(Map II, F7.)

Cocklaw Tower lies in the North Tyne Valley, quite close to the main road to Chollerton from the Hexham direction, and is about a mile to the south-east of Chollerton.

Inquiries should be made at the farm near it by visitors wishing to see the interior of the pele, since it is used nowadays as a farm building.

Literally a tower of strength in a region as lawless as Tynedale was in former days, this sturdy pele still shows a brave face. Built by the Errington family more than six hundred years ago, it was their home for nearly two hundred years before they came into possession of the much more spacious castle of Beaufront, near Hexham. This celebrated Border family took their name from the nearby hamlet of Errington, in its turn named after the Erring Burn flowing past it.

The pele is a large and substantial one as the most cursory of glances will show. It measures about forty feet by fifty feet, and its height on the east side is still thirty-five feet. Its walls, almost as sound as when first raised to dominate the bare, rolling landscape, are of huge ashlar blocks, and are at least six feet thick. Indeed, the south wall is fifteen feet from face to face.

On this side is the entrance, a doorway with a pointed arch, and with holes just within the door-jambs to take the ends of the fall-bar. A door on the right here leads to the newel-stair in the thickness of the wall which originally went up to the roof but is now intact only as far as the first floor. The bottom entrance to the stair was guarded by a door, the hinge-supports and catch of which remain. Opposite to this door is a narrow dungeon, but it was originally walled up here, and the only way in was by a small hatch in its roof, from a similar room above. The main passage leads into the basement, a barrel-vaulted room, only half of which is intact. But the vaulting of that part is very sound, and exhibits splendid craftsmanship.

The first floor has been mainly occupied with a spacious room with some good windows, two of them mullioned, and a huge open fireplace. In the far corner a passage leads in the wall to a latrine; and above the guard-room a step or two leads down into the narrow room already referred to. A loophole here overlooks the entrance; and there are similar loopholes in the large room and on the stairs. A peculiar door on the east side of the tower once, probably, led to a wooden drawbridge communicating with another building, perhaps a chapel, detached from the main one. Further up the interior of the wall some of the corbels remain that supported the beams of the second floor, where the Great Hall was. It can hardly have been a very cheery room in spite of its big fireplace, since there are only two windows, and they are smaller even than those below.

This stout pele has withstood the inroads of time and neglect so well, and it possesses so many interesting features that one feels it deserves official protection. A little judicious restoration would make it a worthy reminder of a picturesque and stirring period in Border history.

TILLIOL

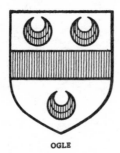

OGLE

COCKLE PARK TOWER
(Map II, E8.)

This ancient tower of the Ogle family stands three and a half miles from Morpeth on the very attractive by-road that runs northward through Hebron and Tritlington. Still in sound repair, the Tower is used as a farmhouse in connection with the experimental farm carried on by the Agricultural Department of King's College, Newcastle.

The Ogles were formerly one of those widespread Northumbrian families who so distinguished themselves in Border warfare. Their original seat was at Ogle, on the other side of Morpeth, and other houses of theirs were at Hepple, Bothal and Causey Park. They were even more pedigree-proud than most ancient families in the North, as a Milburn discovered to his cost in 1583 when, because he insisted on maintaining that the Dacres were of as good blood as the Ogles, four of the Ogles attacked and slew him. Their coat of arms, assumed by Sir Robert Ogle when he was created a baron in 1461, was supported by two antelopes, collared and chained, and these appear on a carved panel, now much defaced, on the east side of the tower, showing the arms of the Ogles quartering Bertram as an indication of their connection by marriage with that family.

It must have been about the time of the first baron that the tower was built, since it was not included in the list of Border fortresses made in 1415. It is mentioned in records dated 1539, and again four years later in a will bequeathing " Cockell Parke and Towre " to Lady Jane Ogle by her husband, the fifth Lord Ogle. He had been commanded " to invade the realm of Scotland in his King's Majestie's wars," and it is not surprising that he thought it wise to put his affairs in order before departing. Perhaps he had a foreboding—only a year later he was slain in the battle of Ancrum Moor.

The northern part of the house, usually called the North Tower, has been least changed. The southern wing had a stair turret added in Jacobean times, and there were later alterations in accordance with a passing craze for Gothic architecture. The North Tower, however, remains a very typical structure, with great corner bartizans overhanging the rugged walls by means of corbelling, and, between them, a projecting parapet pierced with machicolations through which defenders on the roof could command the foot of the tower. In the wall on this side there used to be a large and handsome pointed window but it was removed to Bothal Castle, where it may be seen in the room above the gateway. A newel stair lit by small loops goes up from the entrance on the east side, but the first floor cannot be reached from it now, being connected with the south wing instead, as is part of the floor above. Here the room which lost its window (the recess with a window-seat remains) has also lost its fireplace, part of which has found its way to—of all unlikely places—the *outside wall* of the building, where it was perched on a row of corbels " by way of curiosity and ornament " ! Another of the old fireplaces was taken to Bothal at the same time as the window, which was one of the chief features of the tower. A still higher room is small and roughly vaulted, then the stair emerges on the roof beneath a small gable. Here we are in sight of the sea ; and the dark hills of the Border do not seem much more distant.

CORBETT TOWER
(Map I, B4.)

A mile south of Morebattle, and overlooking the valley of the Kale winding down from the Cheviots, is this small Border tower, once a seat of the ancient Corbett clan. Later it passed to the equally famous Kers, and was in their hands when it was burned by the English in 1522. Lancelot Ker of Gateshaw and his friends had made an extensive raid across the Border, and the result was this retaliatory visit. Again, in 1545, it suffered at English hands. Thirty years later it was reconstructed, and the date, with the initials of the owner in that year and those of his wife, appear on the exterior of the house. About a hundred years ago Sir Charles Ker made still further alterations in which the ancient parapets were removed and the character of the place very much changed.

The old doorway remains, and on its lintel is an unusual inscription that bears out the tradition that the tower once belonged to Melrose Abbey—the sacred monogram I H S (an abbreviated form of the Greek word for " Jesus "). The doorway exhibits signs of having formerly been furnished outside with an iron " yett " in the form of a grille, and a nail-studded door within. Some of the old loopholes remain, too, to aid the imagination to reconstruct the appearance of this old tower in the days of its strength.

†§ CORBRIDGE OLD VICARAGE
(Map II, F7.)

Though there are many peles in the North Country which have been (and still are) used as vicarages, this is the only one standing actually within a churchyard. It forms a picturesque feature of the market-place of this ancient village on the Tyne.

The pele first appears in history as " the Lord's gaole." That was shortly after its erection at the beginning of the fourteenth century, but in 1415 it was inhabited by the vicar, John Brigg. A few years after the Union of the two countries it became ruinous and for long was roofless; then, repaired by the instructions of the late Duke of Northumberland, the old tower took on a new lease of life.

The key is obtainable at the sexton's house. The outside of the pele is extremely typical, with its high-pitched roof, its battlemented parapet crowning the rugged walls, its machicolations through the openings of which the walls could be defended, and, on one side, a projecting garde-robe. The stones are Roman-worked stones brought probably from the neighbouring ruins of *Corstopitum*.

The heavy entrance door is worthy of special notice—it is one of the few ancient grilles extant in the county, the spaces between the bars being filled with oaken planks. The interior of the tower shows domestic arrangements that are rarely seen in such perfection. From the vaulted basement where the vicar stabled his horse, stored his goods, and kept his liquid refreshment nice and cool, a stair mounts in the thickness of the wall to the upper rooms. On the first floor landing is a stone table with a wash basin, and the door beside it leads into the living-room, which has a wide fireplace, some useful wall cupboards, and some attractive-looking window-seats. The floor above, of the study-bedroom, is gone. Near a small window in the west wall is a stone book-rest, so slanted as to catch the light. With so many aids to the imagination, it is not difficult to picture life in this medieval tower.

BAXTER

CORBRIDGE PELE TOWER
(Map II, F7.)

Apart from the vicarage pele in the churchyard, this tower, now part of a comfortable-looking residence, is the oldest in the village. It stands at the east end of the main street, where the road narrows, and is recognisable by the taller tower at one end, and by a sundial, dated 1700, over the entrance.

The tower, which is probably four hundred and fifty years old at least, was built by one of the Baxter family, prominent in Corbridge at that time, and for long was known as Baxter's Tower. One of the Baxters, called Alexander, was a setter and searcher of the watch against the Scots in 1552.

In entering the tower from the adjoining house by the original entrance, there is first a small lobby, from which a straight stair goes up in the thickness of the wall, and a door ahead admits to the vaulted basement, with a loophole in one wall. The window looking on to the road probably occupies the position of another loophole. The stair turns into a spiral in the two upper storeys, and there are loopholes lighting it. The adjoining house, till recently known as the Low Hall, was probably built by one Richard Gibson in the seventeenth century, but later its big mullioned windows and some that had been inserted in the upper part of the tower were replaced with the present smaller ones. At the same time a gabled projection was built on to the rear of the tower. The outlines of the older windows are easily traceable. The window-tax of the period probably accounted for this alteration. Only dwellings with not more than six windows were exempt, providing the tenant was so poor that he could not pay church or poor rates. A little over a hundred years ago the tax was three shillings per window, licensed chapels and dairies being tax free. To escape the tax it was not enough merely to put up shutters or board up the window—the alteration had to be made permanently, after due notice to the Government Surveyor, in brick or stone or material similar to that of which the house was built.

One of the Gibsons took part in the '15 Jacobite Rising and as a result was attainted of high treason, lost most of his estate, and died in the Fleet prison in the same year. An interesting reminder of a remoter period is a slab built into the lower part of the outside wall of the tower. Brought from the neighbouring Roman town of *Corstopitum*, it is incised with part of an inscription in very fine characters to the emperor Marcus Aurelius Antoninus, probably the earliest of that name.

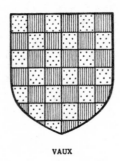

VAUX

WALLACE

COUPLAND CASTLE
(Map II, B7.)

Coupland Castle has a situation that seems to call for a Border tower, and a strong one at that. It stands on the edge of fair Glendale, a frequent objective of Scottish raiders, and at the junction with the Till of the College Water, the valley of which, running far back into the hills, formed an admirable passage for the moss-troopers of Ale and Bowmont Waters. Yet, strangely, there does not appear to have been a castle here till after the Union of the two countries. From early times, however, the Couplands have figured largely in Border affairs, having been mighty warriors. Perhaps the greatest of them was that John de Coupland who commanded a hundred men-at-arms at the battle of Neville's Cross in 1346, and had the honour of capturing the Scottish king. The chronicler of the time records that the knight rushed at King David and dashed the axe out of his hand, but the royal fighter let fly with his gauntleted hand, removing two of the worthy John's teeth. It was an unequal fight since the king was already sorely wounded in the leg and the face. Coupland rode with his prize to Ogle and thence, some say, to Bamburgh ; and was eventually rewarded for his gallant behaviour with an annuity of £600, quite a fortune then. Later he held many honourable positions, among them Sheriff of Northumberland, Warden of the East Marches, Constable of Roxburgh Castle and Sheriff of Roxburgh ; and like many other good Borderers, died " on his feet," but at the hands of an Englishman, not a Scot.

The Wallaces who succeeded the Couplands at Coupland probably built the castle—in one room the long, stone chimney-piece is carved with the initials, G. W. and M. W. (George and Mary Wallace), and the date 1619—sixteen years after the Union, but this only sheds a light on the uncertainty of existence on the Border even then. Subsequent owners of the castle included the Ogles and the Earl of Durham, and they altered the house in various ways in accordance with advancing ideas of comfort ; but the place still forms a picturesque break in the Border

73

landscape beneath the high mass of Yeavering Bell, that fine Cheviots bastion crowned with a Celtic fortress.

The oldest part of the castle consists of two square-built towers with walls six to seven feet thick. The vaulted basement of one tower is now used as a kitchen, and in another the stairway to the cellars is guarded by an iron gate, while the great oven remains in what was once the bakehouse. Upstairs is a private chapel and—a haunted room ! This is the room, already referred to, with the inscribed chimney-piece. The ghost is obscure in its methods. There are, or used to be up to Christmas 1925, " heavy, dragging footsteps," and " things that go bump in the night." A winding stair of peculiar corkscrew design goes up to the leads, emerging from a " pepperbox " turret (an unusual feature on this side of the Border) to give a magnificent view, and an opportunity of picking out some of those " scenes of blood " so enthusiastically listed by Sir Walter Scott on one occasion when he was staying in the neighbourhood—Flodden and Homildon, Ford and Etal and many other unnamed and forgotten spots where English and Scottish slogans rang out above the clash of battle-axe and sword and the thunder of hooves and the whine of the swift arrow.

HORSLEY

CRASTER TOWER
(Map II, C9.)

Craster Tower stands secluded among its dark and clustered trees a little inland from the little fishing village of Craster, which is six miles to the north-east of Alnwick. The house, for such it is now, having been added to considerably from time to time, can be seen from the entrance gates ; but it is a private residence and the interior is not usually shown.

A unique feature of the tower is that it is inhabited by the same family that possessed it in Saxon times ; which means that the Crasters have been in continuous occupation here for at least nine hundred years! After the battle of Hastings Northumbria held out stubbornly against William the Conqueror; and when his knight Robert de Commines, and his followers were massacred in Durham, and York was subsequently taken by storm, William hastened northwards with wrath in his heart. In the north he laid everything waste before him, burning Tynedale and plundering Berwick, and leaving the country between Humber and Tweed such a waste that it was not worth while surveying for the *Domesday Book*, After this terrible vengeance only a very small number of English landowners were allowed to retain their possessions. Among them were the Crasters.

In those times and later, the name was spelt Craucester or Crawster—hence the crest of the family, a raven or crow, embodying a pun on the name. In a similar way, the well-known Northumbrian family of the Greys have a scaling-ladder for their crest, the Old French word, *gré*, meaning a flight of steps.

The oldest part of the house, the ancient tower, like the base of Proctor Steads tower not far away is massively constructed of basalt or whinstone, which is plentiful in the district; and the vaulted basement stable is now used, not unworthily, as a cellar.

CRASTER (OR CRAWSTER)

†§ CRAWLEY TOWER
(Map II, C.8.)

Crawley Tower itself will probably be found rather disappointing. The site, however, is a most interesting one·; and the views from the spot are worth while.

To reach Crawley Tower we follow a green lane from Powburn, on the main road nine miles south of Wooler. The way leaves at the south side of the bridge, twists to pass under the railway, then climbs steeply. The surface is rough, and a better approach, if more round-about, is from the road passing Hedgeley Hall.

At a very early time Crawley was in possession of the Heron family, one of whom in 1343 obtained permission from Edward III to crenellate or fortify Crawley. David Dippie Dixon in his book, *Whittingham Vale*, records that he had the pleasure in 1893 of being entertained by a William Heron, then living in the tower of his ancestors. In the Survey of 1541 Crawley was reported to be in great decay for lack of continual repair, but it continued to be a residence after the union of the two countries.

One tenant in the good old days was the possessor of a remarkably fine white horse—a valuable asset on his frequent excursions " over the Border." So famed was this steed that on one occasion its owner was offered in exchange for it the Crawley estate itself. Said the stout Borderer, " I can *find* lands when I have use for them, but there is no sic a beast i' yon side o' the Cheviot, nor yet o' this, and I wadna' part wi' him if Crawley were made o' gold."

The tower today shows signs of considerable decay, and has been very much altered within. On the south side will be seen some of the small original windows, two of them with lancet-headed lights separated by a stone mullion. The masonry is very massive, but extremely uneven in texture, as if it has been extensively repaired from time to time. The tower stands on the edge of a Roman station, the site, too, of a Celtic fortress, and the ancient ditches, still quite distinct, must have helped in the defence of the stronghold. The Roman road known as the " Devil's Causeway " passes the spot. From this elevated ridge the Vale of Whittingham and that of the Breamish are spread out map-like to the gaze, and the great bastions of the Cheviots rise, dark and forbidding, a mile or two away.

CREST OF THE
BLACK PRINCE

CRESSWELL

†§ CRESSWELL TOWER
(Map II, D9.)

This fine specimen of an ancient pele stands close to the sea, at the south end of Druridge Bay, one of the most beautiful stretches of sand on the Northumbrian coast.

The basement of the tower, which is at least six hundred years old, is a vaulted stable, as is usual in these buildings ; and a wheel-stair goes up to two rooms above, the second of them, which has a garde-robe recess in the thickness of the wall, probably having been the living-room. The roof is in good condition, having been cemented and tiled by the late owner, Mr. Wardill. The doorways in the roof-turret still retain their hinges. Round the turret window is an inscription which is supposed to read, " William Cresswel, brave hero," but has become indecipherable through exposure to the salt-laden winds.

The Cresswells were seated here in very early times, Robert de Cresswell having been in possession of the manor as far back as the reign of Richard I. The manor-house they built in the eighteenth century was demolished to make way for a more modern mansion noted for its remarkably beautiful staircase, but this too has gone, some of the finely-chiselled sandstone blocks having been used in the recent extension of Whitton Tower.

A legend of the Cresswell family takes us back to Saxon times. The lovely daughter of the house and a young Danish prince, an enemy of her country, had lost their hearts to each other. Risking all for an opportunity of seeing his loved one once more and perhaps of carrying her away " over the foam," the gallant Dane came in his ship to the bay. His lady had long been on the tower top, watching and waiting for him, but her eyes had barely brightened in recognition as he stepped ashore when her three brothers rushed down to oppose him, and the young man was slain in the fight that followed. Henceforth the heart-broken lady wished only to die, and refusing all food, soon faded away. But since then the wistful white-clad ghost has often come back to keep vigil on the roof of the old tower.

77

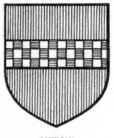

LINDSAY

† DALLY CASTLE
(Map I, E4.)

Dally Castle, on a knoll by the side of the Chirdon Burn, a tributary of the North Tyne above Bellingham, is an interesting reminder of the times when North Tynedale was part of Scotland, and its Sessions were held on the motehill at Wark.

The estate of Chirdon was given in 1221 to a Scottish knight, David de Lindsay, by the sister of Alexander III, who encouraged this knight to build a castle ; and before long Hugh de Bolbec, Keeper of Northumberland, was writing to his sovereign pointing out that the place had remarkably thick walls already the height of the parapet walks, which were completed, and that the intention was to add battlements and surround the place with a moat, in which case it would prove an excellent rallying-post for those of Scotland who had sinister designs on Northumberland. There is little doubt that this was the Scottish King's intention, or that the castle was used in this way by both Wallace and Bruce in their devastating raids on Tynedale before the end of that century.

Dally Castle has its sad legend. Its owner's sister loved and was loved by her brother's enemy, Gilbert of Tarset. A secret assignation was surprised by the lord of Dally, who wrathfully pursued Gilbert across the Tyne and up to the heights of Hareshaw Common, before overtaking him. There on the lonely moor a homeric fight followed—both were men of giant stature—and Gilbert of Tarset was slain. The spot known today as " Gib's Cross " commemorates his fall.

David de Lindsay's stronghold, once so formidable, is now little more than a site, washed by the burn and looking out over the fair vale of the North Tyne.

RADCLIFFE

†§ DILSTON CASTLE
(Map II, F7.)

The ruins of Dilston Castle, perched among its trees high above the Devil's Water two and a half miles east of Hexham, will always be associated with that gallant and tragic young figure, James Radcliffe, the last Earl of Derwentwater, who lost his life in the Jacobite cause. On the night before his execution the Arora Borealis was particularly brilliant in the sky beyond the Tyne. The coincidence was taken as a portent, and ever since the mysterious rays have been known locally as "Lord Derwentwater's Lights."

The young earl had not been long in possession of his estate in the fateful year 1715, when his lady, it is said, persuaded him against his better judgment to ride with the supporters of James Stuart. His heart, however, was in the cause. A Stuart himself (by a natural daughter of Charles II), he had been brought up with the "Pretender" at the court of the exiled James II, and probably did not take a deal of persuading. Only a few months after he bade farewell to his countess and their young baby, and to "pleasant Dilston Hall," and rode off along Dere Street, his embalmed body was brought back to the little chapel hard by the castle; and afterwards the superstitious country folk whispered that his wraith had been seen wandering in the woods beside the Devil's Water, or that a ghostly beacon light had been seen shining from the ruined tower to guide him home.

The Devil's Water below the castle walls is not so sinister as it sounds—it perpetuates the name of the d'Eivills, the owners of the barony in early Norman times. Later their name was altered to Dyvelston, and it was a Sir Thomas of that ilk who, as Sheriff of Northumberland, built the castle in the reign of Edward III. The old fortress was decayed when Sir Francis Radcliffe built his mansion nearly three hundred years later, but he used the site, and a tower of the castle was built into the new house. When, after the Jacobite rising, the vast Derwentwater estates were forfeited to the Crown, the place was neglected and gradually fell into ruin, a process helped by the taking of stone and timber for local building purposes. The "Golden Lion" in Corbridge was built of material from Dilston.

In 1768 the ruins were the stage for an extraordinary spectacle. In the room which had once been the nursery, beneath a tarpaulin stretched across to keep out the rain and with the windows filled with straw or screened with canvas, a woman who claimed to be the great grand-daughter of the last Earl had installed herself with two servants, while overhead from the tower flagstaff waved the banner of the Derwentwaters. The self-styled countess had already vainly petitioned the Government for the return of the family estates, and had now chosen this method of establishing the justice of her claim, which was backed up by her possession of various relics, jewellery, furniture and plate that had belonged to the Radcliffes. Her ladyship, however, was ejected, not without a struggle in which she herself swung a sword right and left. For some time longer she continued to live near the spot in a shed erected at the roadside by her friends; then she was moved on again by the Hexham magistrates. The claims of this remarkable woman were widely believed, and she had the sympathy of many people in the district, as witness the following lines by a local bard:

" To think that a Stuart so strangely should roam
       With a pallet of straw for her bed !
  Then stir up the nation its duty to own,
       For a Radcliffe we know her to be ;
  And her claims must be righted, her wrongs be made known,
       In England the land of the free."

The old castle tower is still standing, with "dungeons" in its basement, and with a pepper-box turret rising high above the battlements. The clearing away of debris in the last century revealed, close to the castle, the massive foundations and parts of the walls of the Norman fortress of the d'Eivills. In some of the rooms there were wooden pegs for the hanging of wall tapestries, in the fashion of those days. Where the ground drops away towards the river on the west side of the tower are the remains of two subterranean passages. One of these is supposed to have communicated with an underground chamber, from which steps led through the rock down to the level of the stream, an arrangement which, if imaginary, may have been suggested by the last Earl's necessity for secretive movement and even concealment in the period before his last venture.

Today the ruins, though fragmentary, are well-cared for, and would be picturesque apart from their romantic situation high above as lovely a stream as flows through Hexhamshire.

MUSGRAVE

† DODDINGTON BASTLE
(Map II, B7).

It is a pity that more care has not been accorded this old house which, now roofless and ruinous, was until fairly recent years a perfect and interesting example of Border architecture three hundred and fifty years ago.

Doddington, three miles north of Wooler, was once quite a considerable place that could supply forty able-bodied horsemen for Border defence, and boasted of a weekly cattle-market, yet it was not till only nineteen years before the peace between the two countries that the house was built. In the same year Sir Thomas Grey of Chillingham, its builder, helped to compile a Report on the castles and towers of the Eastern Marches. The size and style of the place show it to have been more a fortified house than a pele, and it must have supplied a fair degree of comfort, though the windows are rather small. There are three storeys reached by a wheel-stair in the projecting turret on the south side, and the side walls were battlemented, protecting a parapet walk. But the walls were weak—the bonding of the facing-stones with the core was not sound, and in spite of enormous buttresses against the north wall, the whole of the east end of the building collapsed in a gale during the winter of 1896. The days of Doddington Bastle are numbered.

DRAWDYKES " CASTLE "
(Map I, G2.)

A little over two miles from Carlisle on the road to Brampton by way of Stanwix stands this " castle " that is not a castle, but a picturesque and strongly-built pele built in the thirteenth century, and adjoined nowadays by a modern farmhouse. It stands almost on the line of the Roman Wall, a slight hollow in the drive marking the depression of the Vallum. The tower has been partly rebuilt, and the pedimented windows are comparatively modern, but one of the old mullioned windows remains at the rear ; and an inscription over an inner doorway

81

is generally supposed to refer to Alan de Peniton (or Pennington) who was mayor of Carlisle in 1287.

The parapet is adorned with three large busts, popularly but mistakenly supposed to be of Roman origin, and said to portray (reading from left to right) Captain Aglionby (a one-time owner of the tower), a local attorney, and, last but not least, his Satanic Majesty! Beneath the centre bust appear the Aglionby arms (three eaglets) and the date, 1676. Built into the rear wall of the tower is an especial antiquarian treasure—a Roman tombstone probably brought from the Roman station at *Stanwix*. One translation of the epitaph reads: " To the Divine Shade of Marcus Trojanus Augustinus, his most loving wife, Aelia Ammilia Lusima, caused this tomb to be erected." One can make out a lion on each side at the top, and a female head within the pediment, surprisingly clear after fifteen hundred years or so of the English climate.

AGLIONBY

Plate VIII

ALNHAM AND EMBLETON VICARAGES; HOLLOWS TOWER;
PONTELAND TOWER, NOW THE "BLACKBIRD" INN

Plate IX

DUNSTANBURGH—THE GATE-HOUSE

Plate X

WHITTINGHAM TOWER ; LONGHORSLEY PELE ;
COCKLE PARK TOWER

Plate XI

THIRLWALL CASTLE; CAMBO PELE;
SHITTLEHEUGH PELE

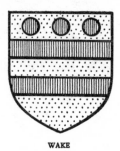

WAKE

† DUDDO TOWER
(Map II, A7.)

Duddo Tower is something of a mystery, though not very much of it remains to be anything at all! Its shattered ruin crowns a prominent position beside the road from Berwick to Ford, and only about three miles from the Border. The rocky knoll from which it gets its name (" dod "—hill; " hoe "—height) commands a fine view of Border country, from the Merse and the Lammermuirs beyond the Tweed round to the Cheviots and Flodden Hill on this side of it.

The mystery referred to concerns the exact identity of this tower. Is it really the old stronghold of the Lords of Till-mouth? That tower was cast down, along with many others in Glendale, by James IV in his expedition to support Perkin Warbeck, a false claimant to the English throne. True, half of it was reported as standing sixty years later, but the present ruin appears to be of later date—indeed, the " pepper-box " turret, corbelled out from the angle above the main entrance, suggests that the present tower was built after the Union of Scotland and England.

From the crudely-built entrance which has been guarded by a stout door, a stair goes up in a square turret projecting from the south side, and now spectacularly rent from top to bottom. Above the doorway and below an arch, is a recess probably intended for an armorial panel. Originally the tower was about thirty-six feet square, and it was protected by a barm-kin. There are coal-workings below the site, and they may account for the ruinous condition of the buildings.

At one time Duddo was in the possession of the Claverings, then it passed to the Greys of Wark. We have a sidelight on the fortunes of William Clavering who was here till 1586. In November of that year he was involved in a skirmish with some of his enemies, one of whom left him " so craysed and sore wounded in his bodye " that he knew his time to be short, and with his dying breath told how he wished his possessions to be disposed of. This solemn declaration had the effect of a will, but in times so violent one would have thought the Borderer would have been already prepared for such an emergency.

LILBURN

* DUNSTANBURGH CASTLE
(Map II, C9.)

Like Bamburgh, Dunstanburgh stands on a high rock on the sea coast. But it has no village beneath its walls. Isolated, remote, encrusted with sea spume, the shattered ruins possess a majesty that is unexcelled.

The castle, which is under the care of H.M. Office of Works, lies seven miles to the north-east of Alnwick, and can be approached from Craster, the nearest village, by a footpath along the coast; or, less easily, from Embleton by crossing the golf-course.

In the romantic swell of its great Gate-House turrets Dunstanburgh is like no other in the North Country; and one is hardly surprised to learn that it was the work of a romantic person, the Earl of Lancaster, High Sheriff of England in the reign of Edward II, who, steeped in ancient lore, dreamed wistfully of recreating the days of King Arthur and of raising on this rocky height a second Joyous Garde. The northern clergy helped him to realise his imaginings; but " o'erweening ambition " brought him into conflict with the king, and Dunstanburgh was barely completed when the Earl was executed as a traitor in the hall of his castle at Pontefract. Under a later distinguished owner, John of Gaunt, "time-honoured Lancaster," considerable alterations were made with a view to strengthening the castle against the Scots; then Gaunt's son made himself King Henry IV, and Dunstanburgh became a royal castle.

But the Wars of the Roses were approaching, which were to spell the doom of Dunstanburgh in numerous attacks. Sir Ralph Percy, the " Falcon of Dunstanburgh," wavering in his allegiance, delivered the castle first to the Yorkists then to the Lancastrians, but later it was recaptured by the Earl of Warwick, that famous maker—and unmaker—of kings. Finally, we hear of lead being taken from the castle roofs for the repair of Wark Castle upon Tweed, a stronghold which was destined, however, to become even more ruinous than Dunstanburgh.

84

In 1550 Sir Robert Bowes reported the castle to be in " wonderful great decay," but little or nothing was done to remedy this, since there were castles nearer to the Border with prior claims to attention ; and Dunstanburgh was finally abandoned.

The main entrance to the castle now faces south. Approaching from Craster, we see the great round towers flanking the gateway, and a long high length of curtain wall

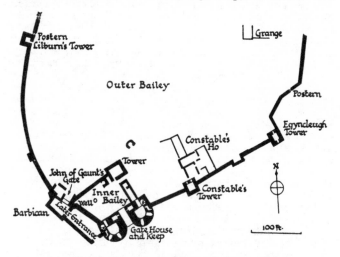

PLAN OF DUNSTANBURGH CASTLE

stretching to the right as far as a tower on the very verge of the cliff. This tower is known locally as " Queen Margaret's Tower " after the heroine of the Wars of the Roses, from a tradition that she made her escape from it during her adventurous wanderings in the north, but the story has, alas! no foundation in historical records. The old name of the tower is " Egyncleugh " after the great chasm nearby, up which in stormy weather the great breakers shoot their spray to a tremendous height.

Returning to the entrance, we must imagine it in John of Gaunt's time to be completely built up, and the only way in then to be a passage to the left of the western tower leading alongside the main wall to a gateway on the west side. An outer wall guarded this approach. The effect of this change was to turn the Gate-House into a keep. Entering it, under the arch near the inner side we notice the grooves of a portcullis. On either hand is a porter's lodge, and on the first floor above is a room from which the portcullis was worked. On the second floor was the Great Hall, a spacious chamber lit by two well-proportioned windows at each end.

Within the Gate-House is the inner ward, where the kitchen and bakehouse stood, and a well, still containing five feet of water, sunk through the basalt by the process of removing portions of the vertical basalt columns. Two dovecote-like structures on the inner face of the Gate-House are the terminations of the chimneys of the porter's lodges—really stone cowls to stop the fires from smoking ! Next to the Inner Ward is John of Gaunt's gateway. It was guarded by a barbican, or external tower. Further along the curtain wall rises the tall Lilburn Tower, probably built when John Lilburn was Constable of the Tower six hundred years ago. Near it is a postern gate made about the same time, and round the base of the tower are clustered some basalt pinnacles, sticking up like great fangs. The wall ends at the edge of the precipitous Gull Crag, then for some distance it has been destroyed by the sea. On the east side the wall recommences, but is of poor construction and materials as far as the Egyncleugh where " Queen Margaret's " Tower stands, a spectacular ruin. Its gateway leads out across the moat, here cut in the rock. One more tower—the Constable's—stands between here and the Gate-House. Behind it are the foundations of the Constable's house. There are traces of other buildings in the huge bailey. One circular structure may have been a kiln ; and on the east side there are remains of what was probably the castle Grange or farmstead, which was described as having a great oak barn. In the grassy hollow to the west of the castle hill is the site of the great moat, eighty feet wide and eighteen feet deep, which was completed by Michaelmas, 1314, the year of Bannockburn. The gateway was going up at the same time. At its southern end the moat is supposed to have communicated with a little harbour, now completely filled up. The " port of Dunstanburgh " is more than once referred to in history. Once part of the fleet of Henry VIII took refuge in it in a storm. This supposed site seems inadequate, unless the level of the land was considerably lower in former days. Can the port, after all, have been that of Craster ?

As a castle, Dunstanburgh had a curiously brief existence compared with the time it has been a ruin. For two hundred years it fulfilled its functions of defence and defiance. It is twice as long since " the tumult and the shouting " died away about its shattered walls.

WALDEN

† EDLINGHAM CASTLE
(Map II, C8.)

Edlingham Castle lies beside that lonely road from Alnwick to Rothbury. In the hollow before the Wooler road is crossed, you see the broken tower a little to the north, beyond the Edlingham Burn. In spite of the latter, the position does not seem very strong, but formerly the barmkin around it was further strengthened by a ditch of water introduced from the burn. A stile beside the church admits to a path to the spot.

Built in the twelfth century, the castle was held in HenryII's reign by John, son of Walden, for the annual rent of a soar-hawk or, in default, sixpence, payable to the lord of the barony. In the sixteenth century the castle passed into the possession of the Swinburnes of Nafferton. An inventory in connection with the will of the son of the purchaser sheds interesting light on the lives of our ancestors nearly four hundred years ago. The furniture of the bedrooms appears to have consisted of little except beds, generally " complete with feather beds, bolsters and pillows." The kitchen was well equipped with " 2 pots, 2 pans, 2 spits, a frying-pan, 15 'peuder platers,' 13 pewter dishes, 7 saucers, 4 plates, a charger or two, a 'basing,' a pestle and mortar, a pair of tongs, 'wan sylver salt, parcell gilt,' and ' wan dozen of sylver spoons '," the whole valued at £8. As for the deceased's dress, it would be accounted effeminate and showy by modern standards. His doublet, for instance, was of satin overlaid with silver lace, and had velvet sleeves ; and a velvet cloak, a velvet hat and a satin gown are also listed. The pride of his possessions however were two " fine horses," a white one being valued at £10, and a black at £8.

When the Swinburnes ceased to reside in the castle they kept an agent in it, and one of these in 1682 had some distressing experiences, for he was plagued by a witch called Margaret Stothard. At least, so the said John Mills deposed before a magistrate, when the alleged witch was brought to trial. Mills solemnly attested that, " lying awake one Sunday night, he, the said informant, did heare a great blast of wind, as he thought, goe by his window, and immediately following there was something fell with a great weight upon his heart, and gave a great crye like a catt, and then after another in the same manner, and just as those was ended there appeared a light at his bedd foot, and did in the same light see Margaret Stothard, or her vission, to the best of his knowledge ; so the poure of this informant's speech being taken from him at the time, and as soon as ever he recovered strenth to speake, he cryd out ' The Witch, the Witch ! ' "

On another occasion, to prevent the hair on his head from standing " on end upwards," he had to jump out of bed and read his Bible. Today such evidence has a humorous side, but it cannot have been anything but a life-and-death matter for the poor old eccentric woman accused. She seems, however, to have been acquitted of the charge.

The barmkin of the castle, enclosing the domestic buildings, has almost disappeared, and a gate-tower is just traceable ; but the ruins of the tower itself have some very interesting features. The basement where Swinburne's two fine horses were probably stabled is barrel-vaulted in the usual manner ; but what is not so usual is that the roof of the room above, perhaps the " brode chambre " mentioned in the inventory already quoted, has been beautifully groined, the arches resting on corbels in the corners. These corbels are quaintly carved with heads. The windows, widely splayed on account of the thick walls, are provided with seats. The fireplace, too, is of great interest—the lintel, now fallen, has been formed of " joggled " stones, like one in Ferniehirst Castle, the stones being designed to interlock one with another. Altogether, this must have been a fine apartment. In a projecting turret on the north side of the castle will be seen the remains of a newel-stair that went to the upper storeys— to the " wainscoted room," the " paynted chambre," and others now indistinguishable in the broken interior.

BABINGTON

HOWARD

§ ELSDON " CASTLE "

(Map II, D–E7.)

Elsdon *Tower* is a more appropriate name for this fortlet. since it is, indeed, a Border pele ; and, moreover, a very fine specimen with some unusual features that make it of outstanding interest, especially as the rector of Elsdon (the tower is the rectory) kindly affords facilities to visitors who wish to see the interior.

The village of Elsdon lies in some seclusion among the hills three miles east of Otterburn, its dwellings fringing the village green dominated by the grey old tower, whose apparent height is increased by its commanding position on the bank of the Elsdon Burn. So for some five hundred years it has with-stood weather and foes alike. It was one of the Norman Umfravilles who built the tower, and their arms, showing a cinquefoil and eight crosses and supported by two wolves each bearing a sword upright, were perhaps placed on the exterior wall in the time of that Sir Robert de Umfraville who was known to the Redesdale men as " Robin-mend-the-market " from the success that attended his forays over the Border. He lived in the fifteenth century, but the Umfravilles had held Redesdale, with Tynedale, ever since the Norman Conquest when William the Conqueror gave these lands to the Umfra-villes " to hold by defending for ever from wolves and enemies with the sword which William had by his side when he entered Northumberland." Hence the wolves with swords as supporters of their arms. The stronghold of those early days was probably a palisaded structure crowning one of the Mote Hills on the other side of the Elsdon Burn. The Umfraville castles of Harbottle and Prudhoe came later. As far back as the fifteenth century the pele-tower was in use as a rectory, as it is today.

Some of the rectors of Elsdon have been men of distinction. There was the Rev. C. Dodgson, afterwards Bishop of Ossery, who was incumbent from 1762 to 1765. His successor, the Rev. Louis Dutens, a Frenchman, was Historiographer to the King, an Honorary Member of the French Academy, and a writer of some note. It was he who was responsible for the lovely plaster work decorating the basement ceiling and made other additions to the amenities of the house, possibly not unforgetful of what his predecessor had written regarding the discomforts of life in a pele-tower: " The vestibule of the castle is a low stable, and above it is the kitchen, in which there are two little beds joining to each other. The curate and his wife lay in one, and Margery, the maid, in the other. I lay in the parlour, between two beds, to keep me from being frozen to death, for, as we keep open house, the winds enter from every quarter, and are apt to creep into bed to one."

Archdeacon Singleton was another distinguished rector here, about a hundred years ago, and it may have been in his time that the comfortable and handsome house was built to adjoin the tower. A high wall round the pleasant garden represents the old barmkin, a defence that formerly must have been essential to a place so near the Border.

The Umfravilles' are not the only arms on the exterior of the tower. One wall shows a very old Percy device—that of five *fusils*; and on another wall will be seen the Percy crescent (the Duke of Northumberland is the patron of the living); and the Howard arms appear high up under the battlements. The Howard arms appear also on the arch of the main entrance. Round the porch here (a later addition) is a curious frieze showing the Percy bugle and fetterlocks; while the Percy lion, the arms of the Umfravilles, and the three pikes or " luces " of the Lucys appear on three shields over the arch. What was once the stable for horses is now a dignified apartment, the vaulted ceiling of which is finely groined in plaster, worked in Italian style into decorative bosses and panels. The newel-stair to the upper floors starts just within the entrance and goes up in the thickness of the wall, which is nine feet six inches thick. The stair winds to the right, not in the usual direction, and only left-handed men could have found it easy to defend, but part-way up there is a trip-step—one higher than the rest—which would surprise an enemy in haste. On the first floor there is more plaster work showing the Percy lion and the Lucy pikes on a series of shields. Above this level two floors have been made into one. A battlemented walk goes along three sides of the gabled, stone-tiled roof, and we can look down on the entrance and note how it is additionally guarded by projecting machicolations, down which hot lead or similar discouragement could be poured. From this airy position, too, there is an extensive view of Border country, almost as lonely today as it was five hundred years ago.

LUCY

EMBLETON TOWER
(Map II, C9.)

Like several other peles in Northumberland, the tower at Embleton is part of the vicarage. The village is almost on the coast, being separated from it only by a low ridge. The great castle of Dunstanburgh is in sight not far away; and the road from Warkworth to Bamburgh passes through the village.

The defensive additions to the tower date from the year 1385 when the vicar was granted leave to crenellate or fortify his residence. The step was a very necessary one. The village, like most others in the county, was in constant danger of Scottish visitations, and only the year before the church and vicarage had been badly damaged by raiders who " lay in the fields of Emeldon and did great destruction "; and subsequently the villagers were advised to remove the roofs from their dwellings, so that an approaching force of Scots would pass them by to seek " pastures new."

At a later period there were still later additions to the tower; but the greatest changes were made a little over a hundred years ago when a large and beautiful wing, to the designs of Dobson the celebrated Newcastle architect, was built. The church is in the patronage of Merton College, Oxford. A former illustrious incumbent was the Rev. Mandell Creighton, later Bishop of London, and a notable writer on historical subjects.

The tower has some very interesting features, among them some ancient fireplaces; and a secret chamber approached by a newel-stair and lit only by the merest crack in the massive walls. The doors to one of the rooms are fitted with *chatières*, i.e. small openings to allow the passage of a cat. From the " dungeons " in the basement, it is alleged, a secret underground passage leads to Dunstanburgh, but such legends, persistently told about ancient buildings, have rarely any foundation.

The exterior of the tower, neighboured by tall trees, is equally interesting, a picturesque addition being the projecting chimney, corbelled at the top. Some of the old windows, now blocked, are traceable, one of them being mullioned. The top of the tower is finely battlemented, and there are projecting spouts for roof drainage. In the glebe near the house stands an ancient dovecote with pantiled roof and a quaint little pent-house on either side.

After nightfall, during evening service, a curious effect may be observed on the rugged wall of the old tower—the shadow of a cross is thrown upon it from the grave of a previous vicar. A striking symbol of an ancient faith !

Visitors who wish to see the vicarage at closer quarters need only apply to the vicar who in his own words will be " only too delighted " to give them permission.

AYNSLEY

† ETAL CASTLE
(Map II, A7.)

The Till, that lovely tributary of the Tweed, slides past no more charming spot than Etal. At the end of the single street of cottages and gardens stands the castle, a solitary ruin these four hundred years and more, since the forces of James of the Iron Belt dismantled it on their way to Flodden Field.

The manor of Etal was held in Norman times by the Manners family, the ancestors of the present Dukes of Rutland, but it was not till Edward III's reign that Sir Robert de Manners, inspired perhaps by the new castle that William Heron, his neighbour, had just completed at Ford, made arrangements with the same masons to build a stronghold on the bank of the Till. It lasted not quite two hundred years. After Flodden it appears to have been allowed to lapse gradually into decay ; and today only the Gate-House, a part of the curtain wall, a tower and the Keep remain.

An interesting incident in the history of the castle occurred just after Flodden, when some of the very guns that had battered down the walls were, by an ironic chance, brought back there as the spoils of war.   At that time there was a bridge across the Till a little further upstream—the road to it from the castle can be traced as a green avenue through the trees.

The castle Gate-House, one of the most interesting in the county, is a massive and gloomy structure.   Above the arch is a time-worn, barred shield—the arms of the Manners family. Formerly the approach to the Gate-House was guarded by a moat and drawbridge.   A door in the wall on the first storey and projecting stones on either side of the arch indicate that formerly there was also some sort of outer defence work—a barbican, or perhaps a brattice (bretesche), a loopholed pent-house of wood attached to the front of the Gate-House.   In their place today are two ancient cannon from one of the " wooden walls " of England—the luckless *Royal George,* which foundered at Spithead in 1782 with the loss of about eight hundred men and officers.   Just within the gateway are the nine-inch square holes to take the ends of four beams, additional obstacles to any attack.   There are guard-rooms on either side of the archway ; and from the vaulted basement of one of them (that on the right, with a curious fireplace) a wheel-stair goes up to an upper chamber that has been well lighted by handsome mullioned and traceried windows.   From the Gate-House a stretch of curtain wall five feet thick runs along to a tower, the basement of which is finely vaulted.   The Keep is a mere shell but its main features are traceable.   It has had a portcullis, an unusual defence for so small a tower.   The basement has been strongly groined.   On the first floor a huge fireplace marks what was probably a kitchen ; and the third storey, indicated by rows of beam-holes in the walls, was very likely the Great Hall ; while the sleeping quarters were higher up still, access being by a wheel-stair on the east side.   On the north wall are a series of garde-robes.   The windows, generally speaking, are small.   Such is Etal Castle today—a romantic ruin in an idyllic setting.

MANNERS

FEATHERSTONEHAUGH

FEATHERSTONE CASTLE
(Map I, G4.)

Featherstone Castle has been described as one of the loveliest strongholds in the county of Northumberland, and few will disagree with this estimate. It lies in wooded seclusion on the south bank of the South Tyne, about three miles to the south-west of Haltwhistle ; and whether its turrets and battlements and ivied walls are seen in the distance or partially through the trees that neighbour it, the result is always a charming picture.

So well are the different portions blended that you would hardly guess that the latest is only about a hundred years old. There is, too, some typical Jacobean work, and at least two other distinct periods represented, the earliest being that of the simple, square pele-tower built by Helios (or Helias) Featherstonehaugh for safety against the raiding Scots. It is said that the name comes from the Feuder Stones, two monoliths on the hill nearby where in feudal times the tenants were wont to assemble. Be that as it may, the Featherstonehaughs were of very ancient lineage and occupied important positions during the Border wars ; and sometimes, too, were involved in local feuds as the well-known ballad by Surtees records. The ballad was a fake (a good one, for it deceived Sir Walter Scott, who used part of it in *Marmion*) but the event it records is historical— the slaying of Sir Albany Featherstonehaugh, High Sheriff of Northumberland, by some of the Ridley clan in 1530. Here is part of Surtees' rollicking poem :

" Hoot awa', lads, hoot awa',
    Ha' ye heard how the Ridleys, and Thirlwalls, and a'
    Ha' set upon Albany Featherstonhaugh,
    And taken his life at the Deadmanshaw ?
        There was Willemoteswick,
        And Hardriding Dick,
    And Hughie of Harden, and Will of the Wa',
    I cannot tell a', I cannot tell a',
    And mony a mair that the de'il may knaw.

．　　．　　．　　．　　．

Hoot, hoot, the auld man's slain outright !
Lay him now wi' his face down : he's a sorrowful sight.
    Janet, thou donot,
    I'll lay my best bonnet,
Thou gets a new gude-man afore it be night."

The Deadman's Haugh is only a mile or so from the castle, across the ford, and in sight from the battlements.

There was one foe at the advent of whom all local feuds were forgotten, and erstwhile enemies fought knee to knee to drive the intruder out, as witness this letter written by the Duke of Northumberland only two years after the killing of Albany Featherstonehaugh :

" The Rotherfordes, Carrs, Davysons, Pryngelles, Halles, Trumbills, Hunters, Robsons, Waughs and Wais, of Tyvydale and the Forest of Gedwurth [Jedburgh], being four hundred in number, . . . upon Tuesday at sunrising ran an open foray at Hawtwesil, within the middle march, seizing all manner of goods in the way as they came. The which manifest by shout and cry unto your inhabitants there nigh adjoining, Thomas Errington, constable of my poor barony of Langley, Alexander Featherstonehaugh, Robert Thyrlewell, with the tenants of Sir Nicholas Ridley to the number of six score persons, came to the rescue, . . . unto which, your Highness's said subjects, it has pleased God to give the victory, who hath wounded to death, as by appearance, six score, the least of them having a piece of a spear in him, or else one arrow, and also slain one Scot outright, called Ways ; and hath taken twelve of them." These twelve were duly hanged " upon Sunday next."

The Civil War, when it came, was to prove the undoing of the Featherstonehaughs, as it did that of many other Northumbrian families. Timothy Featherstonehaugh gained a knighthood from Charles I for his gallantry ; but paid for it later with his life, when he was executed after the defeat of the Royalists at Worcester. The estates, forfeited then, came back to the family, but not for long before they were purchased by the Wallace family whose crest, a lion, is so much in evidence at the castle.

The old tower is a typical pele, with a vaulted basement, and a fine, decorated doorway, with a pointed arch and carved corbels, at least seven hundred years old. After the peace between England and Scotland the castle was enlarged for comfort, but this work and later additions were well done, within and without. The dining-room is an especially charming apartment, with its carved woodwork (it used to be in Carlisle Cathedral), its period furniture, its decorated ceiling, its dignified family portraits, and its views of the lovely gardens.

Like Bellister and Blenkinsopp Castles hard by, Featherstone has its ghostly visitation, not by a solitary wraith, but by a whole party—a bridal party! The lady (legend affirms) had been wedded unwillingly, being really in love with a Ridley, an enemy of her house. After the ceremony in the castle chapel, a gay hunting party set out for the woods, promising to return before nightfall for the sumptuous banquet which was to be laid out in the baronial hall. During the chase, however, they were ambushed by the disappointed lover and his friends and all were slain, even the lovely bride herself in trying to come between her husband and her lover. Crazed with grief, the latter slew himself and his blood ran into a hollow stone, from which the corbies drank it with ghastly relish. Meanwhile in the Great Hall, where the tables groaned with their load, the baron awaited the return of the guests, but it was not till the stroke of midnight that the doors swung silently open to admit the bride and bridegroom and his friends, who silently glided to their seats, their faces ashen, their clothes torn and streaked with blood. To his horror the baron realised this was no earthly company, then as he crossed himself a cold blast swept the ghostly crowd away. Every year at the same dread hour, legend asserts, the hapless bridal party may be seen riding in at the castle gateway.

RUSSELL

§ FENWICK TOWER
(Map II, F8.)

Little remains of the old tower that was once the seat of one of the most celebrated families in the North Country. What is left of Fenwick Tower will be found in a farmyard at the hamlet of Fenwick halfway between Stamfordham and Matfen. It consists of a portion of an extremely thick wall, but it is surprising to find even this amount remaining, for treasure has been found here. In 1775 when the tower was being demolished to make way for a farmhouse, there was discovered beneath the floor of the vaulted basement a box containing over two hundred gold nobles of Edward III, Richard II and one of David II of Scotland. The coins were carefully packed on edge in sand so close together that they gave the impression, to the eyes of William Cooke, the astonished labourer who found them, of being solid bars of gold. The cavity that held the box was beneath a flagstone, above one of the arches of the cellar or dungeon. There the coins had remained for four hundred and fifteen years; for they were hidden by old Sir John Fenwick in 1360. News had come through that the Scottish king had crossed the Border bent on a great raid; and, moreover, two of Sir John's sons had been taken. The old man died shortly afterwards. Did he forget about his hoard? Another curious circumstance is that the coins were all practically new. There is material here for a writer of fiction.

In later years the Fenwicks, by purchase and by marriage, became wealthy landowners; and their clan was widespread. Their battle yell of " A Fenwick! a Fenwick! " was often to be heard in Border frays. In the ballad of *The Raid of the Reidswire* the minstrel records.

> " Five hundred Fennicks in a flock,
> With jack and speir and bowis all bent
> And warlike weapons, at their will."

A jack was a coat of mail.

One of the most popular of all the Fenwicks among his own people was rash enough to incur the intense dislike of his sovereign, William III. One uses the word rash because he appears to have earned that dislike most thoroughly. A staunch Jacobite, Sir John Fenwick was the leader of those who openly rejoiced when William suffered a reverse in his campaign against Louis XIV; and expressed his elation by his boorish behaviour to the Queen, swaggering before her when she took her walks in the royal park and, while others bowed, cocking his hat in her face with an insolent stare. William never forgot these unwarranted slights; and no doubt was swayed by their remembrance when, a few years later, he signed a bill of attainder for the execution of Sir John as a traitor, and remained adamant when Lady Mary Fenwick fell at his feet with a petition for her husband's life.

As it stands today, Fenwick Tower does not seem to have had a very strong position; but its name, which means the town in the fen, reveals that formerly it was protected by one of the best of all defences—an almost impassable morass, the few paths across which would be known only to men of the clan. The Fenwicks crenellated their house here by royal licence in 1378, but they were not here long before Wallington Hall took the place of the old tower as " the chiefest house of the Fenwicks."

§ FERNIEHIRST CASTLE
(Map I, C3.)

A little over a mile from Jedburgh along the Newcastle road that follows the wooded valley of the Jed, a byway to the left winds uphill through the trees to Ferniehirst Castle, a typical and most picturesque example of Scottish architecture at the close of the sixteenth century. It is now used as a Youth Hostel, thanks to the generosity of the Marquess of Lothian.

The *old* castle of Ferniehirst came into existence a hundred years before the present building, and was erected by Sir Thomas Ker. When, following the defeat of Flodden, the Scottish Border was ravaged, the Earl of Surrey reported the castle to be standing " marvellous strongly within a grete woode " (i.e. the Forest of Jedburgh) ; and it was taken only after " long skirmishing and moche difficultie." After the Scottish defeat at Pinkie, Ferniehirst, like many other castles along the Border, was in English hands, and the garrison made themselves detested by the cruelties and oppressions they practised on the country folk. Of the captain it was said by a French officer then campaigning in Scotland that " he never came across a young girl but he outraged her, never an old woman but he put her to death with cruel torture." Retribution came when the Sieur d'Essé with his French troops aided Sir John Ker to regain his castle. At first the garrison seemed like holding out in the keep, then a breach was made in the wall while French arquebusiers protected those who broke through. Seeing that the end was near, the captain of the garrison came out through the breach to try and obtain favourable terms for his men, but unconditional surrender was demanded of him. Meanwhile news of the attack had spread through Jed Forest, and man after man came hurrying to the spot for revenge. A bloodthirsty mob was clamouring in the courtyard when the English captain again appeared, this time to surrender himself to two French officers. Before they could lead their captive away, however, a Jeddart man who had good reason to execrate him sprang forward and with one sword-stroke smote his head from his shoulders. As the trunk sank to the ground other Scots came to bathe their hands in the blood, then they threw the head from hand to hand, and at length placed it on a pole to proclaim their vengeance. This was not the end of as grim and terrible a tale of slaughter as the Borders have witnessed. One by one the garrison were butchered piecemeal, the Scots vying with each other in the skill with which they could lop off limbs without inflicting a mortal wound ; and finally the few prisoners that the French had taken were purchased so that they could be tortured in a similar horrible manner. A French officer's account is that of an eye-witness. " I myself," he wrote, " sold them a prisoner for a small horse. They tied his hands and feet and head together, and placed him thus trussed in the middle of an open space, and ran upon him with their lances, armed as they were and on horseback. When the man was dead they cut his body into pieces and bore the mangled gobbets in triumph on the points of their spears." The writer deprecated the barbarous slaughter but almost thought it justified.

Twenty more or less peaceful years passed, then Sir Thomas Ker's sympathy with the cause of Mary Queen of Scots brought him and his castle under the stern notice of her English rival. He and Sir Walter Scott of Buccleuch and the Earl of Westmorland led a daring raid over the Border, and Queen Elizabeth, furious at the outrage, sent a punitive expedition under the Earl of Sussex and Lord Hunsdon. Ferniehirst received special attention. "We could nott blow up Farnhurst," ran the report, " but have so torne ytt with laborars, as ytt were as goode ley flatt."

Even so, the tough old castle was made defensible again, and would have existed today if it had not been for a rebellious intrigue of its owner with the Earl of Bothwell, as a result of which Ferniehirst was utterly demolished.

The present castle, built in 1598, was restored to its present condition by the Marquess of Lothian about thirty years ago. The exterior of the towered portion is relieved in the characteristic Scottish style with " pepper-box " turrets, one of them extending nearly to the ground in the angle between it and the long wing. Above the main entrance, which is canopied, carved stone panels in the wall bear the initials of Sir Andrew Ker (the builder) and his wife, Dame Ann Stewart, and the date 1598, together with their arms and the devout motto, " Forward in the name of God." The basement is vaulted. Among the many interesting features of this fine old house, there is on the first floor an unusual and magnificent fireplace, the lintel of it being composed of fifteen " joggled " stones (i.e. cut to form an interlacing and self-supporting whole), the total length being twelve feet.

Near the castle stands an imposing chapel decorated with a curious motif of oval bosses, and, as the panel over the door shows, appears to have been built at the same time as the castle, but is now in some decay owing to having been used formerly as a stable. To such base uses . . . !

LEMMINGTON

FORD CASTLE

(Map II, B7.)

Ford Castle is in the centre of one of the most romantic corners of the county—a corner that resounded to the drums and trumpets of Flodden and many another Border fray. At Ford we are only six miles from the Border. In sight of its turrets the Till flows sweetly on its way to the Tweed.

The mansion, built in the thirteenth century by Odinel de Forde, was one of those crenellated or fortified in the reign of Edward III at a time when the Scots, inspired by their victory at Bannockburn, were become very daring in their inroads on English soil. Ten years earlier they had wasted Northumberland with fire and sword to within four miles of Newcastle, and later they dealt with the Bishopric of Durham in like manner. With the king's encouragement, the knights and squires of the English Border began to build towers and curtain walls to defend their homes. The owner of Ford was Sir William Heron, Captain of the castles of Bamburgh, Pickering and Scarborough, Warden of the forests north of the Trent, and High Sheriff of Northumberland for eleven successive years; and, to boot, a doughty knight well able to fend for himself. Once when the Scots plundered him of £600 worth of cattle, he made a counter-foray on which his bag was 320 oxen, 1,600 sheep and £100 in money.

The popular story about Ford is that King James IV lost the battle of Flodden through dalliance with the Lady Heron of the time, and there is even shown the King's Bedroom communicating by a secret staircase with that of the fair lady; but like many such tales, it is not based on fact. Lady Heron spent the time before Flodden in getting the English commander's help to persuade James to spare the castle. James had promised to do this if two of his favourite knights were liberated, but although the Earl of Surrey agreed to the exchange, Ford was burnt after all. As for the King's Room, it probably got this name because it commands a view of Flodden Hill; and the inscription on the chimney-piece: " King James ye 4th of Scotland did lye here at Ford Castle A.D. 1513," is certainly of dubious authenticity. What about the secret staircase, then? Alas! that is merely one of the original stairs which was walled up at the time of the " ginger-bread Gothic " additions carried out by Sir John Hussey Delaval in 1761, and was later discovered when the Marchioness of Waterford restored the castle to make it one of the most beautiful houses in the county.

The estate passed from the Herons to the Carrs in romantic circumstances, following young Thomas Carr's stubborn and successful defence of one of the towers when a Scottish force under the Sieur d'Essé, a brilliant French commander, had battered most of the castle to pieces with four guns. Carr's gallant exploit found him favour in the eyes of the heiress and they were married ; though some blood was spilt before the young couple were allowed to settle down. The Herons wished to retain Ford, and a party of them were on their way to seize it when they were ambushed by Carr's supporters, and in the fray the mayor of Berwick (a Heron partizan) was slain " with xv blodye wounds uppon him."

The north-west tower of the castle, popularly known as King James's Tower, is its strongest part, and is probably the tower where brave Thomas Carr held out in 1549. In the basement is the dungeon, a vaulted room lit only by a small slit, and approached by a stairway covered with a trapdoor in the floor of the passage-way above. A stairway in the thickness of the wall goes up to the " King's Room." Originally the castle consisted of four towers joined by walls to form an inner court, a plan first adopted here in the North Country. The entrance formerly was not on the south side but the west, where the village then lay, close under the walls for safety ; a site now occupied by a garden designed on charmingly formal lines according well with the dignity of this fine old pile.

CARR

TAILBOIS

† GREAT TOSSON TOWER
(Map II, D7.)

The hamlet of Great Tosson looks out over Coquetdale from the side of the Simonside Hills, and can be approached from Rothbury, two miles away, by car or on foot by way of the footbridge half a mile upstream from Rothbury.

" At Great Tosson is a tower of the lorde Ogle's Inherytance, not in good rep'ac'ons." Such was the comment in the Survey of Border Towers carried out during the reign of Henry VIII, and today the pele is the merest shell, raising ragged walls thirty or forty feet above ground. Most of the facing-stones have been removed for local building, only a few remaining high up and fairly well out of reach, yet the rubble core of the walls, composed of small boulders taken from the Coquet and cemented endurably with hot lime, appears tough enough to defy a few more generations of time, that enemy more relentless even than the Scots.

The pele, one of the defensive line of towers and castles along the Coquet Valley, was originally in the Hepple barony, and was held in succession by De Hepples, Tailbois and Ogles, names to conjure with on the Border in the Troublesome Times. When, about the end of the thirteenth century, Hepple Tower was destroyed, possibly by Bruce, the Lords of Hepple held their courts at Tosson, which thus became a place of some importance. It was, of course, primarily intended for the protection of the villagers, and to that end watch and ward were kept so that they could be warned of the approach of the enemy. Under Lord Wharton's system, which he established as Lord Deputy General of the Marches, there had to be maintained at Great Tosson a watch at " the stelle-ende with two men nightly of the inhabitors of Mykle Tosson."

An inspection of the ruin will show slight traces of the vaulted basement and of a spiral stair in the north-east corner, the position of the entrance on the south side (as in most peles), and the enormous thickness of the walls, nine feet at least. There may have been a barmkin enclosing a space for cattle. Close under the walls flows a fine spring of water.

HALTON

HALTON TOWER

(Map II, F7.)

Halton Castle it is often called, and seems imposing enough to warrant that name. It really comprises three buildings— a pele-tower of the De Haltons, at least five hundred years old ; a picturesque manor-house adjoining it, with almost as long a history ; and a charming Jacobean house. A delightful garden adds to the peaceful appearance of this old place.

Halton is about two miles to the north of Corbridge, and almost on the line of the Roman wall. The De Haltons were settled here in Saxon times, and were one of the few English families in Northumberland to be left in possession of their estates after the Norman Conquest. As the years went on the De Haltons became gentlemen of some importance. One of the line, Sir John de Halton who was Sheriff of Northumberland, appears to have done also a " little shifting for a living," for in 1276 he was found guilty of having lifted the cattle of Thomas Fairbairn of Wark and by force of arms driven them to his mansion at Sewingshields ; but he was allowed to buy himself off by the payment of ten marks in silver to the said Thomas Fairbairn.

The last of the De Haltons died in 1345 and shortly afterwards, partly by the marriage of the heiress and partly on the principal that possession is nine-tenths of the law, the manor passed into the hands of the Carnabys, a family of Yorkshire origin with peculiar ideas of *meum* and *teum*. The Carnabys appear to have continued to add to their indifferent reputation. Perhaps the most sinister of them was Sir Reginald de Carnaby who in his official capacity had the power of life and death over any moss-troopers he captured. On one occasion his impatient exclamation of, " Oh, hang the fellow ! " when inquiries were made as to the disposal of a captive was taken so literally that the luckless Scot did not even have the formality of a trial. Sir Reginald (the name has a melodramatic sound) was the inveterate enemy of the Herons of Chipchase and may have been the original of the legendary Sir Reginald Fitzurse who was starved to death in a dungeon at that castle.

It is interesting to read how a Carnaby heir proved his coming of age on the 24th March, 1391. Various witnesses testified to the day of his baptism by relating what they did that same day. While hunting a hare, John Strother met the woman carrying the child to church; Richard Craster's horse came down under him as he was returning to Dilston after the christening; and as Nicholas Turpyn was riding home he saw, or thought he saw, a fox breaking out of a wood with the huntsmen after it.

The tombstone of William Carnaby, on the south side of the church, probably covers the last of the Carnaby race; but a good while before his death the fortunes of the family were low, their estates having been confiscated by the Commonwealth owing to their Royalist activities.

It is interesting to know the contents of the squire's bedchamber in Halton Tower three hundred years ago—" One low bed, with a cannibye [canopy], one mattresse and a feather bed, a paire of blanketts, one coverlett, one greene rug and a Courting belonging to the cannibye, two boulsters, one cubbert and a long sattle bed."

The old manor-house adjoining the tower is a picturesque structure, with tall chimneys, one of which is corbelled at its base below the eaves. Its main room is low-ceilinged and has oak beams. From it the tower can be entered by the original door, set in a pointed arch and with the evidences of " locks, bolts and bars " on its jambs. A second, inner, door leads into the great basement vault, from which a newel-stair goes up to the Tower Room on the first floor, a well-lighted apartment with curious wall-recesses in the corners. The slits in the walls of these recesses can be seen from outside. The second and third floors are now one. A very narrow stair emerges in a turret on the roof, which is battlemented in genuine style, with fine bartizan turrets at the corners. On the east face of the tower is an old shield carved with the Halton arms (two bars and three " roundels "), assumed by the Carnabys in preference to their own—as being more honourable ! The stones of the tower are worthy of particular notice—their size and shape show them to be Roman-worked stones from the nearby station of Hunnum, a settlement compared with which even this hoary tower is a youthful upstart !

§ HALTWHISTLE TOWERS
(Map I, F4.)

There are two old towers in Haltwhistle. As you go up into the town from the east side you see one of them on the right—the ancient " Tower of Hautwysel." It stands back from the road, its small windows and loopholed turret with that watchful look inseparable from old places of defence.

This is the old residence of the Bailiffs of Haltwhistle, mentioned as far back as 1415 in a list of a hundred and fifteen castles and towers of the Border; and over a hundred years

later described as being in the inheritance of Sir William
Musgrave and in measurable good reparations. Bailiffs acted
under the authority of the Warden of the March, and were often
leading figures in counter-attacks when freebooters were abroad
or when feuds had to be settled, as, for instance, is recounted
so racily in Surtees' well-known ballad about the Ridleys and
Thirlwalls " and a' ", who set upon Albany Featherstonehaugh
and took his life at the Deadmanshaugh (see the account of
Featherstone Castle, page 94).

Among the list of Bailiffs of Haltwhistle were Roger le
Tailleur, Nicholas Blenkinsop, John Ridley, who in his will
bequeathed his best ox to Lord William Howard of Naworth,
and Nicholas Ridley. The Ridleys were numerous in this part
of South Tynedale; and Bishop Ridley, the martyr, was a
member of the family.

As it stands today, the tower is still in good repair, thanks
perhaps to some alterations about fifty years ago, when the old
roof of stone flags pinned with sheep-shank bones was replaced,
and wood was substituted for some of the stone-flagged floors;
but even yet the place seems more suited for strength than
pleasant occupation. Though the rooms are large, they are
dim owing to the smallness of the windows, and the winding
stairs are so narrow that bailiffs who were men of girth must
have found them more than a little trying. The tower is still
inhabited, but the visitor need only be tactful to be allowed to
look through it.

The other tower of Haltwhistle is a pele-tower in the main
street, but is not easy to recognise since its front was modernised.
From the yard at the rear, however, its age and character are
revealed. Formerly there were many such peles in the town,
which was very open to raids; but it may well have been from
this one that one of the Ridleys, in May, 1598, shot at and slew
one of the raiding Armstrongs, the son of their chief. The
tower is now the " Red Lion " Hotel, and so here, too, there
will be little difficulty in making the acquaintance of the interior!

STROTHER

BEKERING

† HARBOTTLE CASTLE

(Map I, D5.)

Commanding the western end of a long line of castles and peles in Coquetdale, Harbottle Castle had a position of great strategic importance which is sadly belied by its hopelessly ruined condition today.

The high castle mound partly encompassed by the " Devil's Crook " of the Coquet is seen, like that of Wark-on-Tweed, overtopping the village that once had its protection. The hill appears to have been one of the old Saxon mote-hills, the spot where the elders of the community met in council, and was almost certainly fortified as well, since the name (Here-bottel) means " the station of an army." With the coming of the Normans the site cried out for stouter defence to aid the holding of Northumberland, then a bone of contention between the two countries, and it was Henry II who decided to build the castle, using land which was the property of Odinel de Umfraville, and getting financial and other support from the whole county and from the Bishopric of Durham. The castle withstood the inevitable attacks bravely. In 1296, for instance, it staved off the army, forty thousand strong, of Robert de Ros and the Earls of Athol and Menteith. They killed all the deer in the park, but it was re-stocked with twenty bucks and eighty does, supplied by the King of Scotland in compensation from the estate of John Comyn in the North Tyne Valley. In the next century the castle was showing signs of wear and tear, especially in the years after Bannockburn, and by the middle of the century was so weak that Gilbert de Umfraville deemed it wise to get royal permission to keep his prisoners in his castle of Prudhoe instead. In Tudor times when it was the residence of Lord Dacre as Warden of the Middle Marches (he who distinguished himself at Flodden), an event took place in the castle which was destined to change the whole course of English—and Scottish—history. Henry VIII's sister, Margaret, gave birth to a daughter who was afterwards mother to Lord Darnley and grandmother to the Scottish James VI, the heir to the English throne when Elizabeth died. Though her life was in great danger, the sick woman, with true Tudor love of rich apparel, insisted on having her new gowns held up at her bedside several times a day for her admiration, and added further to her wardrobe " a gown of purple velvet lined with cloth of gold, a gown of bright crimson velvet furred with ermine, three gowns more, and three kirtles of satin."

It was a little later than this that the castle was restored at a cost of " two hundreth & fortye pound," and the garrison is recorded as consisting of a hundred men and their officers, the latter receiving 4s. pay per diem, while the soldiers got " 8d. a piece."

The castle had a high donjon or keep, the base of which, with traces of a moat, remains ; a barbican ; an inner and outer bailey guarded by a towered wall ; and, at the entrance gate, a barmkin for cattle of the district when raids threatened. The keep, on the south side, crowns a conical mound. In the inner bailey to the north-west of the keep is the well and various foundations of a round tower and domestic buildings, such as kitchen, bakehouse, brewhouse, horse-mill, etc. It is interesting to learn that the iron postern gate was 6 feet 9 inches high and 3 feet 9 inches broad, while that at the entrance gate was 10 feet 3 inches high and 9 feet 9 inches broad. What happened eventually to these formidable barriers ? It is possible—but only barely—that they were turned into ploughshares, as James VI ordered after he came to the English throne and the Border castles had become superfluous. As for the stone of the great walls and towers, local building contractors soon discovered that the abandoned castle offered an admirable supply of dressed material. For the rest—

> " On barbican and keep of stone,
> Stern Time the foeman's work has done."

HARNHAM HALL
(Map II, E8.)

As the traveller proceeds on the road to Otterburn from Belsay, after two miles he sees across the fields the high knoll crowned by the houses of Harnham. A narrow road leads to the spot and winds up the hillside to where Harnham Hall looks northward from its high wooded cliff.

The present Hall includes part of the old fifteenth-century tower of the Swinburnes which stood here in early times when Harnham was included in the barony of Bolbeck, and was later held by the Bolams and the Bekerings. Formerly the village was defended at the narrow neck of the ridge by an encircling wall, in which was an iron gate. In 1667 the estate passed into the possession of the Babingtons, a very ancient family of which the present Hall has some interesting reminders. One is their crest in plaster on the ceiling of one of the lower rooms—a dragon's head with a scroll issuing from the mouth, and on it the motto " Foy est tous." The origin of this motto goes back to Henry IV's reign during the French wars, when young John Babington, having volunteered for a dangerous service with five other knights, waved his sword as he left the royal presence and cried, " Foy est tous ! "

Another relic of the Babington family is a strange one— no other than the vault of the beautiful Dame Katherine Babington. Owing to her dissenting beliefs, the vicar of Bolam objected to her burial in consecrated ground, and for ten days after her death her husband tried to get this decision overruled by the ecclesiastical authorities. It was in vain, and a vault was made in the garden on the hillside below the Hall. Hewn partly out of the rock, it contains a rocky shelf where the coffin rested and, at the side, an inscribed board :

> " Here lyeth the body of Madam Babington, who was laid in this sepulchre on the 9th September, 1670.

> > My time is past, as now you see,
> > I viewed the dead as you do me ;
> > Or long you'll be as low as I,
> > And some will look on thee."

Dame Katherine, however, did not sleep well in her garden tomb. Some years after her death, the leaden coffin was stolen by gipsies, and her poor bones lay for a while exposed.

Two more features of Harnham Hall deserve mention— the fine ornamented doorway (the initials are those of one of the Leightons who followed the Babingtons in possession) ; and the chimney look-out, approached by a flight of steps from the leads, whence, looking down into the rocky depths we realise how magnificently situated the old fortalice was to resist " the entree and passage of the Scottes for invadynge this realme or makinge any spoyle in tyme of warre."

THE ARMS OF
CARDINAL WOLSEY

SWINBURNE

HAUGHTON CASTLE
(Map II, F7.)

Haughton Castle has few peers for charm of situation—
from one wooded bank of the North Tyne it looks out across
to the other, and its many turrets strike a romantic note in this
beautiful vicinity.

The best approach to the castle is from Humshaugh, by
a narrow loop road passing within sight of it, reflected attrac-
tively in a little lake ; or by a walk from this road down towards
the ancient ferry, where the other side of the castle is seen at
closer quarters.

In former times the name seems to have had as many
variations as Willimoteswick. Written Halvton, Haluton,
Haluchton or Halgton according to the whim of the chronicler,
the word means a homestead on a meadow, but this hardly
describes the site, which is fairly elevated. The beginnings of
the castle go back to the time when North Tynedale was part of
Scotland. The manor had passed by marriage from Ranulf
son of Huctred to a knight of William the Lion's, then three
generations later to William de Swyneburn who was Treasurer
to the Scottish Queen, and it was he who built the castle,
probably for self-protection, since he had a knack of acquiring
his weaker neighbours' lands. Later the manor passed to that
well-known Northumbrian fighting family, the Widdringtons,
who held it for several centuries.

Of Sir Thomas de Widdrington, who was Lord of Haughton
in the reign of King Harry, the story is told of the Forgotten
Mosstrooper. It had been rumoured of Lord Dacre, Warden of
the Middle Marches, that he was in secret League with the
moss-trooping clans of Liddesdale, and since he had looked into
the dark eyes of Helen Armstrong, sister of the chief of her clan,
that the Armstrongs had been specially favoured. To redress
this unlawful conspiracy, Widdrington was entrusted by other
landowners in Tynedale with a petition to the Chancellor,
Lord Cardinal Wolsey, then at York. He had reached York
and was on his way to the Cardinal's Palace when he discovered
attached to his girdle a great key, the sight of which filled him

with remorse. For it was the only key to the deepest dungeon, which held a captive—no other than Archie Armstrong, the chief of his clan, who had been brought in just before Widdrington's departure—and unless the servants had been able to break in by force, the unfortunate Scot must have been without food or drink for three days. Without waiting to see the Cardinal, Widdrington turned his horse and galloped northward at top speed. His steed dropped dead as he was in sight of Durham, but with another beneath him he spurred on and at midnight, travel-stained and exhausted, he came to Haughton. "The prisoner!" was all he could gasp as the great doors were opened. A torch was brought, the hatch in the roof of the *oubliette* (an apt word in the circumstances) was thrown back, and his worst fears were realised. Armstrong was dead, either from hunger or the foul air or both. He had gnawed his own flesh from his arm in his agony, and there was an unforgettable look of horror on his twisted features. It is said that the spirit of the moss-trooper continued to haunt the dungeon with terrible shrieks that echoed throughout the castle, and it was necessary to get the priest of Simonburn to exorcise the ghost, which he did by the virtue of a black-letter Bible. In 1681, however, when this Bible had been taken away for repair or some such reason the servants were panic-stricken to hear, as before, blood-curdling shrieks of anguish from "Archie Armstrong's Dungeon." The ghost had returned. No time was lost in bringing the Bible back, and the haunting ceased. The reader is left to winnow for himself the false from the true in this weird story.

Whatever the proportion of these, the castle was certainly well-known to the Armstrongs, for they battered down its walls in 1542, and gained an entrance with the help of scaling-ladders. The Tynedale men who helped them were, like many other clans near the Border, not too particular about whose side they took so long as they stood to gain; and on this occasion had won so much plunder in the recent "Pilgrimage of Grace" that it paid them to remain outside the law—a not infrequent position with the men of Tynedale till well into the eighteenth century.

It is hard to believe that the Haughton Castle of today is largely the result of careful rebuilding and restoration by various owners in modern times, and that a hundred and fifty years ago it could truthfully be described as being "chiefly dismantled, some few apartments only remaining habitable." Originally it was a rugged "tower-house," not unlike Langley Castle in conception but on more ambitious lines, with five square turrets breaking the lines of the battlements, and a stout barmkin, now mostly gone but represented by a modern wall and gateway. There are two great parallel vaults in the basement, and in each angle of the castle a newel-stair winds to the roof. The handsome room that was once, probably, the Great Hall has a series of fine windows in arched recesses. The north side of the castle, relieved with projecting garde-robes and corbelling, is the most picturesque; but from whatever angle it is seen, Haughton Castle is capable of satisfying the photographer and artist.

†§ HEBBURN TOWER
(Map II, B7–8.)

Hebburn Tower has puzzled the map-makers. On some it appears as " The Bastile," a corruption of Bastle or bastle-house, which it undoubtedly is, although it is described as a " little tower " in the list of holds of 1541.

Hebburn village is on the south side of Chillingham park. The tower itself stands in the park, near to the road to North Charlton where it is crossed by a gate a short distance above the village.

The site seems a fairly strong one, being guarded on one side by a little cleugh, while formerly, in all probability, a barmkin or surrounding wall would add to the defences.

Hebburn Tower belonged to the Hebburn family, a very old one, who took their name from the estate. Their arms bore " three cressets sable, flaming proper," a reference perhaps to the beacon or cresset maintained on Ros Castle Crag that rises so romantically to over a thousand feet behind the tower. The expense of this particular beacon, which was a very important one, was borne by all villages between the Aln and the Tweed. With others along the Border it was lit to warn the people of any serious inroad of the Scots; and in much later times, when Napoleon was intending to invade the country, the beacons were again called into use.

In 1509 the tower was recorded as being able to accommodate twenty horsemen ready to ride, and thirty years later it was still in " reasonably good reparations." Today, though the place is overgrown and roofless, the outer walls are still fairly intact. The entrance is on the south side nearest the road, and to the right of it will be seen the hollow of the newel-stairway, now almost obliterated. The basement is curiously vaulted, since the top is composed of long flat stones. There is a loophole at each end of it. A smaller vault within has once served as a prison, and from it there descends a still deeper dungeon, reserved doubtless for the incarceration of special prisoners. It is possible to scramble up to the first floor, which has been divided into three rooms, two of which had a fireplace and mullioned windows. A third storey, in the roof, was illuminated by small square windows in the gables.

Ivy provides a picturesque, if insidious, draping for the outer walls, and the first floor is a tangle of trees and bushes, yet enough remains of this very fine old bastle-house to provide us with a type of dwelling once, of necessity, very common along the Border.

† HEFFERLAW TOWER
(Map II, C8.)

Highfarlaw and Heffordlaw are other variants of the name of this tower, but if the writer were asked to make a guess, he would say that the name is more likely to have been Heifer Law— i.e. the hill used for grazing.

There is no doubt about the "law." The Great North Road rises almost continuously from Alnwick three miles away, and on leaving the main road beyond the junction of a by-road on the left, we have to climb again by the side of a plantation for a short distance. It is this lofty position which gives the clue to the purpose of this tower, which is rather small to have been a residence, since it measures not thirty feet each way, and is only three storeys high. One writer calls it a "poor specimen of a Border pele," but this is too disparaging, for it has some unique features. Among these are the sculptured wall panels on the east and south walls bearing the Percy arms—a pair of fetterlocks (or handcuffs) within a crescent. This particular form of the Percy arms was used by the 4th Earl, great-grandson of the famous Hotspur, and fixes the date of the tower to the years 1470–89 ; about the same time that the Earl built the tower in Hulne Priory for its defence.

This tower, too, had an ecclesiastical association, as the crossed crosiers on the panels indicate—it was built as a look-out tower for Alnwick Abbey, two and a half miles away in the valley of the Aln, to warn the monks of any approaching danger. Here we have the explanation of its smallness—it was not a fortified residence, but a military post. A further indication of its connection with the abbey is the canopied niche on the east side. On the abbey gateway, the only part of it now remaining, are several such niches, one of them holding the figure of an angel, another that of a canon ; and some such figure once stood in this niche, perhaps that of the Blessed Mary of Alnwick, or even that of Simon de Montfort, whose uncorrupted foot, preserved in a shoe-shaped silver casket, was the treasured relic and miracle-worker of the monks. The community was enormously rich, and their hospitality almost unlimited—on one occasion they entertained a thousand guests at once. We can imagine some of the brothers, picturesque figures in long white cassocks and cloaks and white felt hats, arriving from time to time, a little breathless from their long ascent, to visit the Earl's men keeping watch and ward in this lonely little pele on the hill.

†§ HEPPLE TOWER
(Map II, D7.)

Hepple is in Coquetdale, five or six miles above Rothbury. In entering the village from this side, we see on the left the broken walls of the stronghold, now relegated to the status of a farm-building.

The barony of Hepple was created by King John in favour of Ivo de Vesci, but later it passed into the joint possession of the De Hepples and the De Tailbois, the latter being descendants of the great Ivo de Tailbois, Baron of Kendal, who traced his descent from King Charlemagne.

There is a curious and interesting record of how one Tailbois heir produced proof of his age at Newcastle in 1372. " Robert de Louthre deposed that the said Walter (the heir) was twenty-one years old on the Feast of the Purification last past ; that he was born at Hephal and baptised in the church at Routhbury. He recollected the day because he was a god-father. John de Walington recollected the day because he had a son baptised there on the same day. John Lawson recollected the day because he had a son buried there the same day."

We do not hear of the tower till the fifteenth century, when it is mentioned in an official record as being one of six Border towers belonging to Sir Robert Ogle ; and was then one of the most important in the line of forts stretching down Coquetdale as far as Warkworth. But it suffered severely from Scottish raids, and, indeed, at one period was so ruinous that the lord of the manor transferred his court to another of his towers at Great Tosson. The lords of Hepple had, among their many rights, the power of life and death and the liberty to erect a gallows. A field on the opposite side of the Coquet, called " Gibbet's Close," marks a spot where many a moss-trooper must have swung from his " hempen caudle."

Some years ago an attempt was made to demolish the tower to furnish building material for a neighbouring farmstead, but the workmen found it almost impossible to separate the stones from their bedding of cement, and the attempt was abandoned. Even so, there is not a great deal left of the old place—a barrel-vaulted basement for horses or stores, and ruinous walls, once forty or fifty feet high, enclosing a roofless chamber, which originally was divided into two storeys. There has been a loft in the roof of the basement, which is lit by a slit set in a splayed recess. Life in this dimly-lit tower must, at its best, have been somewhat primitive, but even the great Tailbois and Hepples and Ogles had to place safety before comfort in those far-off turbulent times.

HEBBURN

†§ HEPPLE WOODHOUSES BASTLE-HOUSE
(Map II, D7.)

In a field adjoining the road from Swindon to Holystone in Coquetdale, and quite close to Dues Hill Grange, rise the weather-beaten walls of the bastle-house known as Hepple Woodhouses. Of many such fortified houses in Coquetdale formerly, this is one of the few remaining in good preservation. It has, too, some extremely interesting features.

The date over the lintel of the door is 1602, but the building is much older than that. In the 1541 Survey we read that, " at a place called the hare clewgh one Rog' hangingeshawes hath lately buylded upon his owne Inherytance a stronge pele house of stone in a convenyent place for resystence of the Incourse of theeves of Ryddesdale, and he ys not able in defaulte of substance to p'forme & fynyshe the same." Harecleugh was the old name of the house. Perhaps the Potte family (whose initials appear beside the date) completed the building when it came into their possession in 1602. " TAM " probably stands for Thomas Potte, another of this one-time influential family. " W.P." was William Potte ; and " B.P." Bartholomew Potte.

It is interesting to note that the house was for defence against the men of Redesdale. They not only had threadbare reputations, but were usually at loggerheads with the Coquetdale men, and were not averse to a little sheep-lifting or horse-stealing in their territory. Not that the Coquet men were not equally adept at doing " a little shifting for a living " ! It was a state of affairs that lasted long after the Union of the two countries, so that in spite of its late completion the house would prove its worth.

It has been suggested that the arch and stone shelf above the original entrance to the house were to allow the throwing of scalding liquids on the heads of unwelcome visitors ; but the arch may be a relieving arch, and the shelf seems more like a dripstone to protect the inscriptions below. There is a loop-hole above the entrance, and within it are the square openings for three bars to secure the door. The basement is vaulted and

Plate XII

AYDON CASTLE—ENTRANCE FROM INNER COURTYARD:
FERNIEHIRST CASTLE

Plate XIII

HERMITAGE CASTLE

Plate XIV

KIRKANDREWS TOWER; HEBBURN TOWER;
CORBRIDGE OLD VICARAGE

Plate XV

NAWORTH CASTLE—GATE-HOUSE, WITH HOWARD TOWER ON RIGHT

furnished with loopholes. A stair winds up to the next floor, illuminated by deeply-splayed windows which have once been guarded by iron bars. A small window has a kitchen sink or drain below it. The floor is flagged ; and there are four wall cupboards. The roof, though not the original one of stone tiles fastened with sheep-shank bones, is sound, and contributes to the curious air of habitation about this ancient bastle-house.

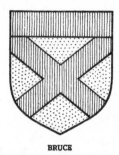

BRUCE

* HERMITAGE CASTLE
(Map I, D2.)

One of the most grimly majestic fortresses in the Border, Hermitage Castle stands four-square in lonely state in a remote glen of Liddesdale. Into Liddel Water a short distance above Newcastleton flows Hermitage Water, and following this up by road to a point where the native woodland of the valley gives place to unrelieved moorland and fell, we see the castle on the further bank. In 1931, Hermitage was presented by the Duke of Buccleuch to the nation, and when it had been repaired by H.M. Office of Works was thrown open to visitors.

There is some uncertainty as to when the castle was built, but it is believed that Nicholas de Soulis, a Norman knight, built a tower here in the thirteenth century ; and two hundred years later the castle seems to have been considerably added to. The De Soulis occupation of Hermitage ended when one of them, Lord William Soulis who claimed to be descended from a natural daughter of Alexander II, plotted against Bruce to gain the throne, and as a result was seized at Berwick and ended his days in Dumbarton Castle. It was this same Lord Soulis who, as Sheriff of Roxburgh, earned the fear and detestation of the Liddesdale people by his oppressions. In Leyden's ballad of " Lord Soulis " he appears as a foul magician, whose fate it is to be boiled in lead, when his captors discover that his charms have rendered him invulnerable to arrow or spear. On the Nine Stane Rig to the north-east of the castle a circle of stones is still pointed out as the place where the " cauldron red " boiled and bubbled with its ghastly broth. It was this same sorcerer, tradition avers, who did to death the famed Cowt (Colt) of Kielder, the Tynedale Hercules. The Cowt wore a talisman of rowan berries to protect him from spells but it was not proof against running water, and Lord Soulis, knowing this, got his men to thrust the Cowt into a pool as he was crossing the stream above the castle. The spot is known as " The Cowt of Kielder's Pool " ; and nearby, beside the ruined walls of a thirteenth-century chapel, is a large mound reputed to be the hero's grave. This chapel, by the way, may be on the site of the original hermitage that gave its name to the castle and stream, and was granted in 1180 " to God and Saint Mary and Brother William of Mercheley."

To turn from legend to fact, the castle's most famous owner was the Earl of Bothwell, that evil genius of Mary Queen of Scots. As Lord of all the Marches he had an encounter with Little Jock Elliot, one of the notorious clan of that ilk. For once Bothwell came off the worse, and was, indeed, like to die of the wound he received from Little Jock's dagger. Hearing of his plight, Queen Mary rode on horsebank from Jedburgh to see him, and returned the same day. Fifty or sixty miles across some of the wildest country in the Border in cold and wet October weather ! No wonder she was gravely ill after returning.

The Earl's successor, Francis Bothwell, used the castle as a centre for his rebellious activities in the district and for his raids into English territory, but eventually was forced to leave the country ; and in 1594 Scott of Buccleuch was made Keeper of Liddesdale and given Hermitage Castle, which remained in the possession of the family till it was handed over to the Government for preservation.

Externally the castle looks a complete and solid structure, with its towering walls broken only by small windows high up, and a few loopholes, and its rows of corbelled openings to take the beams of wooden brattices, from which the walls could be defended. Internally this promise of completeness is not borne out, many of the arrangements being obscured. Unique features are the great arches uniting the towers on the east and west. Strangely enough, it is not certain if they were part of the original structure—they may have been inserted during a restoration of about a hundred years ago. The towers they unite are built at the four corners of an earlier tower, which in its turn encloses the very oldest part of the castle structure, forming a double tower with a central courtyard. An arrangement very unusual, but a sound one, seemingly, yet according to one English military report the castle was " not stronng, but evill to wyn by reasone of the strate ground aboute the same." In other words, there was little cover for attackers. The kitchen of the castle has been in the south-west tower. There is a cess-pool outside the walls here, beside a low arch. On the south side is a little postern gate, the main portcullised entrance being within the western arch. The ditch on the north side was formerly crossed by a drawbridge, but the entrance it guarded no longer exists. In the base of the south-eastern tower, not far from the entrance, is one of two wells, the other being near the opposite corner of the castle. The basement of the north-east tower is solid except for a tiny chamber, five feet by six, entered from an opening in the ceiling. It was in this frightful, windowless *oubliette*, most probably, that Sir Alexander Ramsey, having been captured by his enemy, Sir William Douglas, eked out a miserable existence for seventeen days on grain that trickled down from a store in the room above. Many years ago there were found in this vault a quantity of human bones, a saddle, a bridle, a sword, and a heap of the husks of oats—relics, it is believed, of the tragedy. Sir William Douglas who con-demned his enemy to this death was known as " The Flower of Chivalry," and the tale of his knightly deeds is a long and stirring one. Yet his consuming jealousy of Ramsey's promotion to the Sheriffdom of Teviotdale, a position which Douglas had once held and wished to hold again, awakened the worst side of the " Black Knight's " character. Seizing Ramsey as he held court at Hawick and wounding him before he could defend himself, Douglas carried him off and, wounded as he was, deliberately allowed him to die of starvation. It was a crime for which he went unpunished—indeed, it brought him the position he coveted.

In a strange way Hermitage Castle preserves in this twentieth century the atmosphere of medieval times. It gives, as one writer has noted, an eerie impression of being still inhabited and its gaunt walls look as if they might, at any moment, " pour forth from the great doorway a troop of Border riders with their leather jackets, their steel caps, and their faces set southward."

SCOTT

†§ HETHPOOL PELE
(Map I, B5.)

Hethpool or Heathpool is one of the very oldest peles in the North Country, but it is fragmentary and apt to prove disappointing after the detour needed to reach it. It lies in the College Valley, a mile and a half from West Newton, and the Cheviots rise all round it, leading one to wonder in the first place why anyone should have thought of settling here in former times, and secondly, why the place was not wiped out of existence soon after it was built. It must have been of exceptional strength. It is mentioned in the List of Border fortresses of 1415 as a " turris "; and in the next century as " a lytle stone house or pyle which ys a greate releyffe to the ten'nts thereof." It now stands in the grounds of the country mansion known as Heathpool, and enough remains to show the massive construction. Huge whinstone boulders have been used, and two of the steps that remain of the stair protrude from the east wall like great teeth. Only three walls remain, one of them pierced with a narrow window, and the ruin is almost entirely ivy-covered. The fortress has been more extensive at one time, and probably had a stout barmkin as extra defence.

Hethpool Pele is the spot traditionally associated with the legend of *The Hermit of Warkworth*, as told in Bishop Percy's ballad. Isabel, the heiress of Widdrington, loved and was loved by Sir Bertram of Bothal, but she told him he must " fame the helmet " she had given him before they could be wed. In his quest for adventure over the Border, Bertram was sorely wounded and Isabel, stricken with remorse at the news, set out to reach his side and nurse him back to health. Alas! on the way she was kidnapped; but Bertram's brother, disguised as a Scot, discovered she had been taken to Hethpool Tower, and one night managed to rescue her with the aid of a rope-ladder. They were hurrying from the spot together when they came face to face with Bertram himself, recovered from his wound and bound for Hethpool, where he had learned that his lady was imprisoned. Deceived by the disguise, he struck his brother down; and the lovely Isabel, too, in trying to ward the blow was mortally wounded. The unhappy Bertram made himself a hermitage on the bank of the Coquet at Warkworth, and spent the rest of his days there in penitence. Unfortunately for the truth of this sad and romantic story, Warkworth Hermitage was most probably founded by the first Earl of Northumberland as a chantry for the soul of his first wife; but in spite of this a heart-shaped enclosure on the other side of the valley from the Tower is still pointed out as the very spot where the tragedy occurred.

†§ HETON CASTLE
(Map I, A5.)

Very little remains to be seen of Heton Castle, but it has, at least, a fine setting of which it is a part being on the wooded bank of the Till, that fair tributary of the Tweed. It is approached by a byway from the highway between Twizel Bridge and Crookham.

The Greys chose a fairly strong site when they built their castle soon after the middle of the thirteenth century. A prominent and widespread family on the Border, they made this their principal seat, a fact which is difficult to realise from the slight traces remaining today. Yet they ought to have known that they were tempting Providence by settling so near to Scotland, and that their stronghold would be bound to experience more than its share of the vicissitudes of Border castles. One of the last occasions when we hear of its being " rasen and casten down " was in 1496 when James IV invaded England in support of Perkin Warbeck, an imposter who claimed to be the lawful heir to the English throne. It is said that Warbeck withdrew from the siege of Heton, disgusted at the brutal methods of his allies. The damage must have been severe, for afterwards the castle was more than once reported as being in need of repair ; and in 1541 when Sir Robert Bowes visited it, he found it ruinous. Once two hundred marks was suggested as the sum required to put it in order ; and on another occasion, £300. But not much appears to have been done, though the castle was evidently considered " a very fit and proper place to defend the country and annoy the enemy."

A survey of Elizabeth's reign affords us a good idea of what the ancestral home of the Greys looked like then. " This castle of Heton hath been a pleasant and beautiful building, in manner square, with goodly Towers and turrets, as is yet remaining, the Lyons Tower on the west side thereof at the south coin or corner, and on the north side one mansion [?] of a vault that a hundred horse may stand in."

It is clear from this account and from a sketch accompanying it that the castle was, like Ford and Chillingham, in the form of a quadrangle with corner towers. The main entrance was on the south side, and there was a postern gate on the west. The great Lyons Tower, so called from the gigantic representations of the Grey Lion on its walls, has entirely gone. The single building remaining is probably the " vault " of the above description. At least seventy feet long, it seems capable of holding a hundred horses ready to ride. Stout buttresses flank the entrance, and support the walls ; and the roof is strongly vaulted. When it was converted into a farm building, however, its character was destroyed. The last vestige of the glory of Heton Castle has indeed departed.

HEXHAM MOOT HALL AND KEEP
(Map I, F5.)

The ancient town of Hexham in the fertile valley of the Tyne was a frequent objective of Scottish raiders, especially as it was not walled in like Newcastle and Carlisle. A substitute for such a defence was supplied by the Moot Hall and the Keep, or Manor House, which still raise their dark and massive walls high above the more modern dwellings near the market place. In all probability these fortresses were formerly joined or enclosed by a wall, thus forming a central citadel where the townsfolk could take refuge in emergency.

The Moot Hall, so called because in it the courts of the Regality of Hexham were held, overlooks the market place and consists of a square tower adjoining a tall barbican or gate-house through which runs a low, round-arched passage. At each end of this, within a taller arch, are machicolations from which intruders could be assaulted from above. On one corner of this tower the turret containing the stair is continued higher to form a lookout platform. The Hall itself is square and finished with a parapet supported on corbels and furnished with machicolations on three sides, openings which would enable the defenders on the roof to guard the foot of the walls effectively. The external staircase was added about two hundred years ago, and probably took the place of a low building similar to that outside the Keep at Newcastle. Recently the doorway and windows on the inner side of the Hall were " restored " by the late owner, who also made some unsightly alterations to the parapet.

Not far away is the other tower, the Manor Office, a name got from its use for three hundred years for the transaction of business connected with the manor of Hexham. The masonry of this forbidding stronghold is notably massive, and the walls are eleven feet thick. Many of the stones bear traces of Roman workmanship, and were probably brought here from *Corstopitum*, near Corbridge. Here again the doorway and one of the windows have been modernised. Some of the older windows · are protected with iron grilles. Three rows of corbels support the projecting parapet. This building is the old prison of Hexham, and in its dark dungeons many a bold North Tynedale or Liddesdale freebooting outlaw has awaited his last appearance. Now and then comrades came to the rescue, as in 1536 when Tynedale men forced open the prison and carried all the prisoners off to Scotland ; and again just after Elizabeth's accession, when the gaoler not only liberated his prisoners, but went off with them. These incidents show the terribly disturbed state of the Middle Marches at this period.

§ HOLE BASTLE
(Map I, E5.)

Now used as a farm building, this bastle house, between Woodburn and Bellingham, is a very good example of defensive domestic architecture. The roof is stone-tiled against fire, the foundations are of natural boulders, and the masonry of the walls is almost equally massive. When, recently, one gable was rebuilt, the workmen had to break up the stones before they could manipulate them. Hot lime has been used for cement, and the result is a remarkably stout structure.

A basement with a vaulted roof occupies the ground floor, entered at the end nearest the road, but originally by a door at the other end, now blocked, but with the great oaken beams visible that form the lintel within. A loophole remains over the modern door, and in the roof is a rectangular opening for a ladder to the floor above. A flight of stone steps outside goes up to the living quarters, and the landing at the top is parapeted. The door has originally been suspended not on hinges but with pivots in the lintel and threshold (the holes remain) reminding one of the gateway to a Roman station. Here again, oak logs are used for the lintel within. In the jambs are the holes for a door-bar. At the far end of the upper room is a huge fireplace, massively built and with, again, oak logs used in its construction. Small square windows, one of them suggestively over the door, light the interior ; and a loft occupies the upper part of the room, which must have supplied a considerable degree of comfort and safety.

The sound condition of this interesting bastle-house is due to the care of the Duke of Northumberland, whose property it is.

†§ HOLLOWS TOWER
(Map I, E2.)

In the coaching days the road up Eskdale between Canonbie and Langholm had the reputation of being the most beautiful stretch between London and Edinburgh. About halfway to Langholm and only a few miles north of the Border stands one of the few remaining strongholds of the notorious Armstrong clan. From the highway, a field-path approaches the tower on the bank of the Esk ; and the key is obtainable at the farm hard by.

Just as the Armstrongs were notorious on both sides of the Border, so Johny Armstrong was the most celebrated of that ilk. Sir Walter Scott identified this tower with Johny's " bonnie Gilnock Hall," but it is rather small to have accommodated that freebooter's large following, and, moreover, appears to have been built after Johny's tragic end. A more probable site for his castle is a spot further down the Esk, near the east end of Gilnockie Bridge, where a high rocky tongue projects into a loop of the stream, and a ditch is traceable across the neck of the peninsula. The stone from tower and barmkin more than likely went to the building of the bridge. The Armstrong clan were no worse (and no better!) than others who established themselves in the Debatable Land, that unclaimed waste between the two countries, that No Man's Land where only the fortunate brave could hope to flourish. But the Armstrongs were many, and their numbers grew, and they were forced to extend their " activities " from Liddesdale, their home country, into Eskdale and Ewesdale. Wherever they went, their neighbours found themselves the poorer in livestock; and finally the king himself made an expedition to end the intolerable state of affairs. His subsequent betrayal and hanging of Johny Armstrong and his followers at Caerlanrig is vividly told in the well-known ballad. A later member of the clan, Archie Armstrong of Eskdale (perhaps of Hollows Tower), had more fortunate dealings with royalty, thanks to his native wit. Having been condemned to death for sheep-stealing by James VI at Jedburgh Assizes, Archie pleaded that, as an ignorant wight who had just heard of the Bible, he would like to be reprieved long enough to read it. Though doubtless astonished at this show of devotion, James granted the request; whereupon Archie said slyly, " Then deil tak' me if ever I read a word o't as lang as my e'en are open." So amused was the king at this repartee that he not only pardoned Archie but took him into his employ; and in the next reign Archie was Court Jester to Charles I. But his career ended when at a dinner at which Archbishop Laud was an honoured guest, Archie gave vent to the following grace before meat : " All praise to God, and little Laud to the deil."

Though roofless, Hollows Tower is otherwise in fairly good condition ; the triple corbelling beneath the parapet and the projecting bartizans, ornamented with a rope-like moulding, adding to its picturesque outline. The roof has been a high-pitched one between stepped gables. The south gable is topped with a stone beacon, where a fire could be lit in an iron basket to spread the news of any inroad. Within the entrance, once probably closed by an iron " yett," is a large stone slab known as the " Dead Stane." It was a common practice in the Scottish Border to bury the dead of a chieftain's family within his tower ; and the bones of more than one Armstrong may lie beneath this floor. Such a thought lends an eerie atmosphere to the dank and gloomy vault. A wheel-stair ascends to the upper storeys. On the first floor is a huge fireplace suggesting a kitchen ; while the room above was perhaps the main living-room. Most of the windows are furnished with seats. The parapet-walk which can still be gained, gives superb views of the lovely valley.

GRAHAM

HOLY ISLAND CASTLE
(Map II, A8.)

Crowning the lofty cone-shaped rock of Beblowe on the Island of Lindisfarne, where in the early days of Christianity " a lamp was lit whose flame lighted pagan England," this castle reminds one of an illustration to a fairy-tale. Between the sea and the steep face of the rock a winding path climbs up till, turning, one is confronted with a portcullised entrance that seems too picturesque to be real.

Lindisfarne, half continent, half isle, can only be approached on foot when the tide is out. Cars can be taken over by the track marked by a long line of poles from the coast at Beal ; and cycles can be ridden across ; or one of the vehicles that ply between the mainland and the island can be used.

The castle is not an old one, and was not, as might be imagined, for the protection of the monastery, which had its own defences. It was not till its dissolution that an Order in Council was issued to ensure the protection of the little harbour in preparation for a great raid into Scotland. Robert Rooke of Berwick superintended the first fortifications, which consisted of bulwarks and blockhouses, and there is little doubt that the monastery supplied the stone, since Rooke reported that there was " plentie and sufficient remayning of the olde abbey lately dissolved there to make the bulwark." The following year two hundred troops were landed on the island, and ten battleships lay in the newly-fortified haven. By 1550 the castle was built and was reported upon by Sir Robert Bowes as being very well situated for its purpose. He added that " if there were about the lowe part thereof made a ring, with bulwarks to flancke the same, the ditch thereabout might be easily watered towarde the land." But this additional defence does not seem to have been carried out.

Once England and Scotland were united the castle lost its importance, but continued to be a military station ; and the deaths of certain soldiers, probably of the plague, are recorded in the parish registers. At the time of the Civil War, we get another glimpse of the castle from contemporary records. A young officer of King Charles's suite visited the island and afterwards wrote in his diary : " There is a pretty fort, which upon this occasion was repaired and put into forme. There are 2 batteries on it, on the lower stood mounted 3 iron peeces and 2 of brasse, with carriadges and platformes in good order. On the higher was one brasse gun and 2 iron ones with all ammunition to them. There are 24 men and a captain kept in pay to man it, the common souldiours have 6d. per diem . . . The captain at our being there was Captain Rugg, known commonly by his great nose."

In 1715 an odd incident occurred when two fanatical Jacobites, Lancelot Errington and his nephew, captured the castle for the Pretender. The master gunner, it seemed, practised as well the calling of barber, and Errington was one of his customers. Shortly after his visit, Errington came back with his nephew " to look for the key of his watch," but when the door was opened, presented a pistol in the face of the gunner. A struggle ensued, but the two intruders expelled the gunner and a sentinel (who appear to have been the only two occupants), and held the castle for a few days. Expected reinforcements from the mainland failed to come and the bold Jacobites were taken prisoners and put into Berwick gaol. Their further adventures, even more amazing, included burrowing their way out of gaol and hiding for nine days in a pea-stack at Bamburgh before they gained safety.

Comparatively recently the castle was used as a coast-guard station, then it was acquired early in this century by a Mr. Edward Hudson who enlisted the aid of Sir Edwin Lutyens to superintend the work of restoration. Now period furniture and casement windows enhance the atmosphere of this little stronghold. One quaint fireback is dated 1677 ; and the open fireplace in the vaulted dining-room is ten feet wide. From the courtyard on the summit, whence the stout Lancelot Errington vainly scanned the shore, a fine view discloses itself, not only of the island, but many miles of the coast and the hills far inland.

THE WAKE KNOT

VESCI

§ HULNE PRIORY TOWER
(Map II, C8.)

Hulne Priory is one of those favoured spots whose surroundings have remained unaltered through the centuries,
where time itself seems almost to have stood still. It lies in
the Vale of Aln, in the heart of the vast and lovely park of the
Duke of Northumberland, permits to enter which may be
obtained at the Clock Tower in Alnwick Castle.

The monks of Hulne Priory were of the Carmelite Order,
and this particular monastery was founded about seven hundred
years ago by Ralph Fresborn, on ground given by William de
Vesci, then Lord of Alnwick. There is a story that Fresborn
was a Crusading knight who, having visited the monastery at
Mount Carmel in the Holy Land and wishing to enter the order,
decided to establish it in his native county. With the approval
of the Lord of Alnwick he chose this site because of the resemblance of Brizlee Hill to Mount Carmel, and he was himself
the first abbot. The Carmelites or " White Friars " lived very
austerely; indeed, their existence was morbid. Each friar kept
his coffin in his cell, and every morning dug a portion of his
grave. He slept on straw, crept on his knees to his devotions,
was a vegetarian, and had only two meals a day when he was
not fasting. Some stone figures in the priory grounds show
the style of the Carmelite's white habit. Their sacred vest-
ments, however, were of the utmost splendour.

The present ruins are still entirely surrounded by the old
defensive wall, which when complete had a parapeted top and
a foot-walk approached by steps from inside the grounds. Some
of these steps still remain. At the angles were corbelled turrets,
and one of the two gates was guarded by a strong, three-storeyed
tower. At the other gate there is a look-out and a bell. Such
defences would not, of course, be very adequate against any
raiding Scots; and this was doubtless why the 4th Earl of
Northumberland built a stronger tower within the walls. About
the same time he built Hefferlaw Tower as a look-out for the
monks of Alnwick Abbey. The Priory Tower stands towards

the west of the enclosure, near a sham-Gothic structure of modern date, and was built in 1488, as a tablet in the curtain wall testifies :

" In the year of Christ Ihu MCCCCLXXXVIII
This towr was bilded by Sir Hen Percy
The fourth Erle of Northuberlad of gret hon & worth
That espoused Maud ye good lady full of vertue & bewt
Daughter to Sir Willm Harbr't right noble & hardy
Erle of Pembrock whos soulis god save
And with his grace cosarve ye bilder of this towr."

The builder was not, however, conserved long—the following year a mob, incensed by a war-tax the Earl was raising on behalf of the king, broke into his house near Thirsk and murdered him and some of his servants.

This tablet, decaying though it is, is not the original, but a facsimile. The old tablet, a unique record of its kind, was becoming so badly weathered that it was removed to the shelter of the tower.

It is interesting to know the costs of building in those days. The bill for the tower totalled exactly £27 19s. 8d., and this included the carriage of stone and lead, the price of carpenters' work, *and* a new lock and keys. The sum had, of course, a very much higher value in those times when a calf could be bought for 2s. 6d. ; and a labourer was paid 3d. to 3½d. a day. The basement of this fine tower is vaulted, the rooms are large and well-proportioned, and the battlements are nobly designed. The monks must have rejoiced when they saw the stout walls going up.

§ KIRKANDREWS TOWER
(Map I, F2.)

In the account of Liddel Strength reference is made to Netherby Hall, the seat of the Grahams, and to the inclusion of a pele-tower in its structure. At Kirkandrews we have such another pele of the Grahams, but in this case standing alone. The best way to reach the spot is from the Longtown–Canonbie road, leaving it at Scotch Dyke railway station.

The Scots Dike itself, that great earthwork constructed in 1552 to mark a Border Line across the long-disputed Debatable Land, is a reminder of the precarious position of the tower on the edge of the disputed area. But not so very precarious, perhaps, since the Graham clan made the Debatable Land their own, and, as Sir Walter Scott wrote, " in their depredations on both countries they appear to have been very impartial " ; though impartial is hardly the right word.

KIRKANDREWS TOWER

The tower, built of red freestone and standing on rising ground near the Esk, is the only one of fifty towers in Liddesdale and Eskdale recorded in former days, to remain intact and occupied. In appearance it is not unlike Hollows Tower on the Esk beyond Canonbie, with bold corbelling below the parapets, and a walk round the base of the steeply-pitched roof with stepped gables, a typically Scottish fashion in architectural design. Kirkandrews was built in the fifteenth century, but the Armstrongs destroyed it in 1527, and later it was rebuilt as a farmhouse. The old tower was perhaps intended to guard a ford of the Esk a little further downstream. Not that the Grahams, often in alliance with the Scots, were zealous in the duty of keeping nightly watch and ward as became true Borderers—more than once the Lord Warden had to remind them of their duty to keep the night-watches at the fords here, at Netherby and at Liddel Mote. It is possible, however, that family disagreements were one cause of this slackness, since the Grahams, like the not-so-honest men of the proverb, frequently fell out with each other.

A picturesque addition to the tower, reminding one of bastle-house construction, is the long flight of stone steps giving access to the entrance, now at first-floor level. Formerly a wheel-stair went up from the basement, but the lower part of it has been built up. Beneath the stairs an old, wooden-pegged door, leads into the dim vaulted basement, which has walls more than five feet thick, the foundations being huge boulders. A stone in the wall of the basement is always damp, and like the more famous " Weeping-Stone " in Carlisle Castle is said to have been worn smooth by the tongues of prisoners. From the first floor, access to the roof is by the old wheel-stair. The gargoyles draining the roof are, it will be noticed, shaped to represent cannon. In the high garden wall, which suggests the ancient barmkin for the livestock of the neighbourhood, is an imposing Gothic archway with a battlemented top, but it is of fairly recent construction and, it may be thought, not entirely in keeping with the stern aspect of this fine Border tower.

†§ KYLOE TOWER
(Map II, A7.)

This old pele of the Grey family stands on high ground at East Kyloe Farm, which adjoins the old coach road from Belford to Berwick, and is less than a mile south-west of the hamlet of Fenwick close to the Great North Road.

Though inhabited till 1633, the tower is now ruinous, with only the south wall rising to any height, like a great jagged tooth. The vaulted basement, with a loophole in a round-arched recess at one end, is, however, in perfect preservation, except that the wall has been pierced with a new door at the east end. Corbels in the basement walls show that there has been a loft in the roof, as at Hepple in Coquetdale. The original entrance, now blocked up, is on the side next to the farmyard, and is in the form of a pointed arch. According to the present tenant of the farm, there is a chute, or meurtriere, in the roof of the entrance passage, and accessible from the floor above, but it is not accessible now, nor is the stair, which appears to have ascended in the thickness of the wall from the doorway. The immense size of the ashlar blocks forming the walls eight feet thick show this pele to have been a strong place in its prime. Only a few years ago the west wall was standing high enough to show the corbels, carved to represent human heads, of projecting machicolations. So quickly do walls even as strong as these fall into decay when uncared for.

*LANERCOST PRIORY
(Map I, F3.)

During the Border wars religious houses were not by any means exempt from attack—indeed, the treasures they contained often attracted marauders. At Lanercost Priory, famed for the perfection of its Early English architecture, there are two towers which may be described as defensive buildings. One is the Prior's Lodge, now known as the Dacre Tower, where the Austin Canons doubtless congregated in times of danger, especially in the years after Bannockburn when Scottish raids were frequent. The monastery suffered four particularly savage raids, those of the Earl of Buchan, William Wallace, Robert Bruce and his son, David II. In the last of these the sacred vessels were thrown about, the treasure-chests looted and wanton damage was inflicted everywhere.

The other tower is known as " King Edward's " from its having been the lodging of Edward I on more than one occasion.

The Prior's Lodge and the building adjoining it, formerly containing his library and other rooms, were considerably altered some four hundred years ago when they came into the possession of Sir Thomas Dacre, the bastard son of Thomas Lord Dacre, the hero of Flodden. A Latin verse on a window (now transferred to the church) recorded the circumstances : " To fifty-nine years add fifteen hundred, and in that year Thomas Dacre, Knight, who after the extinction of the religion of this place was the first to come to this house, founded this work. These possessions Edward had given him : Henry, before, had promised them as rewards for long military service." The buildings overlook the cloister garth, but the main entrance is on the other side by a broad flight of steps leading to a parapeted landing. Within is the Dacre Banqueting Hall, a spacious room with a fireplace four yards wide, dated 1586, and tall mullioned windows of about the same period. At one end are the remains of a minstrels' gallery. The roofless tower adjoining, formerly four storeys high, also shows signs of having been adapted as a comfortable dwelling, and a big fireplace with brick ovens marks the kitchen.

King Edward's Tower, forming one end of the Rectory, is well seen from the main doorway of the Dacre Hall. It was perhaps built by the order of Edward I. He and his beloved queen Eleanor lodged in the tower in 1280. He presented a silk cloth to the priory; and during his visit hunted in the adjoining forest of Inglewood, where he killed two hundred stags and hinds. Again in 1306 Edward was here, and spent the winter at Lanercost, but he was an old man and his health was failing. As recompense for the costs of his long stay he bestowed the churches of Mitford and Carlatton (in Cumberland) on the monastery. While he was at Lanercost, two brothers of Robert Bruce were brought to him. He condemned one of them, Thomas Bruce, to be sent to Carlisle, dragged by horses round the city, then hanged, and his head to be put on a spike on the castle wall. The other brother, Alexander, was also to be beheaded and his head to be put over one of the city gates. Though dying, Edward had no intention of softening towards his lifelong enemies. The "King's Room" is on the first floor, its modern window (near the corner) overlooking the lawn at the rear. The tower is battlemented and has a gabled roof. Below the parapet is carved a line of "dog-teeth," a decoration characteristic of the architecture of seven hundred years ago.

THE DACRE KNOT

NEVILLE

LANGLEY CASTLE
(Map II, F6.)

Langley Castle is a feudal fortress of extraordinary interest. As its former owner, Cadwallader J. Bates wrote : " Thanks to its destruction by fire so soon after its erection, paradoxical though it may sound, the castle of Sir Thomas de Lucy retains in an almost, if not quite, unique manner the essential outlines of a fortified house in the great days of Creçy and Poictiers."

This noble structure can be seen through the trees on the road from Haydon Bridge to Whitfield. Its present perfection of outline is due to twenty years of careful restoration and rebuilding by Mr. Bates, who bought the manor in 1882 when the castle was a ruin.

Part of the great barony of Tindale, the manor was in the possession of the De Lucys when, about 1360, the old castle of the Tindales was rebuilt ; and thereafter Umfravilles, Percies, Nevilles and Radcliffes were successive owners. The castle was destroyed only about fifty years after the De Lucy rebuilding, and was to lie a ruin for nearly five hundred years more. It was not the Scots, but our own King Henry IV who laid Langley low when he passed through Northumberland crushing the rebellion of Archbishop Scrope. Langley was then a stronghold of the Earl of Northumberland who had taken a leading part in the rising. The marks of the fire that destroyed the castle are still traceable.

Closely connected with the Radcliffes, who were later Earls of Derwentwater, is the story of the '15 Jacobite Rebellion. When it failed tragically and the young earl had been executed, the estate passed to the Crown ; and was eventually purchased from the Lords of the Admiralty by Mr. Bates who was attracted by its history and its architectural possibilities. During the early stages of the restoration, the owner resided in a tiny room on the first floor on the east side of the castle.

The site is a strong one—between two burns. The foundations do not go below ground—on a base of huge boulders the six-feet thick walls were placed in the form of an oblong, with

a tower at each corner. Adjoining one of these on the east side
is the entrance turret, where the small portcullis, guarding the
only way in, could be let down by a rope passing through a boss
in the vaulting shaped like a man's head. A newel-stair ascends
to the upper storeys; and a finely-designed doorway flanked
with ornamented shafts leads into the Great Hall. A little
traceried window in the east turret marks the chapel, for which
the original permissory document from the Holy See is preserved
in the castle. Mrs. Bates completed the chapel as a memorial
to her husband after his death in 1902. The pointed and
traceried windows of the central portion of the castle are unusual
and beautiful features. It is interesting to note how their
design alters as they ascend, from Decorated style (i.e. belonging
to the earlier Tindale stronghold) to the more elaborate
traceries of a later period.

On the west side of the castle the external arcading of the
south-west turret, marking the *garde-robes*, or latrines, affords
an interesting side-light on sanitary arrangements in feudal
times. The bell in this turret was formerly the big bell in
St. Nicholas's Cathedral, Newcastle.

These are only some of the absorbing features of Langley
Castle, raising its towers and turrets anew above the South
Tyne Valley. One cannot but admire wholeheartedly the
imagination and steady purpose that resulted in restoring to
its former grandeur one of the noblest of the baronial fortresses
of Northumberland.

LEMMINGTON TOWER
(Map II, C8.)

The road westward from Alnwick climbs to the high moors
of ancient Aydon Forest, from which a by-road beyond the
road to Whittingham drops past Lemmington Hall, a magnificent mansion that includes the ancient " Turris de Lematon."

In fairly recent times the place was a ruin, but was rebuilt
and enlarged by Sir Stephen Aitchison to its present state of
splendour. The wide park it faces is dotted with trees and
embellished with a tall memorial column to John Evelyn, the
famous diarist.

The history of the place begins nearly eight hundred years
ago with a Siward de Lemmington (the name has a Danish
sound); but it was probably the Beadnell family who built the
pele in the fourteenth century, and lived in it for nearly four
hundred years. It was a really strong place, higher than it is
now, thirty-five feet square and with walls six feet thick, as
befitted a site so isolated within such easy reach of the Border
hills. It was a place of some importance, too, in the scheme of
defence, and in the sixteenth century a posse of horsemen (among

them foreign mercenaries on one occasion) were stationed here ready to ride. It was at this period that one of the Beadnells was Steward of the Abbot's Court at Alnwick Abbey. It is curious to reflect that this glorious abbey has almost entirely disappeared (only the gate-tower remaining), whereas the humble tower at Lemmington lives on in added security.

After the Beadnells, the Claverings lived at Lemmington; then the tower passed by marriage to the Fenwicks, that widespread and redoubtable family, one of whom probably built the Georgian house adjoining.

At the north-east corner of the mansion stands the old tower, huge and four-square, and little altered from its age-old appearance apart from some carved arcading built into one wall, and the insertion of some large traceried windows; while the battlements are, of course, modern, though in genuine style. In the basement, which is a maze of gloomy, vaulted chambers, darker cement has been used to indicate the new pointing. The old wheel-stair is practically intact, and the Great Hall retains its generous fireplace. The ceiling of this spacious room has been heightened, as the corbels in the walls show. Fine wall panelling, old portraits and period furniture, gleaming copper and pewter, enhance the antique atmosphere. The sturdy pele is more than comfortable in its old age.

† LIDDEL STRENGTH
(Map I, F2.)

Also known as Liddel Mote (or more properly, *Motte*), and formerly as the Pele of Liddel, this magnificent earthwork overlooks from its lofty eminence the junction of the Liddel and the Esk. To reach it, the Longtown–Pentonbridge road is left at a byway sign-posted " Liddel Moat, 1 Mile." The place is a short half-mile from High Moat Farm, and is approached by a footpath.

We have in Liddel Strength a supremely fine example of a Norman fortress of the " Motte-with-Bailey " type, the *Motte* being the highest mound, formerly fortified about its summit with a stout oak palisade, and the Bailey being marked by the vast flanking ramparts and ditches. These latter would originally be filled with a tangle of thorns and briars. There does not seem to have been much stone used in the defences (the " pale and the palisades " are mentioned as late as 1300); but even without any other obstruction, it must have needed stout hearts and strong limbs to storm these steep and grassy slopes.

The line of a Roman road runs near the stronghold from Netherby northwards, and it is very probable that the Romans used this naturally strong site as a station, but the Strength first appears in history in 1165, when it is mentioned in a charter to the Canons of Jedburgh by William the Lion of Scotland. Thereafter it is frequently referred to, showing that it was an important link in the chain of English Border defences. The most stirring and tragic chapter in its troubled history was in 1346 when Sir Walter de Selby, the Royal Constable of the fortress, with a garrison of only two hundred men defied the whole invading army of David Bruce. For some days the gallant defenders held out before being overwhelmed in an assault, then in the barbarous fashion of the times the survivors of the garrison were put to the sword, Selby having the anguish of seeing his two sons strangled before he himself was slain. Having destroyed the defences the Scots marched on—to meet with disaster not long afterwards at Neville's Cross.

But the Mote must have been the theatre for many such scenes of blood ; as when a band of freebooters from over the Border " brent the mote of Liddel and at the same brennyng slew one Gilbert Richardson," a burning which seems to suggest that wood still formed the chief part of the defences. Fifty-five years later, " Arthur Grame of the Mote " was slain in a Scottish raid. The victim was, of course, one of the famous, or shall we say notorious, clan whose headquarters were at Netherby Hall not far away, and his death, it may be sure, would not go un-avenged. Netherby Hall, too, is the scene of Scott's ballad of *Lochinvar*, the dashing hero of which, it will be remembered, bore off the fair Ellen Graham from under the nose of the intended bridegroom and with her arms about his waist galloped off over Canobie Lea, while Forsters, Fenwicks and Musgraves rode and ran in vain pursuit. The clan acquired an evil reputation and after the Union of the two countries got short shrift from James VI, by whose orders they were harried so effectively with burnings and banishments that their power was utterly broken. Ancient Netherby Hall, still the home of the Grahams, stands on historic ground once occupied by a Roman station, and includes an old pele-tower in its structure ; but this is by the way.

The dimensions of Liddel Strength are cyclopean. The external oval measures 282 feet by 305, and the total area enclosed is from 3½ to 4 acres. It is 88 feet from the bottom of the fosse to the top of the central mound, and the width of the ditch here is 60 feet. These figures speak for themselves ! The massive stones in the form of an oblong in the centre of the Inner Bailey may mark the site of the stone tower erected by Sir Thomas Wake in 1348. Near the outer entrance to the stronghold are the grassy foundations of the Gate-House that guarded it. From the far edge of the site the ground drops in a precipitous cliff that was formerly washed by the Liddel. Not far beyond the fork " where the bright waters meet " is the Canobie Lea of the ballad. To the right the stream makes a shining curve over the level meadows; and beyond are the gently-contoured Border hills. A peaceful and lovely prospect now.

LITTLE HARLE TOWER
(Map II, E7.)

The old pele of the De Harles still stands intact and weather-tight, but it keeps such splendid company that it is doubtful if even its builders would recognise it. Today it forms an inconsiderable part of a magnificent modern mansion. Built of freestone in the Early English style, with many embattled towers and a great bay on the south front, fronted by a spacious lawn and sheltered by huge old trees, the house stands on the bank of the Wansbeck (which, lying on the north side, must have afforded a considerable measure of protection to the pele in former times), and is approached by a long avenue from the Newcastle–Otterburn road, about twenty miles out from the city.

In 1541 the tower was described in the Survey carried out by Sir Robert Bowes and Sir Ralph Ellerker for Henry VIII as being " in good reparation." It had then passed into the possession of the Fenwicks, that well-known Northumbrian family, and later was owned by the Aynsleys. Now it forms the western extremity of the mansion, a mere adjunct where formerly it stood in proud isolation, and shut in with trees where once the bare moor sloped steeply down to the Wansbeck.

† LITTLE SWINBURNE PELE
(Map II, F7.)

In the list of Border towers compiled by Sir Robert Bowes and Sir Ralph Ellerker in 1541 there is mentioned as standing at Little Swinburne a little tower which is, in unfortunately chosen words, described as " of thinheritaunce of Thomas Mydleton of Belso esqui' decayed in the roofes." It was, of course, the tower, not its owner, that was decayed in the roofs. It does not appear to have been put into repair again, but it is still standing. Though now a mere shell and in imminent danger of collapse, it contrives to present a fairly imposing appearance.

The hamlet of Little Swinburne lies in that wild area between the Hexham–Rothbury road and the Roman Dere Street, and is about two miles to the north of where those roads cross. A little way from the village stands the tower alone, on a site that does not seem particularly strong. In all probability there was formerly a surrounding barmkin. The south wall of the tower is fairly intact, the others being ruinous with many of the facing stones gone, exposing the rubble core. The entrance is at the north-east corner, part of the vaulting of the doorway remaining. Opposite, within, are the remains and part of the vaulting of the stairway to the upper storeys. On the first floor will be seen a wide fireplace. Few windows remain. On the outside of the west wall are signs that a building has stood against it, and the green foundations of this wing can be traced. The pele is a fairly big one, measuring about eight yards by fourteen, and with its adjoining wing must have formed a substantial dwelling-house some four hundred years ago before the Scots gave it the full benefit of their attentions. The chief seat of the Middletons who owned it was at Belsay. Their magnificent tower there still stands, and the family, too, still reside at Belsay in the nearby Hall.

LONGHORSLEY TOWER
(Map II, D8.)

This rugged pele-tower forms a prominent and picturesque object in the village of Longhorsley, six miles from Morpeth along the Wooler road.

There does not seem to be any record of its building. It was not mentioned in the list of Border towers made in 1415, but was probably built in the century following. Adjoining a little Catholic Chapel, it was for long, until recent years, the residence of the priest; but is now used as an ordinary private residence. The Horsley family, formerly of Brinkburn, built the tower. We last hear of them in the seventeenth century, just before the Restoration, when Sir Thomas Horsley entertained General Monck and his forces. It was in the middle of winter, and doubtless bitterly cold on these high, windswept moors. Sir Thomas's hospitality was lavish, but he admitted that he would rather see the success of Monck's rival, General Lambert, the head of the military party. A month later Monck was in London, to declare Parliament free and open the way for the Merry Monarch's return.

The pele is a large and massively-built tower of four storeys, the basement being barrel-vaulted as usual, with a small room partitioned off from one end in a way that suggests a prison. The original door was on the south side, but has been turned into a window. The present entrance, on the side nearest the village, was probably made when the gabled wing was added to the tower some two hundred and fifty years ago. The room on the ground floor of this wing is known as " The Lady's Room," perhaps after one of the dowagers of the Horsley family, or of the Carnabys who followed them in possession.

A wheel-stair from the basement climbs to the battlements. About twenty years ago when the wainscoting was removed from the first floor room, a fine fireplace with a lintel stone nine or ten feet long was uncovered. The second floor room has two recesses in the wall, one of which has been a latrine. The third floor room is very low. The crenellated battlements, rather low for any serious defensive work, are in a state of almost perfect preservation. Such are the outstanding features of this very fine specimen of a Northumbrian pele.

† MANGERTON CASTLE
(Map I, E2.)

There is some doubt about the identity of the fragmentary but massive pile known as Mangerton Castle, which stands close to the left bank of the Liddel about a mile to the south of Newcastleton. According to Sir Walter Scott, the present ruin is that of a mill built from the stones of the old tower. Be that as it may, there is built into the wall an interesting stone tablet carved with the arms of the Armstrongs of Mangerton (a chevron between three lozenges) and a long broadsword, together with the date, 1583, probably recording the repair or the building of the tower. The initials S.A. and E.E. are those of Symon Armstrong and his wife, Elizabeth Elliot. If the tower was built in the year given, the Laird of Mangerton was the victim of particularly bad luck, for in that same year he was taken in his own house by Lord Scrope's men (Scrope was Governor of Carlisle Castle) without a single English casualty, which was greatly wondered at, " for it was never heard of that a laird of Mangerton was taken in his own house either in peace or war without the hurt or loss of a man. Now that I have him," added Scrope in a letter to the Queen's Secretary, Lord Walsingham, " I trust it will be to good effect to keep the others quiet." It was only a few years after this, however, that Kinmont Willie Armstrong's rescue from Carlisle gaol by the Duke of Buccleuch raised such a stir, and brought down Elizabeth's wrath on Scrope's head.

But the Armstrongs were a constant thorn in the flesh of their neighbours on both sides of the Border, and the following verse conveys the general esteem in which this clan was held :

> " Of Liddisdail the common thiefis,
>   Sa peartlie stellis now and reifis,
>   That nane may keip
>   Horse, nolt, nor scheip,
>   Nor yett dar sleip
>   For their mischeifis."

Of their towers which dotted this district there remain this fragment (if it is one) ; the similar fragment known as Langholm Castle ; and Hollows Tower, the only one at all complete.

§ MELKRIDGE BASTLE-HOUSE
(Map I, F4.)

On the village green at Melkridge, two miles east of Halt-whistle and one of the ancient Twelve Towns of South Tynedale, may be seen as interesting a bastle-house as there is in the North Country. It doubtless owes its perfect preservation to its late erection just after the Union of England and Scotland. Before that happy occasion Tynedale was the favourite hunting ground of the Liddesdale Armstrongs and Elliots and other freebooters from over the Border, and they would not have spared a challenge as obvious as this.

The foundations of the stout walls consist of huge boulders laid upon the ground. The vaulted basement, entered originally only from one end, has loopholes that terminate curiously in circular openings; and an external stair leads up to the first floor, from which formerly a ladder went up to a hatch in the centre of the roof. Similar ladders communicated with the second floor and the loft, from which there is access to a para-peted lookout platform or beacon supported on corbels. From below it has the appearance of a chimney and is decorated with the rope-moulding that appears elsewhere on the house with such picturesque effect. The roof is of stone slabs pegged with sheep-shank bones, and all the floors were formerly flagged—both being precautions against fire. The floors are now boarded but the stout oak balks, black with age and showing the marks of the adze, on which the flags rested, still remain. In the first-floor room the fireplace is nine feet wide, and the original win-dows remain, though two modern ones have been inserted. During the alterations, some small stone cannon-balls were found under the paving of the second floor. This fine old house is still doing good service as the village recreation-room.

VALENCE

* MITFORD CASTLE
(Map II, E8.)

Till recent years Mitford Castle was little more than a romantic ruin, with most of its architectural features veiled under picturesque growths of vegetation, but H.M. Office of Works has now taken the stronghold under its wing, and the excavations in progress will as they develop show more and more of the structure and defences of this finely-situated castle.

Mitford Castle is easy of access. From Morpeth on the Great North Road two miles of winding road up the lovely valley of the Wansbeck bring one to Mitford village, where a byway drops to a sheltered hollow and the castle crowning its high mound.

The site is a strong one and must have appealed to the Norman builders—a plateau guarded on one side by the ravine of the Wansbeck, and on the others by steep slopes lending themselves to an encircling moat that could be fed from the river. There were Mitfords at Mitford in Saxon times, but it was not till the manor passed into Norman hands with the bestowal of the hand of a Mitford heiress by William the Conqueror on Sir Robert Bertram, one of his knights, that the necessity arose for a stronghold. A Bertram of Henry II's time built the present castle at the same time as he built Bothal, five miles down the valley. Almost exactly a hundred years later the Bertrams rebelled against their king and lost their estates, which were given to Aymer de Valence, Earl of Pembroke, of whose family it is recorded that for several generations no father saw his son. This earl, for instance, had the misfortune to be slain at a tournament held to celebrate his wedding.

Strong as it appears to have been, the castle had only a brief existence. It seems to have been a special mark for the Scots, and by the beginning of the thirteenth century it was ruinous, and was never afterwards repaired. It is possible that it was deliberately dismantled after the rebel, Sir Walter de Selby, surrendered it, to prevent its being used again by Northumbrian barons in league with the Scots. For this was the disturbed period after Bannockburn when Northumberland was overrun by Scottish troops, and many Northumbrians threw in their lot with their traditional enemies either for their own safety, or to do some freebooting themselves. One of the boldest of these renegades was Sir Gilbert de Middleton who abused his position as Warden of the March to pursue his get-rich-quick schemes, and filled the dungeons of Mitford Castle with his unfortunate neighbours while he held them to ransom. The feat that closed Middleton's career was the kidnapping of Louis de Beaumont, the Bishop elect of Durham, and his brother. Having surprised them at Rushyford, south of Durham City, Middleton confined Beaumont in Morpeth and brought his brother to Mitford. The ransom demanded was raised by William de Felton and others, and on the day appointed for the final payment, they visited the castle and reported to Middleton that the money was ready in the village. He gave them leave to pass and repass the gate to fetch it, but as they went out they turned on the porters and slew them, then let in a band of their own men concealed outside. Middleton was captured, and later taken to London for execution.

A footpath leads from the bridge up to the castle. To the left of where the bailey is entered will be seen the remains of the original gateway, where, probably, William de Felton and his friends cut the throats of the porters some six hundred years ago. To the right within, and raised on an artificial *motte* or mound, is the keep, of a peculiar pentagonal shape and at one point only a few feet from the outer wall. It is likely that a drawbridge spanned this space formerly. Only the basement of the keep remains. It is approached by a straight flight of steps descending from the first floor and is mostly occupied by two barrel-vaulted cellars that may have been used as dungeons, since the doorway to one of them (opening from the stair) has bar-holes outside. Was this where Middleton kept his wealthy prisoners? A massive, round-headed arch in the curtain wall near the keep gives a charming glimpse of the wooded vale, the church, and the old manor-house of the Mitfords which they built about the time their estates were restored to them by Charles II. On the south side of the bailey a considerable portion of the curtain wall remains, and along one stretch is high enough on the exterior side to give quite a good impression of the formidable nature of the old defences, especially if one imagines the huge moat brimful of water. From the number of human remains found in the south-west corner of the bailey it is supposed that the chapel stood here. Judicious excavation will no doubt solve this and other problems connected with this fragmentary but beautiful ruin.

MERLAY

MORPETH CASTLE
(Map II, E9.)

Not many travellers by the Great North Road through Morpeth catch any glimpse of its castle, though some have been known to mistake the old county prison for it! In truth, little remains of the "fayre castle" of the De Merlays—just the lower part of the curtain walls and the Gate-House which has been adapted as a private residence.

The stronghold was a Norman one, built shortly after the Conquest by William de Merlay, who had fought at Hastings and helped to subdue Northumberland and was rewarded by his sovereign with the barony of Morpeth. The site is strong, occupying the summit of a hill to the left of the highway as we descend into Morpeth from Newcastle, and bounded on the far side by a deep ravine. On the south side a road marks the position of the old moat that cut across the neck of the promontory. Morpeth Castle does not figure prominently in history. In 1138 Ranulph de Merlay entertained here the eight monks of Fountains Abbey whom he had invited to help him to found a new monastery at Newminster. King John in his revengeful expedition against the rebellious barons of Northumberland burnt Morpeth Castle along with several others, but the castle was rebuilt by the last of the De Merlays. The estate then passed by the marriage of his daughter to the Greystoke family, one of whom, William, known as the Good Baron, built the Gate-House at the same time as he restored and extended the defences. Twice more the estate changed hands by the marriage of an heiress, the second bridegroom being the famous "Belted Will" Howard of Naworth Castle, whose descendant, the Earl of Carlisle, still owns the barony.

At the time of the Union of England and Scotland the castle seems to have been in fairly good condition but, ironically enough, the stronghold which had survived the Border wars succumbed to the fury of the Civil War when, in 1644, it was besieged by 2,700 men under the Marquis of Montrose, who was determined "to ferret out his rebellious countrymen."

He referred to a garrison of 500 Scotsmen left by General Leslie to hold the castle for the Parliament. The castle governor banked up the outer gate with earth and sods to prevent its being blown in with a mine, and a fierce attack in the dawn was successfully repulsed. During a respite the garrison sallied out and destroyed some earthworks outside the walls, and also demolished some buildings that might give shelter to the enemy. But they spared a new barn, and in this Montrose placed his cannon, but the thatch of the barn was fired, so he moved his guns to a better position and succeeded in making a breach in the walls. It was promptly closed with feather beds ! In the subsequent mêlée a musket bullet entered the governor's neckcloth and came out at his hat, removing " some of the hide and hair of his head." Finally a flag of truce was raised, and the garrison were eventually allowed to march out with honour, their casualties having been only a tenth of those sustained by the attackers. The Ha' Hill, on the other side of the ravine, is pointed out as one of the positions of Montrose's guns. Two hundred years after the siege, some cannon balls were found in the earth below the castle walls.

The Gate-House has been modernised as regards windows and roof. A wide, slightly-pointed arch pierces the base of the tower, and not far within the vaulted roof of the passage there is the outline of a meurtriere (now blocked), through which attackers could be surprised from above. In peace time it was used for the convenient reception of goods. Gates formerly closed the inner and outer archways, and the square openings for the bars of the outer gates remain. Formerly at two of the angles of the battlements there were tall lookout turrets connected by a gallery. The curtain walls, which are ruinous, are highest on the south and east sides, some of the masonry being very massive, and the bailey they once enclosed is now a peaceful garden.

SELBY

MULTON

† NAFFERTON CASTLE
(Map II, F8.)

Though not a great part of Nafferton Castle remains, or, indeed, was ever built, it is of exceptional interest as an example of an " adulterine " stronghold, one, that is, erected without royal licence in the days when such permission was required.

The reign of John was not famed for its establishment of law and order, and many of the Norman barons took advantage of the king's weakness to build castles in which they could defy their sovereign, or lord it over weaker neighbours. In this case it was the latter motive rather than the former, for Philip de Ulecote, Forester of Northumberland, was in favour with the king and doubtless took his approval for granted. He had, however, overlooked a powerful baron already established in the neighbourhood—Richard de Umfraville of Prudhoe, who resented this challenge taking shape almost at his barbican (the medieval equivalent of a front door), and made such forcible representations to the Crown in the next reign that De Ulecote had to tell his masons to cease work. Daniel, the son of the Constable of Newcastle, and Robert de Whitchester, Sheriff of Northumberland, had instructions to take down the timber and the brattice-tower, and transport them to Bamburgh, though later the place of destination was changed to Newcastle, where the brattice-tower (or bretesche) was re-erected to replace a turret that had fallen owing to weak foundations. In revenge for this set-back, De Ulecote obtained royal letters ordering the destruction of Umfraville's other castle at Harbottle, and there was some difficulty in proving that it was not an " adulterine " stronghold. The building of Nafferton Castle, thus interrupted, was never resumed, and it became ruinous before it had been completed !

The remains of the Keep, sixty feet square, and of the two baileys (now not easy to trace) are to be found among the trees on the west bank of Whittle Dene, just above where it is crossed by the Newcastle–Corbridge highway. A brace of silver-mounted pistols and other relics have been unearthed on the site.

A gruesome legend has grown up round the mouldering walls. The half-finished keep became, it is said, the secret lair of a herculean freebooter called Lang Lonkin who terrorised the district with his unspeakable crimes ; and an old ballad tells how he got into Welton Hall through the treachery of a servant named Orange. The Lord of Welton had ridden to London, not without foreboding that misfortune was hanging over his house.

> " ' Where's the Ladies of the Hall ? '
>   Says the Lonkin ;
> ' They're up in their chambers,'
>   Says Orange to him.
>
> ' How shall we get them down ? '
>   Says the Lonkin ;
> ' Prick the babe in the cradle,'
>   Says Orange to him."

When the mother hurries downstairs to tend to her child, both it and she are slain by the ruffian, and their bodies thrown into a pool in the burn, a pool still shown as " Lang Lonkin's Hole." The freebooter finally closed his career by hanging himself from a tree near the castle, and for long afterwards his skull lay within the ruined walls. The terror inspired by this villain, legendary or not, must have been very real, since till comparatively recent times the name of " Lonkin " was used in the district as a bogey by parents foolish enough to think that their children should be frightened into obedience ; and if a child was disinclined to come into the house at nightfall, its mother had only to jingle a bunch of keys and cry, " There's Lang Lonkin ! " to obtain the desired effect.

Legends are only legends, yet in the dusk, with the arching trees adding to the gloom and the stream making those voicelike murmurs that some streams make, this mossgrown pile can be a very eerie place.

DACRE

§ NAWORTH CASTLE

(Map I, F3.)

As Alnwick Castle holds pride of place among Border holds on the east side of the country, so does Naworth Castle, the seat of the Earl of Carlisle, on the west. As seen in the distance from the main road from Brampton towards Newcastle, its battlements and towers strike a romantic note in an area of spacious park-land. At closer quarters it fulfils the promise, being a storehouse of unique treasures capable of stirring the dullest imagination and of evoking the atmosphere of those far-off times when the Border was a barrier only to be passed at peril to life and limb.

The most famous figure associated with Naworth is Lord William Howard, the " Belted Will " of Scott's poetic fancy, but it is sometimes overlooked that he did not come into his estate until the Union of the two countries, and hence had little or no part in those international frays that did so much to make life precarious along the Border.

It was in the time of the Dacres that the castle served the purpose for which it had been erected—i.e. " to defend the country and annoye the enemye," and it was the Dacres who founded Naworth. In early times Gospatric, Earl of Northumberland, had a " worth," or hall, on this site, but it was probably a wooden structure, and it was not till 1335 that Ranulph de Dacre got a licence from Edward III to crenellate his house at Naworth, which he did by building a tower and enclosing a courtyard with a stone wall. This tower was probably what is now known as the Dacre Tower, or at least the base of it, since Thomas Lord Dacre (he distinguished himself at Flodden and was equally notable as a builder) rebuilt the upper part of this tower and added a storey to it. His arms on the tower mark his handiwork. He also built what is now known as the Howard Tower and rebuilt the Great Banqueting Hall, today little changed. Altogether he made Naworth a redoubtable stronghold. But his work was neglected—his successor preferred to live at his castle at Kirkoswald, and Naworth in course of time was not only uninhabited but ruinous. A chronicler of the time described it as " in very great decay in all parts, and the out-houses and other houses and offices utterlie decayed."

A change came in the fortunes of Naworth when a Dacre co-heiress married her half-brother, Lord William Howard. This scholarly Borderer carefully restored the castle, rebuilt the eastern tower as his own private quarters, bringing ceilings and panelling from Kirkoswald to beautify the rooms, added the picture-gallery ; and in short converted the broken stronghold into a stately mansion. His marriage of convenience at the age of fourteen (his wife was a few months younger !) developed into a real love-match, and " Bessie with the braid apron," as she was called from the ample possessions she brought to her husband, proved herself an excellent wife and mother.

144

They had ten sons and five daughters, most of whom seem to have stayed on at Naworth after their respective marriages, for at one period there were no fewer than fifty-two Howards in the castle. The Great Hall, vast as it is, cannot have been too big for such a family.

The vicissitudes of Naworth were not yet at an end. In 1844 a disastrous fire almost completely gutted the castle. The fine woodwork from Kirkoswald was nearly all destroyed, and only a stout iron door saved Lord William Howard's Tower. The following year Naworth was restored and refurnished by the sixth Earl of Carlisle under the direction of the celebrated architect, Anthony Salvin; and the Morpeth Tower was added. In more recent times the splendid Stanley wing was built to the designs of C. J. Ferguson of Carlisle.

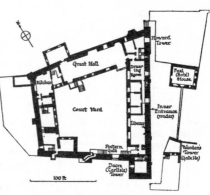

PLAN OF NAWORTH CASTLE

There are, fortunately, considerable facilities for seeing Naworth Castle. The park is always open to the public, and the interior of the castle is shown from May 1st to September 30th on Mondays, Thursdays and Saturdays from 2—5, and on Bank Holidays from 10—12 and 2—5. A shilling a head is charged. Parties consisting of more than twenty should apply beforehand by letter to the Estate Office at the castle. The entrance is by an ancient gateway in the Warden's Tower, over the arch of which appear the arms of Thomas Lord Dacre (quartered with those of Vaux, Multon and Morville) with griffins as supporters, a collared bull as crest, and the Dacre motto, " Fort en loialte " (Strong in loyalty). The inner entrance is not immediately opposite the outer but strategically some distance to the right, near a small detached tower known as the Fuel House, built by Thomas Lord Dacre. It will be seen that the castle is in the form of an enclosed courtyard with a tower at each corner. The tall tower nearest the outer gate is the Dacre Tower, and at the other extremity of the front is the Howard Tower. These, with the great Banqueting Hall, are particularly fine examples of medieval architecture among a great deal of absorbing interest in this wonderful pile. The Dacre Tower, the oldest part of the castle, is a typical pele with red sandstone walls from 7½ to 9 feet thick, and a vaulted basement, from which a straight mural stair goes to the first floor, then a newel stair to the roof. Next to this tower on the north side is the Sallyport, with an oak door twenty feet high. The curtain wall here is seven feet thick.

The Great Hall of the castle, approached from the courtyard by a broad flight of steps, is a room unique in the North Country, both by reason of its size and its furnishings. Measuring a hundred feet by twenty-four, with a dais at one end, a fireplace sixteen feet wide, and an open timber roof supported on corbels enriched with heraldic shields, the Hall has an atmosphere of antique spaciousness. Duplicates of the shields above appear on chairs round the room. Flanking the fireplace are two curious, life-size heraldic figures—the " reed bull " of the Dacres on the left ; the black griffin of the De Vaux on the right ; and at the end of the Hall are two more—the dolphin of the Greystokes, and the stag* of the De Multons. These grotesque banner-bearing figures were brought from Kirkoswald when that castle was demolished. Another treasure from Kirkoswald, a ceiling painted with panel portraits of the kings of England and Scotland, was destroyed in the great fire. One of the rich wall tapestries was originally a marriage gift to Henry IV and Mary Medici ; and among the ancient suits of armour is one worn by " Belted Will " himself. On a side table are three coloured statuary groups, two showing elopements in the history of the family, one being the escape of Ranulph de Dacre with Margaret de Multon from Brougham Castle, and the third representing Thomas Lord Dacre at Flodden, with the Dacre slogan beneath—" A Daker, a Daker ! a reed bull, a reed bull ! " Two of the most interesting of the many valuable old paintings on the walls are the portraits of Lord William Howard and his wife, over the fireplace. An outstanding picture is a full-length portrait of Charles I, by Van Dyck. Other portraits, here and in the Drawing Room, are those of Queen Catherine Parr, Anne Countess of Pembroke, Philip Earl of Arundel, Lord Surrey who commanded the English forces at Flodden, and one said to represent Queen Mary of England. A striking picture of a different type is " A Border Spear," painted by J. W. Glasse, an American artist, and showing a mounted mosstrooper silhouetted against the moon with his spear half raised.

The Library, formerly the Chapel, is panelled with oak and hung with tapestries. Over the fireplace is a plaster panel in relief, the combined work of an artist and a sculptor, both celebrated ; the subject, which shows Lord Dacre leading his troop of horse into action at Flodden, having been designed by Sir Edward Burne-Jones, and the work executed by Sir Edgar

*There is some doubt about the identity of this figure—it may be intended for a unicorn.

Plate XVI

LANGLEY CASTLE;
FEATHERSTONE CASTLE—THE COURTYARD

Plate XVII

TYNEMOUTH AND PRUDHOE CASTLES—
THE GATE-HOUSES

Plate XVIII

WILLIMOTESWICK CASTLE—THE ENTRANCE; FORD CASTLE

Plate XIX

HARNHAM HALL—THE CHIMNEY LOOKOUT;
STONEGARTHSIDE HALL—THE ENTRANCE FROM THE COURTYARD, WITH THE
STAIRS BEYOND

Boehm. There are more pictures, many with Scriptural subjects, in the long Picture Gallery between Lord Dacre's Tower and the Howard Tower. Some quaint old cabinets here are fitted with secret recesses. One cabinet opens out to represent the façade of a house.

The Howard Tower is constructed unusually, not to say daringly, on a series of arches. The end of one of these protrudes from an outside wall, and part of another is visible on the stairway. On the first floor is the stout ironbound door that, during the great fire, barred the flames from what were formerly Lord Howard's private apartments. The door is tremendously heavy, and not easy to swing even on well-oiled hinges. The spot is dimly lit and is not popular with the castle staff. Some of them say that at the time of dusk, to open this door is to have a sensation of one's shoulder being gripped by someone—or something ! We have here the beginnings of a ghost. Soon, doubtless, we shall hear of " Belted Will's " wraith standing guard over his favourite haunt. The rooms are largely as he left them three hundred years ago. Above the Bedroom fireplace, on three shields, are the arms of the Dacres with quarterings, and those of Greystoke and Boteler. The wallpaper is modern and was designed by William Morris, one of the Pre-Raphaelites. The Study, or Library, contains over three hundred of Lord Howard's books, many in their original binding, and all in the old bookcases. A special treasure, most carefully protected, is a huge copy of the " Britannia " of Camden, the famous antiquary with whom Lord Howard was friendly. An ancient leaved screen, done in manuscript on vellum by the monks of Glastonbury, gives the lives of Joseph of Arimathea and other saints. The elaborate ceiling, with recessed panels and bold, heraldic bosses, is one of those brought from Kirkoswald. Adjoining the Library is a little private Chapel, where the Dacre scallop shell is plentifully used in the decorations. The altar is the original one. Facing it is an early sixteenth century panel-painting representing the Scourging, the Crucifixion and the Burial of Christ. In one corner of the Chapel a panel hinges back and a trapdoor in the floor lifts to disclose a little stair descending to a secret room—a " priest's hole," useful in times of religious intolerance. The roof of the tower is furnished with machicolations, through which the foot of the walls could be guarded on the north side.

From this point the disposition of the castle and its defences can be surveyed. A depression across the garden on the south (or south-east) side near the Fuel House marks the line of one of the two moats that formerly linked up the natural moats formed by the Castle Beck and the Capon Cleugh, thus isolating a triangular plateau ideal as a site for the great towers and flanking walls of this superb Border hold.

MARLEY

* NEWCASTLE-UPON-TYNE
(Map II, F9.)

The ancient name for Newcastle was *Pons Aelii*—the Bridge of Aelius. As the first of the Tyne bridges, it demanded defence, and the site for that defence was obviously this high plateau, falling precipitously to the Tyne on one hand and to the present-day " Side " on the other. It is not surprising that both those great builders, the Romans and the Normans, built their forts on the same spot.

Some sort of fort was erected here in the time of Robert Curthose, but the present castle was built by the order of Henry II. He had resumed possession of Northumberland, which had long been in Scottish hands, and the New Castle on the Tyne was one of many he built in anticipation of Scottish resentment. Of the castle of those days only the Keep and the South Postern Gate with a portion of curtain wall remain. The Black Gate, built by Henry's grandson, also stands, separated now from the Keep by the railway. Both Black Gate and Keep are open to the public at a small fee.

Built in five years at a cost of a thousand pounds, the Keep is a fine example of late Norman (or Transitional) work. It played a stout part as " the bridle of Scotland," though after the building of the great town walls in Edwardian times, it was they as often as the castle which withstood attacks. We hear of William the Lion making a fruitless attempt to capture the half-finished fortress, and of various other assaults ; but the greatest chapter in its history was after the Union of the two countries—in 1644 during the Civil War when, the town having been taken by General Leslie and his troops, Sir John Marley the mayor held out for three days longer in the Castle Keep. His resolution did not make him popular with the townsfolk, who were incensed that he should imperil their safety by defying the Scots when the cause was a hopeless one ; and on surrendering himself, he was nearly torn to pieces by an angry mob, and had to be guarded in his own house. Later, for safety, he was put into the castle dungeon, " till the hangman should salute his neck with a blow of Strafford's courtesy."

He was, however, spared that fate and lived to see the Restoration.

When its period of usefulness was over, the castle fell on evil days. For nearly two hundred years it was used as a common gaol, and in 1777 was one of those visited by John Howard, the prison reformer, who was shocked at the conditions the prisoners had to endure. Shortly after this the Keep was at the disposal of a Mr. Fryer, who advertised it as being suitable for a windmill! " To be let, the old Castle in the Castle Garth, upon which with the greatest convenience and advantage, may be erected a wind-mill for the purpose of grinding corn, and bolting flour, or making oil, etc. There is an exceeding good spring of water within the Castle, which renders it a very eligible situation for a Brewery, or any Manufactory that requires a constant supply of water."

Eighty years ago, however, the Keep, and later the Black Gate, were leased by the Newcastle Society of Antiquaries; and, repaired and restored, have been carefully looked after since.

A curious history attaches to the Castle Garth, the space within the walls. When Newcastle was created an independent county in the year 1400, the Castle and its precincts remained part of Northumberland, the advantage of which was quickly grasped by various " wicked persons " in the town who used to go into the Castle Garth after their misdeeds and there defy the town authorities. This nuisance was stopped by a charter, but another thorn in the flesh of Newcastle townsfolk persisted through a very long period. The various guilds of the town could prohibit any unauthorised person from trading in the town, but they held no sway over the Castle Garth, and in course of time all sorts of traders and establishments flourished there— a sword " kipper," a Scotch pedlar, a tavern kept by Master John Pickle, and tailors and shoemakers skilled in " translating old articles into new ones." The decay of the guilds and the sweeping away of old buildings in the Garth finally brought this feud to a close.

The Keep is very massively built, its walls varying from fifteen to eighteen feet in thickness at the lower parts, and at the upper from twelve to seventeen feet. The Great Hall on the second floor is gained by a flight of stairs which pass under a tower. The doorway opening from the landing is an exact copy of the Norman original. The Great Hall is an imposing but gloomy apartment, loftier than it originally was. Adding to its gloom, the banners of notable Northumbrian families hang from the vaulting; and round the walls are various ancient weapons, including bill-hooks (so-called from their shape), vicious-looking weapons which, with bows, were the principal weapons of English infantry in the good old days. On one side a passage leads in the thickness of the wall to the well, which is a hundred feet deep. From basins beside it water could be sent to various parts of the castle, one pipe emerging in the central pillar of the so-called dungeon in the basement. From the window-recess next to the well entrance a passage leads to a wall-room which seems to have been a prison, judging by the bar-holes outside the door. A similar room opens off the basement chamber.

On the opposite side of the Great Hall is a fine mural room known for some reason as the " King's Chamber." It is the most cheerful in the whole building, its windows facing south. The inner door here leads to a garde-robe ; and the decorated fireplace is the original one. Among the objects kept in this room are two fine, iron-bound muniment chests. On the wall opposite the door is carved, 10 : 1644, the date of the last and most famous siege of the castle.

The floors below comprise two large rooms and the chapel, approachable by the great newel-stair in the south-east angle of the Keep. The room on the first floor is a museum, the objects being all carefully labelled and explained, so that no description of them is needed here. The fine horse-shoe table is made of oak dredged from the Tyne. A side-room on the east side was originally entered from the newel-stair, and seems to have been part of the defences of the stairway outside, for two loopholes look that way. Its doorway also commands the entrance to the present museum, which was probably once the Governor's private quarters. It must be remembered, however, that the Keep as a whole was not intended as a residence—there were other buildings in the bailey, such as the hall known as the King's Chamber, more suited as dwellings.

We next descend to the lovely late-Norman chapel, its decorated arches and groined roof, though not altogether symmetrical, giving a rare effect of harmony. The walls of this chapel are thin ; and formerly it was not entered from the Keep at all. Next to the chapel is the room known as the dungeon, probably intended for a storehouse, but used in the seventeenth and eighteenth centuries as a prison. When John Howard, the prison reformer, visited it, it had no roof, but men and women were compelled to spend several nights in it waiting for their turn at the assizes. They were chained to the walls (some of the rings remain), and in rainy weather the water was inches deep. Incredible as it may seem, the townsfolk regarded such sights as entertainment, and paid sixpence a head " to watch the prisoners." This gloomy room is remarkable for its fine vaulting, springing from the central pillar. From it we can go back to the museum on the first floor by a stairway in the north-west octagonal turret ; then regain the great newel-stair and ascend to the battlements ; with an opportunity part way up of looking down into the Great Hall from a mural gallery that extends right round the Keep. The battlements are modern, and not like the original ; and the roof may formerly have had two pointed gables, surrounded by a wall walk.

Part way down the Castle Stairs from the Keep is the very fine Postern Gate, one of the oldest in the country. It has a barrel-vaulted arch, and may formerly have been protected by an overhead tower.

The Black Gate, or Gate-House, has known many vicissitudes. Formerly the chief entrance to the castle, it consists of a vaulted passage guarded by two semi-circular towers, but was greatly altered in Stuart times ; and the outer barbican has been destroyed. Grooves show the position of the portcullis, and beyond it there were open meutrieres in the roof, from which the enemy, held up by the gates, could be assaulted. On either hand here are guard-chambers, with loopholes in the walls to command the ditch, in which the base of the Gate-House rested. Beyond the Gate-House lay a drawbridge spanning a dry moat and then, and not till then, the attackers could reach the north gate into the castle bailey. The dry moat can be seen by visiting the Heron Pit below the curtain wall, an underground prison named after Sir William Heron of Ford, who was Governor of the castle seven hundred years ago. A ladder descends into the moat, and one can go along under the present road. As for the adjoining Pit, it was entered only from above, and was without windows, an *oubliette* of the type to be seen at Alnwick, Warkworth and Hermitage Castles.

In the Black Gate, chiefly on the first floor, will be found the finest collection of Roman stones in the country. The second floor is largely given over to prehistoric and Anglo-Saxon relics. Two models here have particular connection with the subject of this book — one shows a mangonel, a medieval catapult used in sieges ; and the other a reconstruction of the castle, made by Mr. Ventress, which gives an admirable conception of this magnificent fortress in its prime. Here, too, as a frieze round the room, is the copy of the Bayeux Tapestry referred to in the Introduction to this book.

HAGGERSTON

* NORHAM CASTLE

(Map II, A6.)

More than any other castle in the Border, Norham holds the imagination as a symbol of other days. This is largely due, no doubt, to Scott's vivid references to " Norham's castled steep " in the First Canto of *Marmion*, but this fine fortress needs only to be seen to leave a lasting impression of ancient strength.

About midway between Berwick and Coldstream, the castle guarded an important ford of the Tweed, but nowadays a bridge crosses the river higher up, and the old road on the further bank below the castle is a mere green hollow across the fields.

It was a Prince Bishop of Durham, Bishop Flambard, who founded Norham Castle in 1121 in the "Northern Homestead" of the see to protect this part of the county palatine of Durham from the Scots. As may be expected, it had its share of raids and sieges and royal visits—from the sovereigns of both countries ! In early times Northumberlánd was often in Scottish hands, and thus in 1200 we find William the Lion spending Lent in the castle and keeping his fast with fourteen kinds of fish, among them, of course, the incomparable Tweed salmon. As one writer has said, he " spelt his fasts with an *e*." It was at Norham, or rather on a meadow below the walls, where Edward I was accepted by the Scottish lords as the arbitrator upon the succession to the Scottish throne ; and where John Balliol later swore fealty to Edward. After the battle of Bannockburn, when the vengeful Scottish tide surged over the Border, Norham Castle suffered—and withstood—many bitter sieges, thanks to the stout governorship of Sir Thomas Grey and his son ; who gave a stirring account of this period in his *Scalacronica*. From this book Scott probably got the idea for the " Marmion " of his poem. The real Marmion was a Lincolnshire knight who came to Norham to " fame " the golden-crested helmet given to him by his lady, with the command to seek " the daungerest place in England." He had not long to wait to show his mettle—four days after his arrival there drew up before the castle walls a Scottish force under Sir Alexander Mowbray. At the governor's suggestion Sir William Marmion donned his golden helmet, " toke his cursore [courser], and rode emong the throng of ennemyes." But they were too many for him—he was wounded and thrown to the ground, and the governor had to make a sally to rescue him. " With al the hole garison he lette prik yn emong the Scottes, and so wondid them, and their horses, that they were over-throwen, and Marmyon sore beaten was horsid agayn, and with Gray pursewid the Scottes yn chace."

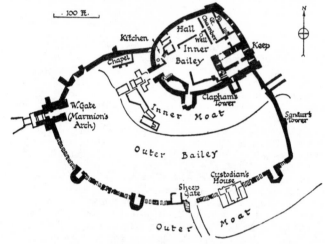

PLAN OF NORHAM CASTLE

When James IV invaded England prior to Flodden, the castle was bombarded with " Mons Meg " (cast at Mons), the famous cannon brought specially from Edinburgh for the occasion. From a fortified position still to be seen in a field on the opposite bank of the Tweed, monstrous stone balls were hurled at the barbican till it was battered to pieces ; and eventually the castle was captured and held—but only for a week or so, for Flodden was fought immediately afterwards. In the 1541 Survey of Border strongholds, Norham was described as being " in muche decay, the outer walls old, thynne and weake," yet it continued to give useful service up till the time of the Union of the two countries.

The excavations carried out since the castle came under the protection of H.M. Office of Works have revealed much of interest—the imposing masonry of the causeway and moat at the West Gate, for instance, where the wooden bridge takes the place of the drawbridge. This gateway, once completely walled up, then later opened out and rebuilt, is known as Marmion's Arch, since it is probably the one from which that knight, a gleaming figure in silver and gold, spurred his charger among the Scots. On the left within this Norman gateway, and of later date than most of the walls, are a series of wide emplacements for cannon, which would lie low on the ground. Many masons' marks are traceable on the stones, which are wonderfully preserved through long burial below ground. An inner wall, defended by a broad deep moat, the drainage system of which is of great interest, cuts off the Inner Bailey where the great red-sandstone Keep stands. At the left end of this moat, against the outer wall, are the foundations of the castle chapel. Little remains of the Inner Gate-House or of its Barbican. The Keep is higher than it was originally, as built by Bishop Puiset in accordance with Henry II's plan for strengthening the northern defences. Richard of Wolviston was the builder entrusted with the work at Norham. Of his work, the two lower storeys remain; and the flat buttresses on two sides of the Keep and the corner buttresses are typical of the architecture of the time. A round-headed door at first floor level on the south wall marks the main entrance, approached by a flight of steps which has disappeared. The walls are twelve to fifteen feet thick, and unusually solid, many of the mural galleries and rooms having been built up. The northern part of the basement is vaulted in sections; and next to it is a long, barrel-vaulted room containing a collection of iron and stone cannon-balls, some of them the offspring of Mons Meg herself!

In the Inner Bailey among the many ruins are those of the sixteenth-century Bishops' residence, comprising a Great Hall opposite the Keep and, adjoining it, a buttery, a pantry and a kitchen. Next to the Hall on the other side is the Great Chamber, and beyond it a lobby and a newel-stair of fifteenth century date.

Returning to the Outer Bailey, the little postern gate at the far (east) end of the inner moat should be noticed. It has two relieving-arches above it. On the other side of the moat is Sandur's Tower, forming a bastion on the outer curtain wall. On the south side of the Outer Bailey there is a series of projecting turrets, formerly rounded, but later made, most of them, with a pointed front. One contains some well-preserved gun-emplacements; and another close to the Sheep Gate is now the custodian's cottage. The mysterious-looking arches in this part of the curtain wall were intended to take its weight, and were formerly below ground. Generally speaking, the outer defences do not appear to have been very strong, and this will explain why the Outer Bailey was taken so often, while the rest of the castle continued to hold out. Before leaving, an ascent should be made of the lookout turret on the west side of the Keep, for its wide views of the Merse and of the Tweed, across which the Queen of Border Castles still looks proudly, even in decay.

OTTERBURN TOWER

(Map I, E5.)

The very name of Otterburn recalls the most stirring of all Border frays—that one fought out under an August moon in the year 1388 ; and the old pele that forms part of the present mansion known as Otterburn Tower figures in the old accounts of the battle. Froissart mentions, for instance, that the Scottish forces, while awaiting the arrival of Earl Percy and his men, tried to take the tower. They began operations at dawn ; but it was " tolerably strong and situated among the marshes, and they attacked it so long and so unsuccessfully that they were fatigued, and therefore sounded a retreat." That night most of the Scottish leaders were for going on across the Border, but Earl Douglas overruled them, saying that the castle must be taken. Before the next morning, however, Harry Hotspur and his men had arrived at Otterburn, and the taking of the tower became a minor and forgotten issue.

At the beginning of the fifteenth century the tower was in the possession of Sir Robert Umfraville, and later passed into the hands of the Halls, a widespread and powerful clan in Redesdale. " Mad Jack Ha' " was one of those " out " in the '15 Rising, and one of those, too, who was executed for his share in it, though reprieved five times. At his trial he pleaded that when he was returning from a Justices' Meeting (he was a J.P.) he was surrounded by rebels and compelled to accompany them. What did actually happen was that he was sitting on the bench at Alnwick Quarter Sessions when he heard that the Jacobites were rallying, and set off in such haste to join them that he left his hat behind.

The old pele is built into the east wing of the house, the wing we reach first in going up the drive. At the rear of it and now within the servants' quarters, is the old well. Formerly there was probably a courtyard surrounded by a barmkin on this side. A spot to the north-west of the house and close to the burn which flows on that side is the traditional site of a still older tower, the foundations of which were once unearthed during gardening operations.

The west part of the house, built about a hundred years ago, is in the same castellated style as the remainder. A handsome stone porch bears the arms of the Umfravilles (the wolf bearing an upright sword was their crest), those of the Pease family who were the late owners, and the initials of Mad Jack Ha'. On the south wall between the porch and the old tower is a bronze tablet giving a brief account of some of the important events in the history of this Border stronghold.

† PONTELAND PELE

(Map II, F8.)

This pele, which stands in the vicarage garden and was itself the vicarage in former days, has seen many alterations from its original structure, some of them obvious owing to being carried out in brick, others dating from fairly recent times when the pele was adapted as a gardener's cottage. A penthouse at one side supersedes an older, similar structure, the weathering of which is visible at the rear of the tower. Here, too, will be seen one of the old loopholes, now blocked. The roof has a double gable. From the cellars, which are now filled up, there ran (according to local tradition) a secret passage to Ponteland Castle, a tradition more credible than most of this nature since the two places are not far apart. It is unfortunate that the tower has lost so many of its characteristics.

UMFRAVILLE

MITFORD

§ PONTELAND TOWER
(Map II, F8.)

Ponteland Tower is one of those Border strongholds which by a happy chance have risen again from their ruins and received a new lease of existence. For long it lay ivy-covered and derelict, but a few years ago the owners of the adjoining " Blackbird " inn restored the ancient tower under expert antiquarian supervision and made it part of the premises without obliterating the characteristic features of the building.

Nowadays known as a cyclists' mecca eight miles from Newcastle, Ponteland is a place of very ancient settlement, formerly in the barony of Mitford. In 1224 it was chosen for an important international conference, where peace was arranged between England and Scotland ; and in the next century it figured in the events leading up to the most celebrated of Border frays. Froissart describes the incident : " On the morrow, the Scots dislodged from before Newcastle ; and, taking the road to their own country, they came to a town and castle called Pontclau, of which a very valiant knight of Northumberland was the lord. They halted there about four o'clock in the morning, as they learned the knight to be within it, and made preparations for the assault. This was done with such courage that the place was won, and the knight made prisoner. After they had burnt the town and castle, they marched away for Otterburne." The very valiant knight of this account was Sir Aylmer de Athol. His family held the tower till the end of the fifteenth century, and later owners were the Burghs, the Mitfords and the Erringtons who, at the beginning of the seventeenth century, built the adjoining manor-house, now the " Blackbird," and at the same time made certain alterations to the castle to make it more comfortable.

The general appearance of the inn today is extremely attractive. To the right we have the Jacobean house with typical mullioned windows furnished with dripstones. A picturesque turret-like structure is corbelled out from the front of the building on the left, and a dignified stone porch shelters

157

the entrance. The old tower at the west end is characterised by an enormous chimney that rises far above the eaves in two square stacks ; and by masonry of a rugged and massive nature, the corner stones being especially noteworthy. The initials of Mark Errington, the builder of the manor-house, appear in more than one place—over the inner door at the main entrance, on the gable of the turret wing, and above a great fireplace in the tower. The basement of the tower is vaulted, the stonework now being plastered over, and the entrance is on the north side by a narrow, weather-worn door. Overhead in the thickness of the wall here is a chute, or meurtriere, down which scalding liquids, even hot porridge in an emergency, could be showered down on intruders. The newel-stair is just within on the left, and is continued above the present first floor, but the second floor does not now exist. Among the alterations to the basement are the addition of a new entrance, a fireplace and a mullioned window. A wide, blocked arch to be seen outside in the north wall was probably broken through when the basement was used as a farm byre. The first floor is a delightfully spacious chamber, with a modern oak-beamed roof. The fireplace, at least nine feet wide, is decorated with a double crenelle pattern, in the centre of which appear the initials, M.E. with a cross between. Some of the ancient wall-openings remain—one high up in the gable, and a loop in the north-west corner, now fitted with diamond panes—and there are various wall-cupboards. Another of the old loopholes lights the stair-way. Old-fashioned wheel-chairs, oak tables and buffet-stools are in keeping with the antique place, and the great red fire beneath the generous chimney-arch adds that touch of cheerful comfort which, rightly or wrongly, we generally associate with the good old days.

PRESTON TOWER
(Map II, B8.)

The modern mansion of Preston Tower lies to the east of the Great North Road a little to the north of Falloden Hall. In the grounds to the west of the house stands old Preston Tower, or rather all that is left of it, which is, however, in excellent preservation.

Originally it was an oblong building with turrets at the four corners, but only two of these turrets and the wall connecting them now remain. The stronghold is an old one, being mentioned in the list of Border fortresses of 1415, when it was held by Robert Harbottle, who probably built it. He was a warrior of some prominence, was in the royal favour, and had been Sheriff of the county and Constable of Dunstanburgh Castle a few miles away. A later tenant had to promise to thatch the roof with " hather flaggs and strawe," and he paid a yearly rent of £8 13s. 4d., an extortionate sum compared with the penny a year Robert Harbottle had paid a hundred years previously for land he held at Preston. Later owners were Thomas Wood, Thomas Haggerston, and the families of Grey, Craster and Baker-Cresswell.

Not only the basement of the south-west tower is vaulted but the first floor as well, which is unusual; and the door at its base is only 4 feet 9 inches high, like most others in the tower. The building is now used as a clock tower, the hours being struck on a sweet-toned bell which was cast in Newcastle. The clock occupies one of the old windows, a fine one more than five feet high and seven feet wide. The initials, H.R.B.C. (Baker-Cresswell) on the south front are those of the restorer of the tower seventy-four years ago. The battlements are modern. On one side of the building may be seen traces of cottages removed about the time of the restoration.

BAKER

PROCTOR STEADS
(Map II, C9.)

Inland from Dunstanburgh Castle and within sight of its ragged towers stands an old pele, adjoining a Carolean house. This is Proctor Steads, or Dunstan Hall. The place is readily accessible, a by-road running past it from Craster to Embleton. The house is tenanted and the interior is not usually shown, unless by special permission, but many of the most interesting features are visible from outside.

It is supposed that the pele was used as an outpost for Dunstanburgh Castle, which could be signalled if necessary, and though in parts it appears to be older than the castle, its name does not appear in the lists of Border strongholds before the fourteenth century, which was the time Dunstanburgh was built. The old tower stands at the rear. The basement, which is vaulted in the usual style, is built of huge blocks of basalt, and seems much older than the upper part which is of freestone. There are traces, on the side nearest the road, of the fortifications that guarded the original entrance. Now shorn of much of its height and ivy-covered, albeit soundly roofed, the tower forms a striking wing to the house.

The later wing is a picturesque structure with pantiled roof and big, broad chimneys. In the gable facing the road are two loophole-like windows, and other windows are stone-mullioned with dripstones above them, some being blocked as if some previous owner had resented the payment of excessive window-tax. The old stone wall of the present garden, with its blocked arch, suggests a barmkin, and there probably would be some such defence, since the site is not naturally a strong one. It is more than likely that this later house was built out of material brought from the ruins of Dunstanburgh.

Dunstan is one of the places claiming the honour of being the birthplace of Duns Scotus, that celebrated thirteenth-century scholar and theologian who as a young man was educated at the Greyfriars Monastery in Newcastle, and at his death was a revered professor in the University of Paris.

There is one other mystery concerning Proctor Steads which the writer finds equally interesting, if not more so—who was the " J.P." (the initials appear very faintly over the doorway) who, three hundred years ago, moved out of the old tower into the new house of stone he had just built next door? What a house-warming that must have been !

COULSON

LAWSON

PRUDHOE CASTLE
(Map II, F8.)

The name, Prudhoe, meaning the high or proudly-swelling mound, conveys an apt impression of this famous stronghold of the Umfravilles. Though ruined, it still looks proudly down from its eminence a hundred and fifty feet above the broad Tyne.

The first Umfraville in England was Robin with the Beard, William the Conqueror's right-hand knight who, for his stout services, was given the barony of Redesdale to defend, with the aid of the very sword worn by William himself, against wolves and the King's enemies. Later the huge barony of Prudhoe was added to the Umfraville possessions, and in Henry I's reign the castle was begun. Odinel de Umfraville, the builder, had excited the hatred of William the Lion of Scotland by refusing to acknowledge his hereditary claims to the county of Northumberland; and when that monarch invaded England, one of his express objectives was Prudhoe. " May I be loathed and disgraced, cursed and excommunicated by priest," he swore, " if I grant any terms or respite to Odinel's castle ! " The siege failed, but William came back the next year, and Odinel, fearing defeat this time, rode himself day and night on his good bay mare to get reinforcements from the Archbishop of York. Though the Scots in their anger spoiled the gardens and cornfields outside the castle walls, and barked the orchard apple-trees, the besieged did not suffer " a silver pennyworth of harm," and the Lion King had to retreat; to be taken prisoner at Alnwick soon afterwards. By an ironical turn of fate, one of the knights who assisted in his capture was Odinel de Umfraville. How the Lion must have roared !

A later Umfraville went to the Crusades with Richard the Lion-Heart, and for his valour was made Captain of Acre. It was an Umfraville, too, who gave the celebrated reply to Edward II at Bannockburn when that monarch commented on the Scots' kneeling, prior to the battle—" You say truth, sire. They ask mercy—but not of you."

In the fourteenth century, Prudhoe passed by the marriage of an heiress into the possession of the Percies. They lost their estates for their rebellion against Henry IV, but later regained them by royal favour, and have retained Prudhoe ever since.

In 1559 this noble pile was described as being old and ruinous, and little seems to have been done to preserve it till about a hundred years ago, when the 2nd Duke of Northumberland carried out some fortunate repairs, together with some alterations, such as the raising of the ground-level within the walls, which were not so fortunate.

The position of the castle is exceptionally strong—only a narrow neck, cut by a deep moat, separates the knoll it occupies from the steep bank of the river, and two of the other sides fall precipitously into a ravine where a burn runs. The present entrance crosses the burn by a dam which originally formed a pond for the working of the castle mill, the ruins of which remain further down the dene. The outer tower, or barbican, was built (the mason marks on it show) by the same masons as Bothal Castle, which fixes its date at about 1343, much later than most other parts of the castle. It was built by the nephew of that same Gilbert de Umfraville who, when his other castle at Harbottle was smashed by the Scots, had to get royal permission to hold his Border prisoners at Prudhoe.

The Gate-House at the end of the rising battlemented causeway is enormously solid—one of the walls is fourteen feet thick, and there are no doorways to weaken the Norman archway. Strange to say, there has been no portcullis here, nor in the barbican. There were, instead, iron lattice gates. A picturesque outside stairway mounts to the first floor occupied by the Chapel of St. Mary, which has a unique feature—its oriel window which, so far as is known, is the earliest of its kind in England. Projecting on corbels, it has three lancet-shaped lights, and held the altar. According to Bates, the historian, the window was carried out beyond the walls and the priest's lodging above because it was undesirable to have any inhabited structure above the most sacred part of the chapel. Another interesting feature of the Gate-House is the twin-headed corbelling supporting an inner arch, which is similar to some in Durham Cathedral.

Within the massive, loopholed curtain walls, ten to twelve feet high and reinforced with bastion towers, stands the ruined Keep, incongruously neighboured and largely obscured by a modern dwelling. At the door of this house is a large shield showing the Umfraville arms—" a cinquefoil within an orle of crosses patonce."

Older than any other keep in the county except Norham, this Norman structure still conveys an impression of unassailable strength. A tall turret soars up from one angle. A wheel-stair ascends to the first floor from the basement (which is not vaulted), then the ascent is in the thickness of the walls towards

the south-east turret. As for the other buildings in the bailey—
the Great Hall, the kitchens, the bakehouse, the brewery, etc.—
all have gone, even their foundations being covered.

Within, Prudhoe Castle may be disappointing. From
without it preserves more than a semblance of that impregnable
fortress which was for so many centuries the *beau ideal* of Border
holds.

* QUEEN MARY'S HOUSE, JEDBURGH
(Map I, C3.)

It is related in the account of Hermitage Castle how Queen
Mary rode over from Jedburgh to visit Bothwell, lying wounded
there. The picturesque house where she lodged in the town,
and where she lay sick almost unto death after her arduous ride,
still stands, and is open to the public as a museum.

Its five hundred years sit lightly upon it, and the garden
sloping down to the Jed is as pleasant a place as when the
unhappy Queen walked its paths. Queen Mary had come to
Jedburgh officially, in order to preside at the " Justice Eyres "
and to deal with the depredations of moss-troopers. At the
time of her visit the house was comparatively new, as were
most of the dwellings in the town, which had been completely
devastated fifty years previously by the Earl of Surrey in the
raid he made after Flodden. The house was rebuilt as a bastle-
house, probably in 1523, by Andrew Ker of Ferniehirst Castle,
and a brass cannon preserved is one presented to another
member of this clan by the Queen in recognition of his services.
Formerly the house was thatched, but is now red-tiled. It has
a typically Scottish " corbie-stepped " gable, and a pepper-box
turret filling the angle between the two wings that form the
L-shaped plan. Over the doorway is a manorial panel bearing
the arms of the Wigmore family, prominent in Edinburgh civic
affairs in the fourteenth century.

The vaulted basement of the house has a cobbled floor,
and at one end is the kitchen, with meat-hooks in the ceiling
and a generous fireplace eloquent of ancient hospitality. Behind
the panelling of the ante-chamber of the Hall there is, tradition
says, the beginning of a secret passage-way running to the abbey,
but like most of such stories it has not been substantiated.

The room is, of course, the Queen's Room—a small upper
room in the turret, where for nine days her fever developed
until she lay rigid and cold, so that they took her for dead and
opened the windows according to the superstition of the times.
" The Earl of Moray," wrote the Queen's secretary, " began
to lay hands on the most precious articles, such as her silver
plate and jewels. The mourning dresses were ordered, and
arrangements were made for the funeral." But the royal patient

recovered, and actually left Jedburgh a fortnight later, with the Earl of Bothwell himself among her brilliant train. Among the most interesting articles preserved in the house is the Queen's watch. Its history is an amazing one. During her ride the Queen's horse was bogged at a spot since called the Queen's Mire, and in her desperate efforts to free herself she lost her watch. There it lay buried for over two hundred years. Then, the bog having been drained, the watch was brought to the surface by the burrowing of rabbits and found by a shepherd. Its astonishingly good condition is due to the preserving power of the peaty earth in which it lay. A spur of ancient design also found near this place may well have been the Queen's or that of one of her company. The town of Jedburgh is to be congratulated on the care it has accorded this ancient house and its historic memories.

BOTHWELL

SWINHOE

ROCK HALL
(Map II, C8.)

Four miles to the north-north-east of Alnwick the charming hamlet of Rock lies at the gates of Rock Hall, a most picturesque manor-house with battlemented, ivy-covered walls and mullioned windows. It includes an ancient tower supposed to have been built in Norman times (a little private chapel of that period seems to confirm this) but probably greatly altered in Elizabethan times. The central part of the Hall is the oldest, comprising an oblong tower with two smaller towers adjoining it.

The De Rocks held the manor in Norman times under the barony of Alnwick; then it passed in turn to the De Tughalls, the De Swinhoes and the Lawsons to the famous Salkeld family, whose arms appear over a blocked doorway in the front of the house together with a sundial and the date, 1690. Colonel John Salkeld, the most prominent member of this family, was a staunch Royalist devoted to the Stuart cause and, according to his epitaph in the nearby Norman church, served Charles I " with a constant, dangerous and expensive loyalty as volunteer, captain, and colonel of horse." But his dangerous career was never nearer to being cut short than when, at the age of twenty-seven, he killed Mr. John Swinburne of Capheaton near the gates of Meldon. At the inquest a verdict of wilful murder was returned against him, but somehow he escaped the penalty. A later owner of Rock Hall, Mr. John Fenwick, was involved in a similar affair, arising out of a feud, when during a duel with Ferdinando Forster near the White Cross, Newcastle, he treacherously stabbed his opponent through the heart as he lay on the ground. Not so fortunate as Salkeld, Fenwick was executed a month later.

The hall was burnt down in 1752 and remained a ruin for nearly seventy years, before being restored by the Bosanquet family, who built the wing with " crow-stepped " gables. The wing at the other extremity of the hall was added to the old tower in the seventeenth century, in the time of the redoubtable Colonel Salkeld, who probably also planted the avenue of limes and chestnuts that adds to the dignity of this attractive old residence.

GILPIN

† ROXBURGH CASTLE

(Map I, B4.)

A mile and a quarter from Kelso, the road to Melrose passes close to the foot of a long, high ridge fringed with broken walls. These are all that remain of what has been the residence of five Scottish kings, and worthy to be ranked with the great castles of Edinburgh and Stirling.

As far back as Saxon times there was a fortress on this naturally strong position between Tweed and Teviot, but when the castle was built is not known. In the twelfth century it was the royal residence of David I, and the four kings that followed him lived here, too, some of their charters being issued from Roxburgh Castle.

The fortress was lost to Scotland by William the Lion, who had to surrender it along with Edinburgh and Stirling castles as a guarantee that his ransom would be forthcoming. A savage and protracted raid through the English Borders had terminated in his capture outside Alnwick Castle, and he was conveyed to Normandy and his ransom fixed at £100,000, an enormous sum in those days. But Roxburgh came back to Scotland, establishing peace between the two countries, and in 1225 the castle was the scene of unprecedented festivities when Alexander III entertained his father-in-law, Henry III of England. At that time there lay below the castle walls a considerable town—the royal burgh of Easter Roxburgh, which had a city seal and a mint, and held its annual fair of St. James. Now in the green meadows there is no single trace of its protecting wall or its dwellings, its convent, schools or churches. It is almost incredible that a town should have vanished so completely.

Edward I received the castle from John Balliol, and for nearly a hundred years after this it was a thorn in the Scottish side, and the object of repeated attacks. William Wallace tried in vain to take it. A later attempt by Sir James Douglas achieved by guile what a direct attack would have failed to accomplish, since he had only sixty men. One Shrove Tuesday evening an English sentry on the walls saw in the gathering dusk on the meadows below what he took to be a herd of black cattle, and went on his round unsuspecting. The " black cattle " were Douglas's men creeping on all fours beneath black cloaks which concealed their armour. Below the walls a soldier called Syn hooked a rope ladder to the parapet and, mounting, slew the sentry on his return, then signalled the coast clear to his comrades. The result was that the garrison were surprised in the castle hall in the middle of their Fastern's E'en revels, and a great slaughter ensued, though the captain and a few men held out for a day in the keep.

A later assault on the castle was by the Scottish James II, but he lost his life during the siege through the bursting of a great gun called " The Lion," a primitive piece of Flemish ordnance constructed of longitudinal bars of iron; the king's thigh being " doung in twa . . . be the quhilk [which] he was strickin to the grund and dieit haistilie thereof, quhilk grettumlie discuragit all his nobill gentlemen and freindis that war standand aboot him."

This was practically the end of Roxburgh—town and castle. The former was razed to the ground before the siege; when the castle was captured it, too, was levelled by the Queen's orders, and a long-standing source of annoyance and danger removed. Though we hear of Roxburgh again after this, it had no great military value. Today we can only trace the outlines of the great corner towers, and of the moat on the west side, fed by the river which was formerly dammed; and there are some fragmentary stretches of curtain wall on the side overlooking the Teviot, the views of which are exquisite.

RUTHERFORD

RUDCHESTER TOWER
(Map II, F8.)

Not a great deal remains of the old seat of the Rutherfords, who for so many generations figured largely in Border affairs. What does exist is built into an eighteenth-century farmhouse. The tower took its name from the Roman camp beside which it stood, a mile and a half to the west of Heddon-on-the-Wall. The name, Rudchester, means Red Camp, the stones of the Roman station being reddened by burning, as they must more than once have been in this outpost of the Roman Empire.

The date when the tower was built is preserved in an interesting way—in ancient times a man coming of age had to give proof of his birth or baptism by means of the affidavits of various witnesses, and on such an occasion Simon de Rudchester testified that he was building his hall in the same year, 1285. Of that hall, the only parts identifiable are the very thick walls at the east end of the present farmhouse. An old fireplace has a stone mantel embellished with a triangular design flanked with shields. Within the recess there is a smaller one with stone lintel and carved jambs and, at the bottom, a Roman centurial stone from the Wall, where it originally recorded building or repairing done by Pedovius's century of the third cohort.

The Rutherfords acquired Rudchester in 1419. They were a warlike race. One of them, known for his fiery temper that would brook no argument, is referred to in Scott's *Lay of the Last Minstrel* as

> " A hot and hardy Rutherford
> Whom men called Dickòn Draw-the-Sword."

The Rutherfords quarrelled with their kinsmen almost as readily as with their foes, and the history of their family is remarkable for the number of law-suits, generally connected with the inheritance of property, in which they were involved. On one occasion, in accordance with the custom of the time, two Rutherfords hired champions to decide the point at issue by trial of combat which, the law decided, was to take place " on Tuesday next after the feast of St. Denis."

Large families were common formerly, but the Rutherfords were outstanding in this respect. One Rutherford had thirty children by one wife. Nineteen of his twenty sons were, however, killed in the Civil War in King Charles's service. The family's devotion to their sovereign ruined them. The Hall was sold soon afterwards, and their long connection with the old tower came to a close.

FAWCETT

§ SCALEBY CASTLE

(Map I, F2.)

This interesting and most picturesque pile, which shows the development through four hundred years from simple pele-tower to moat-surrounded castle and then to manor-house, stands six miles to the north-east of Carlisle in beautiful but rather neglected surroundings. From a lodge-gate in the village an avenue of ancient oaks leads through the park to the castle, part of which is occupied as a farm where permission may be obtained to visit the older and unoccupied portions.

The De Tilliols were at Scaleby in Norman times, and held the manor for more than three hundred years. In 1307 Robert de Tilliol is recorded as fortifying his house here by royal licence. It was then that the pele was built. Later owners were the Colvilles, the Musgraves, the Gilpins, and the Fawcetts, each of whom made their additions to the structure, so that besides the pele there is a fifteenth-century Gate-House, and a comfortable-looking manor-house. Of the three moats, the outer still contains water and is now crossed by a stone bridge, but traces of the ancient drawbridge remain; while a portion of the inner moat forms an ornamental pond in front of the castle.

The fortress, however, does not seem to have been strong enough to stand a siege. It was taken easily in 1645; and again three years later when Sir Edward Musgrave garrisoned it in the cause of Charles I, only one shot was fired from the castle walls before it surrendered to a detachment of General Lambert's army, who afterwards, it is said, set fire to the place. Musgrave was so impoverished by his loyalty to his king that he was obliged to sell a large part of his estates. Richard Gilpin, the subsequent owner, did a great deal towards restoring and rebuilding the castle as a residence, and his arms appear over the entrance gate, below those of the De Tilliols. On one side of the narrow archway is the door of a guard-room. Here one of the ancient gates is preserved. Flanking one side of the Gate-House is a tall, narrow, lookout turret, and on the other an octagonal structure with loopholes directed upon the entrance.

Next to this is the old pele, roofless and ruinous, and its upper floors gone, but giving an impression of massive strength. The thick walls of its barrel-vaulted basement, which is twenty-four feet by fifteen, are pierced with deeply-splayed loopholes. On the far side of the inner courtyard is the handsome entrance to the manor-house, on the site of a sixteenth-century hall, and rebuilt, as the date over the door records, in 1737. The façade adjoining the lawn presents some finely-proportioned mullioned windows, and is supported at each end by colossal, stepped buttresses rising nearly to the eaves.

SHANKS CASTLE

(Map I, F2.)

On the bank of the River Lyne, which flows from the ancient " Waste " of Bewcastle on the south-west flank of the Cheviots, stands this ancient tower, for tower it is essentially, and not a castle in the usual sense of the word.

It is an odd place, in that it is almost without any recorded history. Practically the first mention of it is in James I's reign when Sir William Hutton, Steward to the Earl of Cumberland, built a " neat house " here, and that he lived here to subdue the freebooters of the district, who continued to flourish in this wild region long after the Union of the two countries. It is probable that he made his residence by adapting the tower that had been here for a century at least, perhaps two.

The tower, fifty-two feet by twenty-four and four storeys high, is well suited for self-contained security. The walls are five feet thick and the original entrance is on the first floor, ten feet from the ground, the basement being reached by a newel-stair. A feature of the interior is the number of mural chambers and garderobes, the presence of which give a clue to the probable age of this lonely stronghold.

COLVILLE

SHILBOTTLE PELE
(Map II, C8.)

The old pele-tower that now forms part of Shilbottle vicarage is not the least attractive feature of this quiet village, which lies three miles to the south of Alnwick.

The tower of "Schipilbodille" is mentioned in a fifteenth-century list of Northumbrian fortresses. It was not originally a vicarage, like some in the county, and when it was given to the benefice by the lord of the manor is not known, though it must have been after 1526, since in that year a tenant called Charles Watson paid a rent of 12d. The adjoining house, with its fine stone porch surmounted by a cross, is, of course, a comparatively modern addition.

The front of the tower is rendered more attractive by the projecting corbelled turret on the left. The upper part of the walls, however, was only added in 1863, when Mr. Roberts, then vicar, modernised the whole house and heightened the tower to its present proportions, the effect being in keeping with the general character of the building. The arched entrance to the tower is on the west side, from the adjoining house, into a vaulted chamber which has had two narrow windows, and two wall cupboards. There is no trace of any stair to the upper apartments, and probably they were gained by a wooden stairway outside, which could be drawn up for greater safety. The first floor was formerly flagged, but the stones were replaced with boards towards the end of the eighteenth century. The tower is also well seen from the churchyard which it overlooks, and on the wall on this side is a stone panel inscribed with the heading, "Turris de Schilbotal," and a verse which has probably been taken from an old tombstone to be seen at Melrose :

> " The earth builds on the earth
> Castles and towers,
> To earth saith the earth,
> All shall be ours."

There is the common tradition of an underground passage from the tower—it is said to communicate with the church in this case.

Though Alnwick and its great castle lie between Shilbottle and the Border, the village was definitely in the danger zone, and the pele must often have been needed. In 1538 a night watch had to be maintained in the district by ten men from Shilbottle, Whittle, Sturton Grange, Birling, High and Low Buston, Wooden and Bilton ; and close to the village is a Beacon Hill, where often the cresset must have flared its warning far and wide.

MONTAGU

† SHITTLEHEUGH PELE
(Map II, D6.)

This shattered relic of former times, standing on high ground to the north of the road from Otterburn up Redesdale near where it meets the Roman Dere Street from Woodburn, commands an extensive view of the valley, and the height of Blakeman Law just behind it affords an excellent lookout towards the hills. The pele stands near the crossing of two old hill tracks—one through Hopehead to Holystone; the other up the Durtrees Burn—ways that were doubtless once well frequented.

The best way to reach the spot is to take the field road to Shittleheugh Farm, to which the pele is quite near. Only the two end walls are at all intact, but nevertheless there are some points of interest. The unusually massive construction, for instance, exemplified in the doorway, which is formed of a huge trilithon. The holes for the drop-bars remain; and just within the doorway lies a broken stone trough, part of the equipment of the basement, the vaulting of which is traceable. Of the two loopholes, one is level with the ground outside; and in the upper storey there are three wall cupboards. Life cannot have been secure in this perilous position on the very edge of the vast " Waste," which was the nightly haunt of mosstroopers and outlaws.

SHORTFLATT TOWER
(Map II, E8.)

Two miles to the north-west of Belsay stands Shortflatt Tower, which is now a private residence. Though well removed from any main highway, it is seen at close quarters from the footpath between Harnham and Bolam Low House, close to Bolam Lake. A fine distant view of it, among its sheltering trees, is got from the field road going northward from Harnham, a road practicable for motors.

The manor of Shortflatt was in early times held by a family with the odd name of Gosebek, then it was transferred to Robert de Raymes, a member of a Suffolk family. The transaction was done illegally without royal permission, and before De Raymes could enter into possession he had to pay the very considerable fine of £60. That was in 1296. A few years later he received the royal licence to crenellate his manor-houses here and at Aydon. In this case the crenellation appears to have meant the almost entire rebuilding of the houses, which are very similar in their style and internal arrangements. Aydon, however, developed into a miniature castle, whereas Shortflatt, while certainly a strong place, does not present so many military features.

Sir Robert de Raymes's active military career did not permit of his enjoying much of the comforts of either of his two splendid houses. He saw a good deal of service in Scotland, where he fought against the redoubtable William Wallace. Eventually he was taken prisoner and had to leave his son in Scottish hands as a hostage until his own ransom of five hundred marks was paid. This same son died of the dreaded " Black Death " in 1349, and his widow came to Shortflatt to live. Later the house came into the possession of that famous Northumbrian family, the Fenwicks. Their " chiefest house " was, however, Wallington Hall not far away. At the time of the '15 Rising a dog was trained (local tradition affirms) to take provisions from Shortflatt to a cave at Shaftoe Crags, where Lord Derwentwater was in hiding ; and that he was fed for a fortnight in this way.

Finely and solidly built of stone, Shortflatt, though con-siderably altered to give more comfort and convenience, retains many of the characteristic features of its period. One square tower, higher than the rest of the building, suggests an ancient pele. Huge chimneys from equally generous and quaintly-fashioned fireplaces ; handsome windows ; a courtyard that reminds one of Aydon ; a high wall recalling the ancient barmkin—these are some of the features of this dignified house that Robert de Raymes first raised beside the How Burn more than six hundred years ago.

RAYMES

BACON

† SIMONBURN CASTLE
(Map I, F5.)

From Simonburn, a retired hamlet on a tributary of the North Tyne between Humshaugh and Wark, a lane leads westward for about half-a-mile to Simonburn Castle, standing on a strong position between two ravines, in a setting now of beautiful woodland.

This is the castle or tower which, built by the Herons of Chipchase about six hundred years ago, was recommended by Sir Robert Bowes, military adviser to Henry VIII, as a suitable residence for the Keeper of Tynedale, who was to have fifty horsemen ready to ride against the Scots. It is not easy to believe this in the face of these ruined walls and broken vaults.

The chief remaining portion is the northern end, which is a picturesque fragment nearly as high as the parapet, with turrets corbelled out beyond the walls, and on the second floor a handsome three-light window with a " dog-tooth " decoration typical of the period when the tower was built. The lower windows, also pointed, are smaller and more suited to defence. A local tradition of buried treasure in the castle has been the cause of much of its dilapidation, many a countryman having in the past delved hopefully among the ruins for the hoard that is supposed to be worth the whole of Northumberland.

†§ STAWARD PELE
(Map I, G4.)

This ruinous tower has an almost impregnable site in what is one of the most beautiful corners of the North Country. It stands near Staward Station on the brink of the thickly-wooded ravine in the depths of which the Allen flows, and is shut off on another side by a tributary of the Allen. The remaining side, the narrow neck of the oval promontory, was defended by a ditch, traces of which remain, and by a wall of earth and stone. Very little of the tower remains, but it has obviously been a very strong place. The Gate-House, formerly possessing a drawbridge and a portcullis, is built of Roman stones.

The pele was probably built in the fourteenth century, for it was given in 1386 by the Duke of York to the Eremite Friars of Hexham for an annual payment of five marks. When that monastery was dissolved with other religious houses, the tower was lived in by the Bacon family, a branch of the same family as that of the famous Lord High Chancellor in James I's reign. In later times, probably when it was ruinous, a free-booter called Dicky of Kingswood made it his lair. He seems to have been a sort of Robin Hood who lived by his wits. Once, the story goes, he stole a fine pair of oxen at Denton Burn, near Newcastle, and at Lanercost sold them to a farmer, who was the possessor of a beautiful mare. Over the bottle of wine that followed the deal Dicky warned him to watch his animal closely, as there were horse-thieves in the neighbourhood. Sure enough, next morning the mare was gone — and Dicky too! On his way back to Staward he met the late owner of the oxen, and told him where he would find them. The farmer thanked him, then said, "You ride a good mare. What about selling her to me? I've had enough of tramping." After some bargaining, a price was agreed upon, and the owner of the oxen arrived in due course at Lanercost. "Look 'ee here," he said to the Lanercost farmer, "those are my oxen in your field." "And I'm durned," retorted the other, "if that bain't my mare you're astride of!"

STONEGARTHSIDE HALL

(Map I, E2.)

" There was a wild gallant among us a',
His name was Watty-wi'-the-Wudspurs,
Cried, ' On for his house in Stanegirthside
Gin ony man will ride wi' us'."

The house, or one on its site, referred to thus in the ballad of *Jamie Telfer of the Fair Dodhead*, stands high on the left bank of the Liddel, two miles south of Kershopefoot, and within the ancient Forest of Nicholl. The word " garth " means an enclosed yard, and there are references as far back as 1276 to the garth here, probably a strong barmkin with a tower where the hall now stands ; a supposition borne out by various carved stones built into the walls of the present Hall. On its west side there is still a field enclosed by a strong wall. About three hundred years ago the Hall was the seat of the Forsters or Fosters.

A feature of the fine stonework is its decorative finish, not only in the moulding of the doors and windows, but at the angles of the building where the stones are carved with an intricate alternating device that gives the effect of a wavy band running from ground to eaves. The two wings, bearing the date 1682, enclose a courtyard, the door to which is overlooked by an embrasured parapet. The yard was formerly roofed over and covered with lead which, it is said, was sold for the silver it was found to contain. Within the courtyard an inner door admits to a lobby and a flight of broad, well-worn stone steps mounting easily to the upper storeys. The upper part of the house is unfinished, the story being that the property belonged to three brothers who could not agree as to its completion. One room here has not been opened for years. Can this be the ghost room from which the figure of a Cavalier has been seen to issue on occasions and gaze anxiously about him till a lady materialises in a dress of the same period, when they embrace and fade away. The windows of the Hall have all been iron-barred at one time; and a vast quantity of massive oak timbering, bearing the marks of the adze, has been used in the construction. It will be noticed that the gables are " crow-stepped " in Scottish fashion. The Hall has its dungeon—opening downwards from the end of a cellar, which itself is lit only by the scanty light from a curious, heart-shaped loophole in the outer wall.

GIBSON

COMYN

† TARSET CASTLE
(Map I, E4.)

There is little more than a massive green mound left of this ancient stronghold on the North Tyne four miles above Bellingham. Its builder was a Scottish knight—John Comyn, Lord of Badenoch, generally known as the " Black Comyn." At the time there were exceptionally good relations between the two countries, due to the marriage of Henry III's sister with the Scottish king ; and this accounts for Henry's permission to Comyn to fortify his mansion, with the curious proviso that it should be " enclosed and embattled like the camera of Adam de Gesemuth " (Jesmond, in Newcastle). Not long before this, however, the Keeper of Northumberland had been very suspicious concerning the erection of Dally Castle nearby by another Scot. From the park at Tarset in Comyn's time twenty bucks and eighty does were, by order of the Scottish king, sent to Harbottle Castle to re-stock the park there, as compensation for damage done by a besieging Scots army.

His son, the " Red Comyn," gained an unlucky prominence in history by being assassinated by his rival to the throne, the famous Robert Bruce, who thus made himself " at a stroke " owner of Tarset and one step nearer to the crown. In the Survey of Border Castles made in 1541, the castle was described as " the Hall of the Lord Burrowes' inheritance, the which was burnt by the said Tyndalles sixteen years since and more, at a tyme when Sir Rauffe Fenwick lay with a certain garrison in the tower at Tarset Hall for the reformation of certain misorders in the said country of Tyndale." The reference was to an armed expedition into Tynedale by the said Sir Ralph to apprehend one William Ridley, probably one of the Haltwhistle clan concerned in the murder of Sir Albany Featherstonehaugh, High Sheriff of Northumberland. Led by William Charlton of Bellingham, the Tynedale men, always " agin the law," not only deterred Sir Ralph " from hys purpose of attackinge the sayd Ridley, but alsoe chased the sayd Sir Rauff out of Tyndaill, to his great reproache."

177

One could hardly imagine such clansmen to have been unduly devout, yet only the previous year when they were under excommunication by Cardinal Wolsey, one of the Charltons (Hector Charlton of the Bower) took the sacrament from Bellingham Church at Easter, together with a firkin of wine and eight hundred " breads," so that he and his comrades could hold their own communion service at Tarset Castle with the aid of a Scottish friar, one of those wandering clerics known in the Border as a " Book-a-bosom." Hector himself served the wine and received the parson's dues.

During the Fenwick episode, Tarset Castle was burnt down, and was never rebuilt. A local tradition asserts the existence of a subterranean passage between here and Dally Castle, a little over a mile away, and the writer has spoken with a local workman who says he saw part of it unearthed near the gateway of Tarset Hall, but the evidence is not at all conclusive ! The tragic legend of Gilbert of Tarset is related in the account of Dally Castle. It is almost forgotten by the people of the district; as is the old war-cry of North Tynedale, heard and feared in many an ancient fray :

> " Tarset and Tarret Burn
> Hard and heather bred
> Yet, yet, yet ! "

WIDDRINGTON

Plate XX

PONTELAND PELE;
SCALEBY CASTLE—THE GATE-HOUSE;
LEMMINGTON TOWER

Plate XXI

"THE PELE TOWER," CORBRIDGE;
WELTON HALL;
PROCTOR STEADS

Plate XXII

KING EDWARD'S TOWER, LANERCOST;
WHITTON TOWER

THE BARBICAN, ALNWICK CASTLE

Plate XXIII

THIRLWALL

† THIRLWALL CASTLE
(Map I, F3.)

Three and a half miles west of Haltwhistle and hard by the Roman Wall, from the stones of which it was built, stands the broken castle of Thirlwall. Part of it has fallen down into the Tipalt Burn at its foot, and the remaining part does not look as if it would last a great deal longer, yet the ruins have an appeal that many a larger and more complete pile does not possess.

We first hear of Thirlwall in the thirteenth century when it was part of Scotland, together with North Tynedale. The Prioress of the nunnery at Lambley had been pasturing cattle on some disputed land claimed by the Baron of Thirlwall, and went so far as to challenge him to combat to settle the issue; a proceeding not so humorous as it may sound, since it was the custom then for disputants to hire champions to fight their battles. In this case all arrangements were complete for the meeting of the champions when the Prioress, perhaps unwilling to risk a man's life, agreed to pay ten pounds in silver for damage done, together with twenty shillings in connection with another little affair—a matter of inciting a shepherd to burn down a house on the Baron's estate.

But the Thirlwalls were not in the habit of accepting challenges from women. They were noted for their warlike activities and their gathering-cry, " A Thirlwall ! a Thirlwall ! " rang out in many a fight on both sides of the Border. One Thirlwall lost his life in holding a pele on the bank of the Forth against Sir William Wallace who, when the place was stormed, seized an iron-pointed shaft from a watchman and laid the Northumbrian knight low. But another member of the family had the satisfaction of being at Falkirk where Wallace's power was finally broken. Young John de Thirlwall was only twenty-one at the time, yet he had had five years' military experience. He lived to the ripe age of eighty-five, at his death was the " oldest esquire of all the north," and was sixty-five when his youngest son was born.

The castle was probably allowed to fall into decay after the Restoration, when the family left the neighbourhood for a pleasanter house near Hexham. Eleanora, the last heiress of Thirlwall married Matthew Swinburne of Capheaton Hall, then Thirlwall was sold to the Howards of Naworth.

In its prime, the castle consisted of a main building, with a tower on the east side ; and from the entrance, guarded by an iron gate, stairs went up in the thickness of the wall (here measuring nine feet) to the first floor of a turret, the basement of which, only 6 feet 5 inches by 5 feet, was probably the dungeon. But it can hardly have been much more gloomy than the castle itself, with its windows hardly bigger than loopholes. Amid the shattered walls there is no trace of the " Dwarf's Well," where, legend asserts, a misshapen creature guards a golden table thrown there by him when the Scots once took the castle and put the garrison to the sword. The dwarf, having supernatural powers, closed the well mouth by a spell, which can only be broken by the coming of one who is the only son of a widow.

BLAKE

† TWIZEL CASTLE
(Map I, A5.)

Twizel Castle, looking down on the Till where it is crossed by the road from Berwick to Cornhill, is a monument to eccentricity, one of those " Follies " which are to be found in every corner of the country.

This is not to say that the foundation of the castle is not an ancient one. There was a pele here in very early times, and strong though the position is, high up on the edge of a ravine, the tower suffered severely in the Border wars. It was burnt in 1496 by James IV when he invaded England to support Perkin Warbeck in his attempt to gain the English throne ; and again about fifty years later. Yet it survived till the Union— only to meet with a curious fate, when it was sacrificed to a grandiose scheme on the part of an eighteenth-century baronet,

Sir Francis Blake, to build a castle that was to be the wonder of the North Country. When he died, his son continued the work with even more enthusiasm and lack of judgment, and for fifty years building went leisurely on, but still the castle was not finished, and was not destined to be.

Some amazing stories are told of the erection of this " white elephant." Sir Francis (the son) was his own architect, inspector and clerk of works, and the men employed were all on day wages. Some served their apprenticeship there, and it is said that the foreman mason became a wealthy man out of the honest profits he made, while some of his men, not so scrupulous, used to make furniture in the baronet's time and out of his well-seasoned timber to sell in the neighbourhood.

The castle was planned to be six storeys high, and the lower apartments were vaulted to guard against fire, but the upper floors were never completed. A gallery ninety feet long and twenty-two wide was intended to accommodate the valuable family collection of pictures. Sir Walter Scott, who had a distinct leaning towards Gothic (as witness Abbotsford) thought the castle a splendid pile, but he appears to have been one of the few admirers of it.

These protracted building operations plus Sir Francis Blake's passion for electioneering contests finally reduced him to penury, and to escape his creditors he took refuge in the debtors' sanctuary within the precincts of Holyrood Abbey ; but sometimes on a Sunday he would hire a postchaise and drive southward to take a look at his creation from afar, then hurry back to get across the strand at the foot of the Canongate before midnight.

Today a thick growth of trees on the hillside almost conceals the castle. The walls are ruinous and overgrown with a dense covering of ivy which has overflowed to the ground round about. There are two wings, and circular towers at the four corners. The interior, dim and forlorn, is a melancholy reminder of mistaken ambition.

COUPLAND

MOWBRAY

*TYNEMOUTH CASTLE
(Map II, F9-10.)

The history of Tynemouth Castle is, of course, intimately connected with that of the Priory which for many centuries it protected, both being on the same rocky headland at the mouth of the river, with the castle at the neck of the promontory.

The proverb regarding an ill wind applies to Tynemouth Castle. A fire that gutted it in 1930 led to its being taken over by H.M. Office of Works, and from being a barracks with many mean additions it has assumed something more like its ancient nobility of form and setting.

The naturally strong and commanding site has just as naturally attracted those who were military-minded. The Romans had a fort here (excavations have revealed its remains on the south side of the Priory); and the Norman Robert de Mowbray chose this Heaven-sent site for his castle of wood on an artificial mound, and in it later defied his sovereign, William Rufus, who found the stronghold a hard nut to crack. But crack it he did, and Mowbray ended his days in prison.

The present building was probably finished in the early years of the fifteenth century, and with a garrison of eighty men-at-arms was vested in the Prior of the convent for the protection of all under his charge. The great Gate-House then built was, however, just a logical extension of the defences of the monastery, which had already been fortified as early as Henry II's reign.

Tynemouth has figured prominently in history. In earlier days notable people like Queen Margaret and Edward II sought sanctuary within the " Peace of St. Oswin," which extended for a mile round his shrine in the monastery; and in later times the castle was an important strategic point. Thus, during the Civil War, Charles I took care to order the strengthening of the fortress; but in spite of this it was taken the following year by General Leslie, Earl of Leven, and his Scots. It was then held by Colonel Lilburn for the Parliament, but he turned his coat and released all his Royalist prisoners, with the eventual sequel that his head appeared on a pole on the castle battlements.

Thirty years later the castle was reported to be ruinous, and during a subsequent period was so neglected that one Leonard Smelt was allowed to convert it into a private residence, which he did, hideously, with the aid of red brick.

Like Bothal, Dunstanburgh and Bywell, Tynemouth Castle is of the gate-house type of fortress, the Gate-House serving also as a keep. Defending the entrance is a barbican, as at Alnwick. The present moat-like depression before the castle is said to have been due to the activities of the contractor who built the pier when he tried in vain to locate a supply of building stone. The portcullis-slot at the entrance remains, then there are two great oaken, iron-studded gates filling the pointed arch, the vault behind which has been recessed to allow the doors to swing back. A large pivot-hole and curved groove from it in the passage-wall on each side here are rather puzzling. One authority has suggested that they are evidences of an apparatus by which the portcullis could be raised at the same time as the drawbridge was being lowered. A doorway on each side of this dim passage leads into a vaulted guard-chamber lit by a small window at one end, and with a fireplace in one.

The archway piercing the base of the Gate-House was guarded by three more doors, the second and third of them closer together, with a roofless space between them that was under fire from four chutes or meutrieres high overhead on the face of the building; so that an enemy who had passed the drawbridge, the portcullis and three doors was still not out of the wood! The entrance to the Gate-House is by a small, pointed door on the first floor, approached by a modern ramp on the right-hand side as we enter the Bailey. The room above the arch is a large and stately apartment with a generous fireplace. On the floor above is a similar room which appears to have been the principal one of the Keep. The large windows are pointed within and rectangular without. In one corner there is a latrine; and on the east side there is access to a wall walk and to the mouths of the afore-mentioned meutrieres. Here, too, begins a straight stairway in the thickness of the wall. It is continued round to the west face where, in a turret projecting from the main wall, it links up with the head of a newel-stair going down to first-floor level. The structure on the south side of the Gate-House has been considerably adapted, and in the future some attempt may be made to restore it to something more like its original form. The tall round look-out tower, a feature of the castle as seen in the distance, is also a modern addition.

Further defences of the castle were, of course, its curtain walls which formerly extended right round the priory church, the monastery and various domestic buildings, represented today by ruined aisles and fragments of walls—very lovely, if scant, remains of a glorious structure—and by the purely utilitarian erections connected with modern military occupation. Soon, doubtless, these latter will go, and the hallowed enclosure left again to " its ancient, solitary reign " in the shadow of its grim guardian.

§ WALLINGTON HALL
(Map II, E7.)

There are few mansions in the county more pleasantly situated than this seat of the Trevelyans, which contains part of the ancient stronghold of the De Strothers. The Hall stands a mile to the south of Cambo, on the edge of a spacious park sloping down to the Wansbeck ; and the road past it is an old coaching route into Scotland. The gardens on the east side of the road are always accessible to the public ; and the Hall is shown on Saturdays and Sundays and public holidays, from Easter to the beginning of October. The present owner, the Rt. Hon. Sir Charles Trevelyan, Bart., has during his lifetime made over the entire property to the National Trust to be preserved for the nation.

More famous owners than the De Strothers were the jovial and hospitable Fenwicks, who made Wallington their chief seat when they came here from Fenwick Tower. They added a Gothic mansion to the old pele, and lived here till the middle of the eighteenth century, when Sir William Blackett bought the estate and built the present Hall, a plain structure externally, but of great interest within.

Among the fine portraits is a Gainsborough-Reynolds, showing the work of both of these celebrated artists ; and the remarkable picture gallery, built at the suggestion of John Ruskin, is decorated with some cartoons by William Bell Scott illustrating Northumbrian history. One called " The Spur in the Dish " shows the presentation of the Charlton Spur on a trencher to the chief of the Charlton clan by his wife—a hint that the larder was nearly empty, and it was time to ride again over the Border to replenish it. The room shown is in the castle at Newcastle. The Charltons, however, were a North Tynedale clan, seated near Bellingham. Of the medallions above, portraits pertaining to the subject of this book are those of Bishop Ridley, Belted Will Howard, and Lord Derwentwater ; while in the angles and spandrels of the upper arches are eighteen illustrations of the old ballad of " Chevy Chase," from the " Departure " to " The Return to Alnwick with the dead." There are, of course, many other objects of historical and artistic value.

Of the ancient fortress, the portion remaining is at the south-west corner, where there is a long, vaulted cellar, and the basement, also vaulted, of the old tower.

CHARLTON

† WARK CASTLE
(Map I, B4.)

As you approach Wark from the Cornhill direction, you see a gigantic mound overtopping the village. This is all that remains of what was once the mightiest fortress along the Tweed ; the castle that was without a parallel " for surprises, assaults, sieges, blockades, surrenders, burnings, restorations, slaughters " ; the royal pile that was visited by most of our English kings up to Henry IV and, of course, by many Scottish ones ! It would be a long task to trace in any detail the varied fortunes of the castle through more than four hundred years of service, as its battered walls changed hands again and again, as garrison after garrison were surprised or starved into surrender, sometimes slain in cold blood. The old couplet tells the story with grim brevity :

> " Auld Wark upon Tweed
> Has been mony a man's deid."

The castle was one of the earliest to be built in North-umberland. Only Bamburgh, Norham, Newcastle and perhaps Alnwick and Morpeth are older. Guarding one of the main fords on the Tweed, arrogantly raising its walls within a bowshot of the enemy, it was, as may be expected, soon the centre of considerable activity. Within a decade it was razed to the ground by the plaid-clad troops of David I, the founder of Holyrood, Melrose and Dryburgh Abbeys.

The castle had hardly been rebuilt before it received the attentions of the redoubtable William the Lion who, when held up at the inner gate, brought a catapult to bear against it. " Unless our engineer's a liar," roared the royal lion, " we shall gain the bailey without delay." But the first stone went wide of its mark, felling a Scottish knight, and others were hardly more useful. We do not learn what happened to the engineer. An attempt at burning the castle was equally fruitless, and next day saw the king and his Flemish mercenaries retiring to the sound of fanfares and songs of triumph from the garrison. King John burnt Wark. Edward II assembled his troops here on his way to Bannockburn. In 1341 we have the most pictur-esque of all incidents in the story of Wark. The beautiful

Countess of Salisbury was holding the castle with the help of her nephew, who after two days' desperate defence got through the Scottish lines one night and rode to Newcastle to warn his sovereign, Edward III, of the position. The enemy retreated when the royal army approached ; and to celebrate the occasion a ball was held in the castle hall. During a dance with the king, the countess's garter fell to the floor, and there were smiles from the onlookers, but the king rebuked them with the words, " Honi soit qui mal y pense," and fastened the garter round his knee. Such, tradition says, was the origin of the noble Order of the Garter. The story has a considerable amount of historical backing ; and Froissart's highly romantic tale (in his *Chronicles*) of Edward's love for the fair lady, and his sadness when she entreated him " to drive from his heart such villainous thoughts," seems also to be founded on fact.

The bloodiest episode that Wark has seen was in the reign of Henry V. Sir William Haliburton of Fast Castle captured Wark and slew the defenders to a man ; but a few months later Sir Robert Ogle, a former Captain of Wark who knew the place intimately, got his forces to enter the castle kitchen through a sewer, and the castle was won again. This time it was the turn of the Scottish garrison to be put to the sword.

After Flodden, Lord Dacre, determined to make the castle " the strongest he had ever seen," raised the keep to four storeys and enlarged the outer ward to accommodate a thousand horses and cattle.

In 1560 the walls were still twenty-four feet high. Today a mere heap represents the mighty keep, and the curtain walls are fragmentary. The site is badly overgrown. Twenty years ago the writer thought he identified the sewer up which, probably, Ogle's men forced their unsavoury passage ; but on a subsequent visit the spot was unlocatable. There are traces of steps leading down from the keep to the outer ward, and various other indications of strength, but it is amazing how little of the " Honour of Carham " remains.

SOULIS

ELLIOT

* WARKWORTH CASTLE
(Map II, D9.)

Standing sentinel on the neck of a peninsula formed by the River Coquet near where it enters the sea, this ancient stronghold of the Percies rears itself formidably at the head of the main street of Warkworth. It is only by chance that Warkworth Castle is not the seat of the Duke of Northumberland today—when the estate came into the possession of the Duke of Somerset by his marriage with the heiress of the last Earl of Northumberland, he hesitated between restoring Warkworth or Alnwick before he chose the latter. The choice was in a way fortunate, since Warkworth escaped any risk of injudicious restoration, so that the Keep remains a unique and almost unspoiled example of medieval architecture, planned for domestic comfort as well as defence.

In 1922 the late Duke of Northumberland placed the castle under the care of the Commissioners of H.M. Works, and apart from a small private suite in the Keep which was restored under the direction of the celebrated architect Anthony Salvin, the whole castle is now accessible to the public.

The origins of Warkworth Castle go back to a very early period. It is probable that a " worth," or hall, occupied the site in Saxon times, but it was not till after the coming of William the Norman that any stone defence was erected—and then by a Scotsman, Henry, son of David I of Scotland, who had been created Earl of Northumberland. But on his accession Henry II reclaimed Northumberland and gave Warkworth to Roger-fitz-Richard for his bravery in battle. His descendants held the castle for nearly two hundred years, then it passed by royal grant to the Percies, whose seat it became. Of this great line the most celebrated were the first Earl of Northumberland and his son, Harry Hotspur, the reckless hero of Otterburn and Homildon Hill. Their conspiracy against their king ended in disaster—Hotspur was slain at Shrewsbury and his father had to surrender Warkworth after it had been battered by the king's cannon. The Percy estates, forfeited then, were restored by royal clemency to Hotspur's son, who became the second earl and Warden of the Eastern Marches, and later showed his devotion by giving

187

his life in the royal cause during the Wars of the Roses. For
some generations the castle was in constant use, but the Rising
of the North to restore the Catholic faith brought the Percies
again into conflict with their king, and their estates were again
lost to them ; and subsequently the castle was so plundered by
Sir John Forster, Warden of the Middle Marches, for his own
use, that it was ruinous when the eighth earl regained his estates,

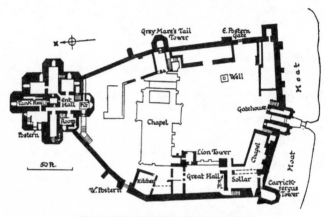

PLAN OF WARKWORTH CASTLE

and when James I visited the place in 1617 he vowed that it was
only the great Percy lion on the keep that held it together.
Still further damage was done in 1672 by one John Clark, the
estate auditor, who took away 272 waggon-loads of lead, timber
and other materials to build his manor-house at Chirton. In
view of such wholesale depredations it is amazing that so much
of the castle remains, and one can only think with regret of
what a " marvellous proper " place it must have been when
intact.

In approaching the castle from the south side we see a long
stretch of curtain wall pierced by an arch, over which frowns
a magnificent Gate-House built in the Early English style.
A ditch crossed by a bridge forms additional protection on this
side, but originally there was a drawbridge that could be swung
up to cover the archway. The recess into which it fitted can
be seen. Higher up there are machicolations, openings projecting on corbels, through which the defenders could fire
arrows or pour down hot lead or scalding liquids. The square
holes high in the walls were for the support of a projecting
wooden staging, or brattice, with openings and loopholes in its

floor to command the walls. In the archway, as further obstacles, were a door, a portcullis and an inner gate, while the passage was commanded by loopholes from the guard-rooms on either side. Quite a warm corner for intruders !

To the left within the Gate-House are the ruins of a chapel, and beyond, against the curtain wall, the remains of the Great Hall, 57 feet long, and the Solar, or private apartment, above a cellar in the corner next to the Carrickfergus Tower at the angle of the curtain wall. The base of this tower is loopholed on each side and was intended to hold a " nest " of cross-bowmen. A room in the west wall of the Solar (on the first floor) is most probably the " closet " that figures in an interesting little incident of the days of William Wallace. The battle of Stirling, won by that hero, created a panic in Northumberland, and the rector of Ford, who kept the Custom House there, sent a large sum of money in leather bags to Warkworth Castle for safety. The Constable himself, with his son, carried them to a closet opening off the hall, and remarked how heavy they were. But later part of the money was missing, and it was never traced. The rector blamed the Constable who, in turn, blamed Robert-fitz-Roger, the lord of the castle.

The Great Hall has a Norman fireplace at one end. The building was taken down by orders of the seventh earl, who intended to rebuild it but was executed in the meanwhile for his share in the Rising of the North. The main entrance was by the handsome porch below the Lion Tower, so called from the fearsome beast on the face of it. The collar on the animal, which was probably originally painted blue, shows the Percy crescent and their motto, " Esperance." Above the archway is the " littyl chamber " where the seventh earl lived and died. Of a large, tub-shaped blue stone close to the tower the tale is told that a former custodian of the castle dreamed persistently of treasure hidden beneath it. When he did finally investigate, he found a gaping hole beside the blue stone, and in the light of this he must have been exasperated when a neighbour, to whom he had confided his visions, blossomed into sudden and mysterious prosperity.

The ruins of a kitchen and a buttery lie beyond the Great Hall ; and in the centre of the bailey opposite are the foundations of a chapel, intended by the first Percy earl to be a college of secular canons, but apparently never finished. The vaults which remain may have been intended as a secret treasury. The Eastern Tower on the curtain wall is particularly interesting for its five loopholes, sixteen feet high and passing through two storeys, since they are, according to Bates, the finest examples in Europe of loopholes designed for cross-bow shooting. Some curious carvings in one embrasure may have been the work of a prisoner when the tower was used as a lock-up. The curtain wall between here and the next postern gate is of massive Norman masonry. The postern gate on the other (north-west) side of the bailey is a very old one. It was guarded by a shouldered portcullis, and its door opened outwards as was the custom in early times, an old Roman fashion.

The elaborately planned Keep is entered by a flight of steps mounting the side of the *motte*, or mound, on which it stands. The unique feature of the building is its central "lantern," intended to give light and to supply rain water for an extraordinarily up-to-date system of flushing the various garde-robes. The system of tanks and conduits by which this was done can be seen on the ground floor on the far side of the "lantern." The other rooms on this side were provision, wine and beer cellars. At the main entrance to the Keep there is a pit, a bottle-shaped *oubliette*, beneath the wooden floor, the only opening in it being the hatch in the roof. Here a man could well be forgotten, with only the tramp of feet overhead to remind him of the outside world. The Porter's Room is to the right, in the wall ; and to the left, round the corner, is the Guard Room, also with a pit beneath its floor. From the dark entrance hall, broad steps go up to the ante-room of the Great Hall, which extends to the roof. One of the big windows is fitted with a stone sideboard ; and there is a gallery high up at one end leading to a similar gallery looking down on the Chapel next door, the most decorative part of the Keep. Occupying the other (western) side of this floor are the Buttery, the Pantry and the great Kitchen with two enormous fireplaces that suggest roasting oxen, and a smaller kitchen with oven and set-pot. A narrow passage from the Great Hall leads to two rooms with a fine outlook towards the sea ; and there are two similar rooms above reached by a newel-stair. The remainder of the second floor contains the private suite of the Duke of Northumberland, used when he visits Warkworth, and is not shown. There is, however, access to the slender lookout tower that rises thirty-two feet above the roof, and is such a prominent feature of the castle. From this height the view is as wide as it is lovely. At hand the Coquet, winding between wooded banks, makes a shining loop about castle and village ; a mile or two away is the sea and Coquet Island ; and westward the varied landscape of central Northumberland stretches towards the Cheviots.

BOWES

§ WELTON HALL
(Map II, F8.)

The name Welton may have once been Wall-town, since the hamlet lies close to the Roman Wall where it passes the Whittle Dene Reservoirs on the Military Road from Newcastle ; though the ancient name of the place was Waltheden.

The Hall, which is built entirely of Roman-worked stones, consists of a fifteenth century pele, now roofless and a mere shell, though the walls are intact ; and a fine and solidly-built Jacobean house, which is used as a farmhouse. As one enters the farm-yard, the dark, square bulk of the tower catches the eye. The modern entrance to it can be reached through the archway to the right of it. At the doorway on the south side it will be seen that the walls are at least a yard thick. The vaulted basement is unusually low in height. At the far end is the original entrance. It once led into the adjoining house but is now blocked, together with the stair that formerly went up in the thickness of the wall to the upper storeys, the first of which has a window with a trefoil head. This window and a similar one to be seen on the north side of the house have an ecclesiastical look, and may be relics of the chapel of St. Michael that was standing hereabouts in the thirteenth century. From the south side the great chimney of the house is seen to advantage. It is corbelled on one side, and " crow-stepped " in its upper portion. A picturesque feature of the south front is the magnificent bay of mullioned windows going the height of two storeys, and in perfect preservation after more than three hundred years.

On the other side of the house, in the angle between the wings will be found the back entrance, which has a moulded head and a dripstone. Above the doorway are the initials W.W. and the date, 1614, carved in shapely characters. W.W. stands for Will o' Welton, perhaps the most noteworthy of the long line of Weltons who lived here for over two hundred years, from the time of Henry IV. Will o' Welton was celebrated for his enor-mous strength, and remarkable stories are told of him. A rather tall one concerns his old age when he was blind, and his mental faculties, too, were perhaps failing him, though his muscle had not. He was sitting at the door of his house when he called a passing plough-boy to him, saying that he wanted to feel his arm, to see what sort of bones folk had in these days ; but the boy, knowing his master, wisely held out an iron plough coulter instead. Promptly breaking it in two in his great hands, the old man said disparagingly, " Men's banes are nought but gristle to what they were in my day."

It will be noticed that some of the mullioned windows in this north-east angle have been built up, probably to avoid the ancient window-tax (it is only recently that one has been re-opened) ; and there is the outline of a door in the west wing. An interesting decorative feature are the corbels of the low gable on the north-east corner, which are naively carved to represent human heads.

The old Hall of the house is now the farmhouse kitchen, and its window is the great bay already referred to. It is an enormous room, twenty-five feet by eighteen, with a flagged floor ; and matching its size is a fireplace nine feet wide, the lintel of which is a single, massive stone that must have rejoiced Old Will's heart. Wide, stone steps ascend to the upper storey, and from them there is communication with a large room between the house and the tower. This is the Haunted Room, but the present tenants have not yet seen the ghost, which is said to be that of the unfortunate Lady of Welton who, with her infant child, was murdered by " Lang Lonkin," the freebooter of Nafferton Castle, as related in the chapter on that stronghold.

Apart from its ancient pele, Welton Hall is particularly interesting as an example of the transformation of an old house to a comfortable modern dwelling, without any loss of dignity or any undesirable additions.

COLLINGWOOD

FENWICK

WEST BEECHFIELD TOWER
(Map II, F8.)

This old fifteenth-century Fenwick pele lies on high ground a mile and a half to the south-west of Belsay along a field-road, or can be approached from the Black Heddon road by a new drive constructed by the present owner when, recently, he restored and rebuilt the tower and the Jacobean farmhouse adjoining it to form a modern residence.

In the seventeenth century Bitchfield was the seat of Robert Fenwick, a son of Sir John Fenwick of Wallington Hall, and his initials, with those of his wife and the date 1622, appear over a doorway in the original east wall of the house. In earlier history we have a brief glimpse of " Bechefield " as it was then (and has become again) with the recorded abduction of Denise de Bechefield, a wealthy widow of this place, by Walter de Sweethope, as she was returning home one August day in 1271. He took his captive over the Border to Jedburgh eventually, intending that she should marry his brother, but the fair widow was not to be persuaded, probably scorning a man who could not even do his own wooing.

A handsome stone wing has been built on to the east side of the Jacobean house, and the pele has been restored and modernised within. The battlemented parapet is not the original. The tower is now entered from the adjoining building, and at the far end of the vaulted basement a stair in the thickness of the wall mounts to the first floor.

The handsome doorway of the south front of the house is a fine specimen of seventeenth-century work, and the windows, too, are noteworthy. There are the foundations of a barmkin round the place, and distinct traces of the old moat on the south side. A grove of tall old trees shelters the spot, which from its eminence commands a wide view, including a glimpse of the sea.

§ WHITTINGHAM TOWER

(Map II, C8.)

One of the pleasantest and most picturesquely situated villages in the county, Whittingham stands on the old coach road which continues through Glanton. The main road from Morpeth to Wooler now runs two miles to the east. In the centre of the village and overlooking the wooded dene where the Aln flows, rises the old pele tower, its rugged walls and casement windows providing a fine picture.

The time of its erection goes back more than six hundred years, for in 1317, we read, one Roger Purvays " resisted the King " in Whittingham Tower. He was finally taken prisoner and his captors earnestly petitioned the King and Council that " this open traitor and one of the greatest evildoers in the March " should be hanged and drawn. The tower originally belonged to the Heron family, then passed to the Collingwoods, and today belongs to Lord Ravensworth of Eslington.

For over a hundred years the tower has been an almshouse for elderly people connected with the Eslington estate, as the inscribed panel above the doorway records—" By the munificence and piety of Lady Ravensworth this ancient tower which was formerly used as a place of refuge in times of rapine and insecurity was repaired and otherwise embellished for the use and benefit of the deserving poor. A.D. 1845." The doorway facing the road was made at the time of the alterations. The original doorway remains on the south side, and from it one can enter the vaulted basement (there are traces of an arch here) with its remnants of stalls for horses. From this basement, stairs once ascended to the upper storeys, probably straight stairs in the thickness of the wall, here nearly nine feet thick. The present stairway is modern. Surmounting the tower are modern corbelled battlements, and at one angle a sort of enlarged bartizan which carries a flagstaff—and a flag on special occasions. The weight of this turret appears to be too much for the old walls, strong as they are, for they show signs of cracking below. The original roof was quite different in appearance—it was double-gabled and covered with red pantiles, drained by projecting spouts. A defensive barmkin probably shut in a few outbuildings round the base of the tower.

The tactful visitor will have little difficulty in obtaining access to the interior. The apartments are large and well-lit, and some of the views are exquisite. The casement windows, however, are in bad repair and have to remain closed, which is a drawback to what otherwise must be a pleasant existence within the stout old walls.

WHITTON TOWER
(Map II, D7.)

Till recently the residence through many centuries of the rectors of Rothbury, Whitton Tower stands on the south side of the Coquet, half a mile from the town, and like Tosson looks out across the valley to the hills where the danger once lay.

A few years ago the tower was acquired by Sir Angus Watson who spent a considerable sum in turning it into a hospital for needy children of Newcastle-upon-Tyne. The beautiful grounds shut in with well-grown trees can be visited on application to the Matron, and doubtless the interior also by those particularly interested and sufficiently tactful.

One of the finest peles in the county, Whitton Tower dates, along with other fortlets in Coquetdale, from very early times, being mentioned with Cartington and Hepple in a list made in 1415. In 1541 it was described as " a toure and lytle barmekin " and as being in good condition, but later it became ruinous. Successive rectors, however, repaired and extended the building, the chief of these being Canon Harcourt who held the living from 1822 to 1870. It is his coat of arms with a peacock as crest that appears above the entrance to the handsome and spacious porch.

Owing to the trees about it, the old tower can be well seen only from the garden. The massive nature of the masonry, especially that of the lowest and oldest stage, is noteworthy. The battlements are modern. Within there are some unusual features, for the first floor is barrel-vaulted ; and there is a well in the basement, lined with stone and fifteen feet deep. The basement, or " dungeon " as it is sometimes called, is entered from outside, and was guarded by a double door. In the roof a hatchway communicates with the room above. From the first floor a newel staircase in the thickness of the wall goes to an upper room where, in an alcove, is a carved piscina of early date, and a recess in the wall that may have been a secret room.

A shield built into the west wall and carved with a coat of arms has caused some controversy among antiquaries. Some say it bears the arms of the Umfravilles, but others think the arms are those of a one-time rector who repaired the upper part of the tower five hundred years ago. Whitton, like other places along the Border, kept a constant look-out for the enemy, whether from Scotland, Tynedale or Redesdale. The station in 1553 was at a quarry, which still exists a little to the south near the round tower known as Sharpe's Folly. There, " at the quarie yate " [quarry gate], two men kept nightly watch and ward.

LESLIE

WILLIMOTESWICK CASTLE
(Map I, F4.)

This oddly named stronghold is equally out-of-the-way
as to its situation. It lies along what is very much of a by-road
through Ridley and Beltingham on the south side of the South
Tyne about halfway between Haydon Bridge and Haltwhistle.
In approaching there is an impression of a great, square tower
with other buildings to the left, and on coming nearer it is seen
that the road passes beneath the tower into a courtyard where
one is confronted with an old manor-house flanked at one end
with a remarkable-looking tower. This is the ancient seat of
the Ridleys, and the traditional birthplace of that Bishop Ridley
who with Latimer suffered at the stake in Oxford, and by their
martyrdom " lit a candle " in the cause of Protestantism.

Regarding the name of this castle, there is some disagreement
among philologists. Bates has it that it means the " wyke," or
fortified house, of a Saxon thane called Willimont: others talk
of a Willimont being the Northumbrian name for a guillemot,
a species of bird that used to frequent the marshes nearby.
The spelling, too, is delightfully varied ; but all this is comparatively unimportant beside the inherent attractiveness of
the place.

The great entrance-tower, with walls upwards of seven
feet thick, is a fine specimen of medieval architecture, though
not the oldest part of the castle. The upper hinge of the gate
which closed the archway still remains, with the holes for the
sliding-bar that reinforced it. Within one of the doors on the
right, a newel-stair goes up to the battlements, now somewhat
decayed, which are corbelled out to overhang the walls. In one
of the rooms there is one of the original fireplaces, a yawning
structure nearly eleven feet wide. The spouts draining the roof
are peculiar—they have been made to represent cannon to impress
unwanted strangers. The windows are nearly as small as the
loops, mere oblongs that would hardly illuminate the darkness,

but afford all the less chance of attack. Above the entrance is an empty recess that once, doubtless, held the arms of the Ridleys. The manor-house in the courtyard has been much altered during its three hundred years (or so) of habitation, but the great fireplace remains, and there is the outline of one of the old Gothic doorways. The walls are very thick as if intended for defence. The building forming the east wing, probably the oldest part of the castle, has unique features in the two tall, tapering towers which are just wide enough to take a spiral stair. They seem to have been used chiefly as look-outs, though they have had corbelled battlements. On the south side a little dene, a charming spot today, completes the defences of this extremely interesting block of buildings known as Willimoteswick Castle.

The Ridleys appear to have come into possession of the manor towards the end of the thirteenth century, but not to have lived here till two hundred years later. For many generations the family occupied a very important place in the affairs of the district, especially as regards the defence of the Border. One Ridley was one of the Commissioners for assuring the truce with Scotland in 1484; and others were setters and searchers and overseers of the nightly watch and ward kept against invasion at places such as " the ford of Hawtwesyll " and " the Crawecragge." These two danger-spots are mentioned in the ballad of *The Fray of Hautwessel*, in which the Ridleys receive special mention for their valour during a raid by the Liddesdale Armstrongs, when one Ridley thrust his spear right through Sim o' the Cathills, and Wat Armstrong, the leader, fell a victim to the redoubtable Alec Ridley.

> " Then Alec Ridley he let flee
> A clothyard shaft, ahint the wa';
> It struck Wat Armstrong in the ee',
> Went through his steel cap, heid and a'.
> I wot it made him quickly fa',
> He would na rise, though he essayed;
> The best at thief-craft or the ba',
> He ne'er again shall ride a raid."

It is interesting to know what the best parlour at Willimoteswick contained four hundred years ago. The owner then was Nicholas Ridley, grand-nephew to Bishop Ridley and Sheriff of Northumberland. An inventory taken at the time records the following : Twenty pairs of double linen sheets, ten pairs of ' strakinge ' sheets, ten pairs of ' harne ' sheets, six ' wishons,' six ' worset wishons,' six candlesticks, a new cupboard, a ' hurle ' bed, a new ' presser,' seven chests, two ' carping ' cloths, two cupboard cloths, four new sacks, the ' Boke of Marters,' and a Bible.

The Ridleys were always ready to repel the intruding Scot—they were equally ready on occasions to " bang it out " with their own neighbours. Sometimes worse happened, as when the Ridleys and the Thirlwalls set upon Albany Featherstonehaugh within a bowshot of his own castle, and left him dead. We do not know now what lay behind this attack, but doubtless the old sheriff had made himself unpopular by some attempt to impose law and order upon men who, brought up in a rough school, found it hard to " brook a bridle."

RIDLEY

BIBLIOGRAPHY

GENERAL

ARMITAGE, ELLA S. *The Early Norman Castles of the British Isles*, 1912. This is the great book on the mount-and-bailey castles in which Mrs. Armitage, on a basis of inspired research, proved definitely their Norman origin and laid the foundations of our modern knowledge of the early history of the castle.

ASHDOWN, CHARLES H. *British Castles*, 1911. A very excellent book for the general reader.

BRAUN, HUGH. *The English Castle*, 1936. The most recent of the books for the general reader, this brings the castle to life most vividly. Particularly good is the treatment of the mount-and-bailey castles and of the domestic life within the castle. (Batsford, 7/6.)

CAMDEN, W. *Britannia*. Trans. by P. Holland. (London: 1610.)

Carey, Memoirs of Robert, ed. by G. H. Powell. (London: 1905.)

CARLETON, G. *Life of Bernard Gilpin*. (London: 1636.)

D'AUVERGNE, EDMUND B. *The English Castles*, 1926. An account, for the general reader, of upwards of fifty of the principal English castles. (T. Werner Laurie, Ltd.)

HARVEY, ALFRED. *Castles and Walled Towns of England*. (Antiquary's Books. Methuen.)

LANG, A. *A History of Scotland*. (Edinburgh and London: 1912.)

LANG, A. & J. *Highways and Byways in the Border*. (London: 1914.)

OMAN, CHARLES. *Castles*. A clearly written and beautifully illustrated account of the castles on the Great Western Railway System, 5/-. (G.W.R.)

STENTON, F. M. *The Development of the Castle in England and Wales*. (1910.)

THOMPSON, A. HAMILTON. *Military Architecture in England during the Middle Ages*, 1912. A most scholarly, detailed treatment, with frequent references to Continental practice, this is the most valuable of all works on castles in general.

TECHNICAL AND ARCHAEOLOGICAL

Medieval England. A standard text-book, invaluable to the student of medieval life generally, containing useful and well illustrated chapters on military architecture, arms and armour. (Oxford: Clarendon Press, £1 1s.)

Archaeological Journal, Vols. 28—39. One of the best sources of information on the science of fortification and siegecraft as practised in the past.

Royal Military Academy Text Book of Fortification, Part ii. (London : 1893.)

OMAN, CHARLES. *A History of the Art of War in the Middle Ages,* 2 vols., 2nd edition, 1924. A great work, by our foremost authority, on the strategy and tactics, arms and armour, of the Middle Ages, it includes much matter relevant to castles and shows them in their true perspective as facets of the art of war.

BARNARD, FRANCIS PIERREPONT. *Companion to English History (Middle Ages).* An excellent guide, for the general reader, to the life and arts, in war and peace, of the Middle Ages.

CLARKE, GEO. T. *Medieval Military Architecture in England,* 2 vols., 1884. Clark was the great 19th-century authority on castles and his two volumes are still invaluable store-houses of architectural detail. Unfortunately he was a stalwart protagonist of the school of history which assigned all mount-and-bailey castles to pre-Norman times; they could be anything from Ancient British earthworks to Anglo-Saxon " moot-hills," but not Norman fortresses. The result of this obsession was to throw wrong much of Clark's chronology, but his work yet remains a quarry of exact and painstaking research in which only too many subsequent writers have delved without the courtesy of acknowledgment. The unfortunate results of the blind copying of Clark are easily seen in many modern guide-books where the mount-and-baileys are ignorantly ascribed to " our Anglo-Saxon forefathers," " pre-historic races " or, better still, as " village meeting places " ; one such book, published within the last two years, leaves the reader with the impression that the Anglo-Saxons had nothing better to do than pile up huge mounds of earth and then sit gossiping on top of them !

LE DUC, E. VIOLLET. *L'Architecture Militaire au Moyen Age* (Paris : 1854). (There is an English translation of this fascinating work.)

Instruction in Military Engineering, Parts i, ii and iv. (London : 1900—1908.) British Official Publication.

MACGIBBON, D. & ROSS, T. *Architecture of Scotland.* (Edinburgh : 1887–92.)

ARTICLES : " Fortification and Siegecraft " ; " Castle." *Encyclopaedia Britannica,* 11th Edition.

BIBLIOGRAPHY

Proceedings of the Newcastle Society of Antiquaries. (Newcastle : 1857- .)

Transactions of the Cumberland and Westmorland A. and A. Society. (Kendal : 1874- .)

Transactions of the A. and A. Society of Durham and Northumberland. (London : 1862-1905.)

TOPOGRAPHICAL

Archaeologia Aeliana. (Newcastle : 1816- .)

ARMSTRONG, R. B. *History of Liddesdale.* (Edinburgh : 1883.)

BATES, C. J. *The Border Holds of Northumberland.* (Newcastle : 1891).

    ,, *History of Northumberland.* (London : 1895.)

CREIGHTON, M. *Carlisle.* (London : 1889.)

CURWEN, J. F. *Castles and Towers of Cumberland and Westmorland.* (Kendal : 1913.)

DIXON, D. D. *Upper Coquetdale.* (Newcastle : 1903.)

    ,, *Whittingham Vale* (Newcastle : 1895.)

DOUGLAS, G. B. S. *History of the Border Counties.* (Edinburgh : 1899.)

ELLIOT, G. F. S. *The Border Elliots.* (Edinburgh 1897.)

FERGUSON, R. S. *Guide to Carlisle.* (Carlisle).

    ,, *History of Cumberland.* (London : 1890.)

GAUL, H. D. *Brave Borderland.* (London.)

GRAHAM, P. A. *Highways and Byways in Northumberland.* (London : 1920.)

HARTSHORNE, C. H. *Feudal and Military Antiquities of Northumberland.* (1852.)

HODGKIN, T. *The Wardens of the Marches.* (London : 1908.)

HODGSON, J. *History of Northumberland.* (Newcastle : 1820-58.)

Howard, The Household Books of Lord W. (Surtees Soc. Durham : 1878.

MACK, J. L. *The Border Line.* (Edinburgh and London : 1926.)

Northumberland County History. (Newcastle : 1893- .)

PEASE, H. *The Wardens of the Marches.* (London : 1913.)

ROSS, T. *Castellated and Domestic Architecture of Scotland.*

SCOTT, J. *History of Berwick.* (London, 1888.)

TOMLINSON, W. W. *Northumberland in the Sixteenth Century.*
(London.)

,, *Guide to Northumberland.* (London.)

WEDGWOOD, IRIS. *Northumberland and Durham.* (London.)

ARMS AND ARMOUR

DEMMIN, A. *Arms and Armour.* (English Edition, Bell, 1894.)

FFOULKES, C. J. *Armour and Weapons.* (1909.)

FFOULKES, C. J. *The Armourer and his Craft.* (1912.)

LAKIN, SIR GUY. *Arms and Armour*, 5 vols. (1920—22.)

HAINES. *A Manual of Monumental Brasses*, 2 vols. (1861.)

BOUTELL. *The Monumental Brasses of England.* (1849.)

GAWTHORPE, WALTER E. *The Brasses of our Homeland Churches.*
A useful and reliable account for popular use. (Homeland
Association Ltd.)

COLLINSON

A Short Glossary

of

Medieval Arms, Armour and Architecture, Heraldry, etc.

ADULTERINE—A term used to denote those fortifications which were erected without royal licence during the anarchy of Stephen's reign ; most of them were levelled by Henry II. (See page 5.)

AILETTE—An epaulette of steel or *cuir bouilli* displaying the badge of the wearer. It was fashionable during the 13th and 14th centuries and primarily worn to protect the neck from sword thrusts, but later it served merely for the display of heraldry. (See under PAULDRONS.)

AKETON (HAUKETON : HAKETON). A quilted garment worn in the early medieval period under the hauberk, to provide additional protection from sword thrusts and to prevent chafing. It was also known as the Gambeson. (The wool stuffing was sometimes known as the Wambeys or Wambais.) (See page 205.)

ALLURES—(See under BRATTICES).

ANELACE (ANLACE)—A short double-edged dagger tapering to a point, usually suspended from the girdle. It features in innumerable church monumental brasses of knights up to the close of the 15th cent. (See also under MISERICORDE.)

ANGLO-SAXON CHRONICLE—This, "the first history of any Teutonic people in their own language ; the earliest and most venerable monument of English prose," is an invaluable record of events kept in various monasteries from A.D. 755 to 1154.

ANTE-MURAL (see under BARBICAN).

ARBALAST (ARBALEST : ARBLAST : ARBALIST—the Classical *balista*).—A medieval weapon operated on the same principle as the mangon (q.v.) consisting of a large bow mounted horizontally on a stand.

ARCHERY—(See under Bows).

ARMET—(See under HELM).

ARMING-POINT—The " points " or ties of defensive armour. (See page 205.)

ARQUEBUS (ARQUEBUSE : ARCUBUS : HARQUEBUS : HACKBUT : HAGBUT)—First introduced early in the 16th cent., this instrument was an improvement on the first type of hand-gun. It was the first fire-arm to be worked by a trigger and was the successor to the cross-bow and the immediate predecessor of the musket, passing out during the close of the 16th cent. There were two types—the match-lock and the wheel-lock.

ARROW SLITS (Balistraria : Arbalisteria : Arbalistina : Loops)—Narrow openings, used in medieval fortifications, through which arrows and other missiles could be discharged. They did not come into general use in this country until the early 13th cent. and then were designed for use with the cross-bow, Later, with the coming into use of the long-bow, which was an ideal weapon for the defence, they were provided in greater numbers and were elaborated to allow of simultaneous use by as many

TYPES OF ARROW SLITS

as three archers. The slits seen in 11th and 12th-cent. keeps and towers were usually only for the admittance of light and air. Arrow slits took various forms.

ASHLAR—Hewn and squared wall stone laid in courses as distinguished from that which is unhewn. (See under Rubble.)

AULA—The timber-built house of a Saxon lord or an early type of Norman manor house. Such houses were not castles since they lacked elaborate fortifications.

AVANTAIL (Ventaile)—The front part of a late 13th-cent. helm which could be lifted at will. It superseded the Norman nasal and preceded the visor.

BAILEY (Ballium)—(1) The fortified base-court of a mount-and-bailey castle, which see. The name often lingers long after all trace of the thing itself has disappeared, e.g. the Old Bailey in London, St. Peter's in the Bailey in Oxford, the Old Baile in York. (2) An open space, or ward, within the walls of a castle. The large outer baileys of the peles or fortified houses of the Border country were known as Barmkins. (See pages 1 and 7.)

BAINBERGS—Shin-guards worn over chain armour in the 13th-cent. They preceded the greaves or jambarts of the 14th cent.

BALISTRARIA—(See under Bartizan : Arrow Slits).

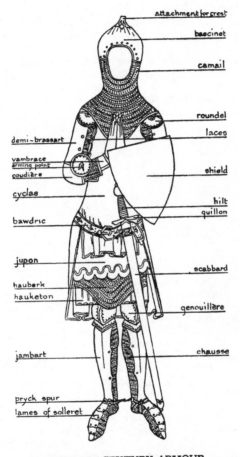

attachment for crest
bascinet
camail
roundel
laces
demi-brassart
vambrace
arming point
coudière
shield
cyclas
hilt
quillon
bawdric
jupon
scabbard
hauberk
hauketon
genouillère
jambart
chausse
pryck spur
lames of solleret

LATE 13TH-CENTURY ARMOUR
as represented in contemporary monumental brasses shewing
many features noted in the accompanying Glossary

205

BALLISTA—(See under MANGON and TRÉBUCHET).

BALLIUM—(See under BAILEY).

BARBETTE—A specially constructed gun-emplacement or platform of earth or timber, to facilitate firing over a parapet.

BARBICAN (ANTEMURAL : BARMKIN)—A defensive outwork designed to protect the main entrance to a castle. (See page 5.)

BARMKIN (BARMEKYN)—(See under BAILEY).

BARONIAL STYLE—The Scottish baronial style of architecture became the vogue in the late medieval period, the most distinguishing feature being the so-called " pepperbox " corner turrets and crow-stepped gables, reflecting the Continental influence of the period prior to the Union of the Crowns in 1603.

BARREL-VAULT—One that resembles the inside of a barrel.

BARTIZAN (BRETISE)—An overhanging watch-turret designed to project from a curtain wall. (See also ARROW SLITS).

BASCINET—(See under HELM). (See pages 205 and 207.)

BASTION (REDOUBT)—High towers and walls were very vulnerable against cannon and in the 16th century we find fortifications being made low and squat in defence against the new weapon. The round, flanking towers of the Middle Ages were replaced by projecting, solid earthern banks, their faces revetted by stone walling : these are true bastions. Early examples can be seen in the walls of Berwick-on-Tweed, *circa* 1558. The term is often used, though loosely, for such medieval towers as consist of a core of earth or rock faced with a wall of stone.

BASTLE or BASTEL HOUSES—Fortified houses in the Border country between England and Scotland. The ground storey is usually stone vaulted. They were used as places of refuge for women and cattle during Border raids. (See pages 1 and 8.)

BATTER—Said of a stone wall which tapers toward the top. Many Norman towers and Castles (e.g. Bamburgh) and churches shew this tendency.

BATTERING-RAM—A huge tree trunk furnished with a solid iron head (sometimes fashioned in the form of a ram's head) used for breaching a stone wall. It was impelled either by a body of soldiers or was suspended from a timber framework and swung to and fro under cover of a penthouse, or *testudo*, known as a " cat " or " sow."

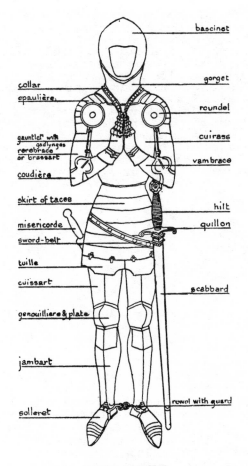

bascinet

collar

epaulière,

gorget

roundel

gauntlet with
gadlynges
rerebrace
or brassart

cuirass

coudière

vambrace

skirt of taces

hilt

misericorde

quillon

sword-belt

tuille

cuissart

scabbard

genouilliere & plate

jambart

solleret

rowel with guard

PLATE ARMOUR

as illustrated in monumental brasses of the second
half of the 14th century and onwards

GLOSSARY

BATTLEMENT (CRENELLATION: EMBATTAILMENT: BATELING
Ancient adjectival form BRETEXED)—Of very ancient origin,
the term is applied to the parapet about 6 feet high surrounding a castle (or church) wall which has portions cut
away at regular intervals to permit the passage of arrows
or missiles. The embrasured openings are termed
"crenelles," the uncut parts of the parapet cops or merlons.
This system of defence is sometimes known as a crenelle.
During the medieval period it was imperative to obtain
permission of the king to build a castle, fortify a house
or extend fortifications: this was the familiar "licence
to crenellate." In medieval battlements the crenelle was
usually one third the width of a merlon. Sometimes
the merlons themselves were pierced by a loop-hole.
(See under ARROW SLITS: EMBRASURE.)

BAUDRIC (BAWDRIC: CINGULUM)—The leather (*cuir bouilli*)
belt from which the sword was suspended as represented
in many sepulchral monuments and brasses of medieval
knights. It was often highly ornate. (See page 205.)

BAVIER (BEAVER)—The chin piece of a medieval helm. (See
under Helm.)

BEAVER—(See under HELM).

BELFRY (Siege Tower)—A movable wooden tower mounted
on wheels or rollers which was pushed forward by the
besiegers towards the curtain wall of the castle. Its
height gave advantage to the archers in its fighting top
while a bridge could be let down on to the top of the
wall and an assault launched over it. (See opposite
page.) (See also under MALVOISIN.)

BERM—A ledge between the rampart or curtain wall and the
edge of the ditch.

BILL—A sharp-pointed weapon or concave battle axe mounted
on a long pole and provided with hooks for unhorsing
armoured knights. (See also Guisarme.)

BOMBARD. The earliest form of cannon first used in the
14th cent. It was employed to project stone and iron
balls and other heavy missiles. Two examples of this
early form of siege engine are to be seen at St. Michael's
Mount, Cornwall. Typical medieval siege balls are to
be seen in Norham and Newcastle Castles; London-
derry Cathedral; at Scarborough, Helmsley and Knares-
borough castles and elsewhere.

BORE—(See under "MOUSE.")

BOUCHE—The name given to the slit or small opening cut
away from the dexter side (the right hand side as used,
but the left as seen by the spectator) of the shield to allow

free play for the sword. A similar rounded opening is seen in the jousting or tilting shields for resting the shaft of the lance. The bouche forms a conspicuous feature of the somewhat fanciful shield frequently used in heraldic design in the Renaissance period.

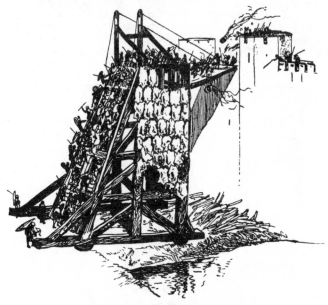

A BELFRY OR SIEGE TOWER

BOWS—The origin of the bow and arrow is lost in the mists of antiquity. It was certainly known among the ancient Egyptians.

The archers at the battle of Hastings in 1066 used the SHORT BOW, which was drawn only to the chest and had little penetrative power; it was never considered a weapon of very great value and is unmentioned in an Assize of Arms of 1181. The favourite missile weapon of this period was the CROSS BOW; it had great stopping power but was clumsy and slow in use. Its bow was bent upon a stock with a notch to which the cord was stretched, being released by a trigger; sometimes it was wound up by means of a crank known as a moulinet. Its missiles were quarrels (short, heavy arrows or bolts . . . Cadrelli or Carreaux) and stones.

A MEDIEVAL LONG-BOW MAN

The appearance of the famed English LONG BOW—originally a Welsh weapon—in the Assize of Arms of 1252 marks the turning point in our medieval military history. Prior to this the feudal horseman had been the decisive factor on the field of battle, but the new weapon, with its amazing accuracy, low trajectory, long range, great stopping power and speed in action, completely turned the tables and gave to the English infantry a superiority over all other arms which lasted a full hundred years. Edward I was the first leader to perceive its tactical possibilities, and used it with great success in his Welsh and Scotch wars; Edward III and Henry V vanquished with it the feudal nobility of France. Crecy, Poictiers and Agincourt were the triumphs of the English bowman.

The length of the long bow was usually equal to the height of the archer; it was drawn right back to the shoulder and discharged an arrow a cloth-yard in length. The "self-bow" (i.e., one made from one piece of wood as distinct from "backed" when it was made of two or more strips glued together) was almost always fashioned from yew. The effective range was fully 250 yards. (See under ARROW SLITS.)

BRASSARTS (RERE BRACES : DEMI-PLATES: DEMI-BRASSARTS)—Plates of wrought-iron or steel laced to the forearms over the Hauberk for additional protection.

BRATTICES (HOURDS : MANTLING : BRATTISH : BRETESCHE : "HOARD-INGS ")—In the early medieval period before the days of gunpowder, it was imperative that strict watch be kept for the

A MEDIEVAL
CROSS-BOW MAN

activities of hostile engineers at the foot of the castle wall. It was impossible to command a clear view of the base of the walls from the ramparts or embattlements without risk of exposure. It therefore became necessary to provide a safe means of survey. This took the form of a portable hurdle of wattle supported by brackets attached to the crenelle. As time went on they became larger and more solidly built, with apertures in the flooring through which missiles could be dropped on the enemy below. Subsequently these allures or "hoardings" as they were termed became a permanent feature of the stone embattlement, taking the form of massive brackets corbelled out from the walling and known as machicolations, which see.

BRIGANDINE—(See under JAZERINE).

BUHL—Furniture ornamented with inlay work of unburnished gold, brass or mother-of-pearl.

BURGONET—(See under HELM).

BURGUS—An enclosure surrounded by a ditch and stockade or wall, inhabited by a community of people on special terms of tenancy.

BURH—(See INTRODUCTION, page 2.)

BUTTERY—A store-room for provisions, especially liquors. One of the three rooms usually at one end of the medieval Hall. The other two were the Pantry and the Kitchen.

BYRNIE—(See under HAUBERK).

CALTRAP (CALTHROPS : CALTROP : GALTRAP). A small iron instrument devised with four sharp points designed in such a way that when thrown on the ground would settle on three of them, the remaining point pointing uppermost. Scattered over the battlefield, these cheval-traps as they are sometimes called proved very effective in impeding the progress of cavalry. (See page 213.)

CAMAIL—A tippet of chain mail laced to the rim of the helmet and falling on to the shoulders to give protection to the face and neck. (See page 205.)

CAMDEN, WILLIAM—Born 1551, died 1623. He was one of the earliest of the English antiquarians and his *Britannia*, published in 1586, gives us valuable information on the state of the castles at that time and enables us to reconstruct many details which have since disappeared.

CANBERIA—(See under JAMBART).

CAPUT BARONIAL—The principal home of an important family ; the chief house and administrative centre of a barony.

CASQUE—(See under HELM).

CASTLE GUARD—The method by which the medieval castle was garrisoned. The military tenure of some tenants and officers of the king, or a lord, took the form of providing a contingent of men for the defence of a castle. Frequently a specific portion of the defences was assigned to each tenant and in some castles, as at Dover, we find the towers still retaining the names of the families charged with their manning.

" CAT "—(See under BATTERING RAM).

CATAPULT—A war-engine for the projection of heavy darts. (See under TRÉBUCHET and MANGON.)

CHAMFRON (FRONTALE : TESTIERE : CHANFRON). A frontlet or headpiece (usually of steel) designed to protect a war horse's head. Known to the ancient Greeks and Persians, it was introduced into Europe in the 15th cent. Most of the specimens preserved as museum pieces were wrought by Continental craftsmen and are extremely fine, most often bearing elaborate chased designs.

CHAUSSES (CHASTONS : CHAUSSONS)—Tight-fitting breeches or leg-coverings (usually of linked mail) further protected by the jambarts (q.v.). (See page 205.)

CHEVAL-DE-FRISE (ERICIUS—" hedgehog ")—A long iron barrel or heavy log of wood studded with sharp-pointed spikes or spears employed to impede the progress of infantry or cavalry. It seems to have had its origin in the thorn hedge or " hedge-hog " placed, in early fortifications, on the outer edge of a ditch as the outermost defence on the " lists."

CHEVRON—A V-shaped ornament characteristic of early Norman architecture.

CINGULUM—(See under BAUDRIC).

CINQUEFOIL—In Heraldry, representing a flower of five petals, shown full-faced and without a stalk.

CLEUGH or CLEUCH—A steep-sided ravine.

COIF DE MAILES—(See under HAUBERK).

COINTISE—(See under MANTLING).

CONCENTRIC CASTLE—The concentric plan of fortification involved a series of two, sometimes more, curtain walls, one within the other and so designed that the inner, and higher, wall commanded and supported the defences of the outer, and lower, wall. The first British castle to be planned on truly concentric lines was Caerphilly, begun about 1267, but the finest examples are Harlech and Beaumaris, built by Edward I at the close of the century ; the Tower of London became concentric in the course of its long evolution. The concentric idea

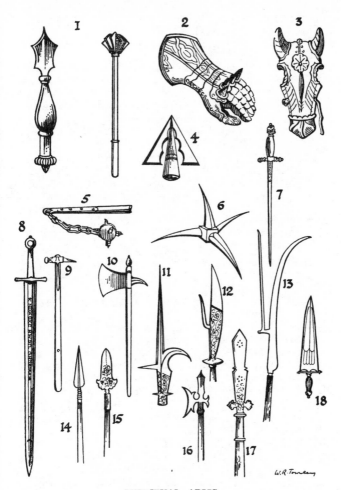

MEDIEVAL ARMS

1. Types of maces used by ecclesiastics who were forbidden by their sacred calling to carry arms.
2. An armoured knight's gauntlet with the knuckles further protected by gadlyngs.
3. Chamfron designed to give protection to the head of a steed.
4. Pheon, the cross-bow missile.
5. "Holy-water sprinkler," or flail.
6. Caltrap or galtrap.
7. Misericord.
8. Sword of the 14th century.
9. Martel-de-fer.
10. Battle axe.
11. Late medieval Bill.
12. Glaive.
13. Guisarme.
14, 15. } Pike heads.
16. Halbert.
17. Langue-de-bœuf.
18. Anelace.

represents the highest pitch of medieval military science, though the plan was originally developed in the Byzantine Empire where the magnificent triple walls of Constantinople were raised in the 5th century. (See opposite page.)

CORBEL—A bracket or piece of timber or stone projecting from a wall to support a weight, and often decorative in the form of a human head, coat of arms, etc.

CORBIE-STEPPED—Applied to gables which are stepped ; a common Scottish fashion. (Scots, *corbie*, a crow.)

COUDIERES (COUTES : COUTERES). Steel plates protecting the elbows. In the late medieval period these became elaborated to an absurd degree as depicted in innumerable monumental brasses of the 15th and 16th centuries. (See pages 205 and 207.)

COUNTERSCARP—The outer slope or edge of the ditch.

CRENELLATE, LICENCE TO—Royal permission to furnish with battlements and otherwise fortify. (See under BATTLEMENT.)

CRENELLATION (QUARNELLUS : CASTELLATION)—(See under BATTLEMENT).

CRESSET—An iron basket, jar or open lamp filled with combustible materials, for use on a beacon.

CREST—Figure of a man, beast, bird or monster worn by knights on their helmets, and later adapted to heraldry to appear over the shield.

CROSS BOW—(See under Bows).

CROSS PATONCE or PATONCEE—In heraldry, a cross the limbs of which expand towards the ends, which resemble a *fleur-de-lys*.

CROW-STEPPED—(See CORBIE-STEPPED).

CUIRASS (CUIRIE : LORICA). This was originally a two-piece suit of leather to protect the body, consisting of breast-plate and back-plate. In the late 16th and early 17th centuries it became a highly ornate affair (covered with elaborate hand-chased design) for purely ceremonial wear. Below the cuirass were suspended the taces consisting of articulated steel plates forming a flexible skirt to protect the hips and thighs. Hinged to the lowest taces were further steel plates known as tuilles. (See page 207.)

CUIR BOUILLI—Leather boiled in oil or soaked to soften, impressed or moulded with an artistic design or inscription, heraldic badge, etc. It was used extensively throughout the medieval period in conjunction with both mail and plate armour and also for other purposes,

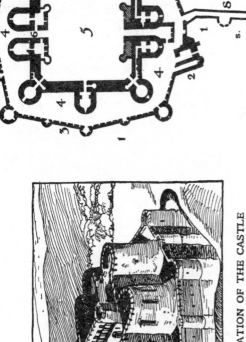

CONJECTURAL RESTORATION OF THE CASTLE
SHOWING THE MOAT AND CURTAIN WALLS

PLAN OF BEAUMARIS CASTLE

1. The Moat
2. Main Entrance with barbican and portcullis
3. Outer Curtain Wall
4. Outer Ward
5. Inner Ward
6. Great Hall
7. Chapel
8. Gunner's Wall

BEAUMARIS CASTLE, ANGLESEY

One of the finest of the Concentric Castles, this was commenced by Edward I in 1295.
Note the two well-flanked curtains, the inner one commanding and supporting the outer

e.g., book, ivory and instrument cases, sword and knife sheaths, bottle and casket covers, etc.

CUISSARTS (Cuisses : Cuish)—Steel plates provided for the protection of the thighs. Often further provided with pourpoint and iron studs. Originally articulated, they were later made in one piece. (See page 207.)

CULETTES—Plates of armour devised to give protection to the back of a mounted knight (cuirassier). They were usually worn from the waist-line to the saddle.

CULVERIN (Colubrina)—A portable firearm which in the 14th cent. marked the transition between the cannon and the hand-gun. By the 16th and early 17th cent. it had developed to a cannon some 9 to 12 feet in length firing balls weighing 18 lb. apiece. It takes its name from the handles which were usually in the form of snakes. A demi-culverin had a 4 in. bore, according to Meyrick.

CURTAIN or CURTAIN WALL—Strictly this is the stretch of wall between two towers but the term is frequently used to denote the whole wall, with its included towers, bounding any portion of the castle. The Cross-Curtain is the wall dividing the principal enclosure of the castle in two wards. (See also page 215.)

CYCLAS (Armilausa)—The long sleeveless garment worn over the armour. It was derived from the surcoat, from which it differed inasmuch as the whole of the front was cut away up to the middle of the thighs and the sides were slit up to the hips, drawn in to the body and laced to the righthand side. (See page 205.)

DAIS—In the medieval Hall, a raised floor at the upper end where the high table stood, at which the lord of the house and his family and friends dined, the retainers eating at the lower table.

DEAD ANGLE—A part of the field in front of a fortification into which it is impossible for the defenders to direct their fire without unduly exposing themselves. Much of the development of the art of fortification has been concerned with the elimination of such dead angles.

DEBATABLE LAND—An area on the Border where the exact course of the Line was not fixed, or was in dispute. Also known as " Threapland."

DEMI-CULVERIN—(See under Culverin).

DEMI-JAMBES—(See under Jambart).

DEMI-PLATES—(See under Brassarts and Vambraces).

DOG-TOOTH—A moulding characteristic of late Norman and Early English architecture, consisting of a series of ornamented and sometimes undercut conical projections.

DONJON—Ancient name for a castle keep. (See page 2.)

DOUBLET—A tightly-fitting body garment reaching from the neck to a few inches below the waist; worn from the fourteenth to the seventeenth centuries. It took its name from the fact that it was double and padded.

DRAWBRIDGE—A movable wooden bridge across a moat, sometimes so arranged as to cover the adjoining archway when raised.

DRIPSTONE—A moulding projecting over doors and windows, its purpose being to divert rainwater.

DUNGEON—(See page 2.)

EMBRASURE—The inward splay of a window opening, doorway or crenelle. (See under BATTLEMENT.)

ENCEINTE—The whole principal enclosure of a castle.

ENFEOFFMENT—Conferment of land, possessions or title upon a person by the sovereign or overlord.

ENFILADE.—A fire, of arrows, musketry, etc., which sweeps a line of works or men from end to end; hence a part of the field which can be so raked from the fortifications is said to be " enfiladed."

ENTABLATURE—In Greek architecture, the upper part of a building, above the capitals of the columns.

EPAULIÈRES (EPAULLETS: EPAULETS)—Metal shoulder-pieces affording protection to the shoulders and neck from sword thrusts (see page 207). The name is now applied to the ornamental shoulder knots worn since the 18th century by men of fashion and liveried servants and naval officers, etc. (See also under AILETTE, PAULDRONS).

ESCUTCHEON—A shield showing a coat of arms.

FACADE—The exterior front of a building.

FALL-BAR—The oak beam used to secure a door from inside. It swung or " fell " from one side into an opening in the opposite jamb.

FEE, FIEF—A heritable estate held on conditions of feudal service to the king or a superior lord; a lordship.

FIELD—The area of operation of an attacking force before the walls of a fortress.

FIRKIN—A measure equal to the fourth part of a barrel and equal to nine gallons.

FLAIL (" HOLY WATER SPRINKLER ")—Used extensively on the Continent, it was also known in England throughout the medieval period. It consisted of a hand-shaft to the end of which were fastened several whips (like a modern cat-o'-nine-tails) on the end of each of which was an iron point. Some flails (as depicted in the " Doom " window of Fairford church, Glos.) had a chain fastened to the handle on the end of which was a ball studded with iron spikes. (See page 213.)

FLANK.—To attack or threaten from the side ; hence any part of the field where an enemy may be subjected to a fire from the side is said to be " flanked," e.g. besiegers attacking a stretch of wall between two projecting towers.

FLANKER—A fortification commanding the flank of an attacking force.

FLYING BUTTRESS—An arch-like support for a wall, usually designed to resist the thrust of a stone vaulted ceiling.

FORTALICE—An early medieval term for a fortress. The term is now generally applied to an outwork of a fortification.

FOSSE—A ditch or moat, with or without water.

FRESCO (Italian, *fresh*)—A painting done in water-colour on fresh plaster.

FUNDIBALUS (FUNDIBALUM)—A war engine for hurling heavy missiles. (See under MANGON and TRÉBUCHET.)

GADLINGS (GADLYNGS)—(See under GAUNTLET).

GALTRAP (See under CALTRAP).

GAMBESON—(See under AKETON).

GARDE DE BRAS—An additional protection fastened to the elbow piece of the left arm of a jousting suit of armour.

GARDEROBE—Properly this is a wardrobe but has unfortunately become the accepted euphemism for the medieval latrine. It consisted of a mural recess with an external outlet.

GARGOYLE—A projecting spout conveying the water from a roof clear of the wall, and often carved into curious forms, e.g. cannon.

GATE-HOUSE—Being the principal entrance to a fortress, it combined every defensive feature in its design. When the drawbridge was raised the moat would have to be crossed under a rain of arrows from bowmen from the embattled parapets. Reaching the Gate-House, the massive portcullis would have to be stormed under a shower of hot liquid through the machicolations. Gaining the entrance to the passage under the Gate-House, this would have to be negotiated amid a constant shower of huge missiles dropped through the meurtrieres from above and arrows from side loopholes and finally a massive portcullis at the other end. (See pages 5 and 219.)

GAUNTLET—An armoured glove to defend the hand from sword-thrusts, etc. In the early medieval period it was constructed of mail, being an integral part of the hauberk (q.v.). It was sometimes made of leather, covered by metal scales (laminated steel plates). After the introduction of plate armour in the late 14th cent.

A LATE MEDIEVAL GATE-HOUSE

shewing embattled parapet, machicolations, loop-holes, portcullis, and drawbridge over moat.

the gauntlet became a most ingeniously designed system of minutely articulated steel plates covering the back of the hand and each finger and the thumb *separately*. The knuckles were additionally furnished with gadlings —spikes or knobs—which converted the gauntlet into a very handy *offensive* weapon! (See pages 207 and 213.)

GENOUILLÈRES (GENOVILIER : GENOUILLIERES : POLEYNS)—
A leather or metal defensive covering for the knees, either an articulated part of the leg protection or separately fastened over the chausses, thus forming a connection between the greave and thigh-piece. (See pages 205 and 207.) Genouillères is sometimes applied to the sides of Embrasures (q.v.).

GIROUETTE—A piece of sheet metal fixed to an upright pole to act as a weather-cock or vane. Knights banneret were permitted to display square shaped girouettes, whereas simple knights' girouettes were pointed.

GLACIS—A part of the approach to a castle so designed that every part of it could be swept by fire from the main fortifications.

GONFANON (GONFALON).—The small ensign or standard which was hung beneath the head of a medieval knight's lance.

GORGET—That portion of a medieval suit of armour which protected the throat and/or upper part of the breast. Extant specimens are of both mail and plate. In the late medieval period a chin piece was attached to the gorget. This is known as the mentonnière. (See page 207.)

GOTHIC—A style of architecture with highly-pointed arches, clustered columns, etc. The term was applied in reproach at the time of the Renaissance (which see).

GRAFT—The medieval term for a ditch or moat.

GREAVE—(See under JAMBART).

" GREEK FIRE "—(See page 2.)

GRILLE—A lattice or openwork of metal used to enclose a doorway or protect a window.

GROIN (ARRIS)—An angular curve formed by the crossing of two interior arches, or vaults.

GROUTING—Filling up with a coarse mortar containing a larger proportion of water than is usual.

GUIGE—The strap from which the knights' shield was suspended from the saddle or hung round the neck over the right shoulder.

GUISARME.—A medieval iron weapon combining a scythe with a bill, fixed to the end of a long pole and used by foot soldiers for unhorsing cavalry. (See page 213.) (See also BILL : PIKE.)

HABERGEON—(See under HAUBERK).

HALBERD (HALBERT : HALBARD : PARTIZAN)—A late medieval infantry weapon. It consisted of a staff some 5 feet or 6 feet in length surmounted by an axe combined with a pick. During the Civil Wars of the 17th cent. it was much in evidence and lingered on into the reign of Charles II, but thereafter its retention was purely for ceremonial purposes, halberdiers becoming the royal bodyguard known to this day as the Yeomen of the Guard. Halberds became, consequently, highly ornamental. (See also PIKE.) (See page 213.)

HARNESS—Formerly the armour for a man or a horse.

HAUBERK—Descended from the mail Byrnie, this garment was almost invariably worn by knights of the Norman period. It consisted of a long narrow tunic or shirt of leather or woven material with long sleeves and hood or coif (the *Coif-de-Mailes*) covering the whole head. This garment was covered by metal rings attached separately (or interlinked and thus forming the chain armour or mail about which so much has been written but about which so little is known). The hauberk was divided at the bottom to provide protection for the legs when the wearer was mounted on horseback. Mail armour persisted into the late 15th cent. when it was superseded by plate armour under which the hauberk was sometimes worn. The Habergeon was the name given to the short light mail skirt sometimes worn to protect the throat and breast. (See page 213.)

" HEDGEHOG "—(See page 1.) (See also CHEVAL-DE-FRISE.)

HELMS (HELMETS : HEAUMES)—The development both of the casque and helm as defensive covering for the head affords an interesting study. In the famous Bayeux Tapestry (c. A.D. 1100) depicting the history of the Norman Conquest of 1066, are shewn knights wearing the close-fitting pointed or cone-shaped headpiece with fixed nasal typical of the 12th cent. These simple close-fitting caps or casques were usually made of *cuir bouilli*, or wood covered with mail or imbricated (scale) plate and worn *over* the hood of the hauberk. Sometimes ear-pieces and a neck-guard were added as additional defences, (See page 223.) After A.D.1100 development follows two distinct courses. The casque ultimately becomes the pointed bascinet characteristic of the 14th cent and familiarized in many contemporary monumental effigies and engraved brasses which have survived, especially the famous latten effigy of the Black Prince at Canterbury Cathedral.

On the other hand the curious and cumbrous Chapelle-de-fer was evolved. First, after about A.D. 1180, we find those ponderous cylindrical flat-top affairs as seen in the Temple Church, London, covering both the head and the neck, leaving mere horizontal slits (Ocularia) for the eyes and ventilation. These cumbrous heaumes were carried suspended from the saddle-bow and only used in the hour of need. When the jousts or tournaments became the fashion in the second half of the 14th cent. these heaumes were preferred and thereupon were made heavier and more elaborate, the bascinet being reserved for active service on the field of battle only.

Early in the 15th cent. the salade or salley was introduced (see page 223). It was used extensively in the latter half of the Hundred Years' War. The simpler type was worn by the archers and pikemen. The more elaborate pieces were worn by knights and men-at-arms. Protection to the chin and neck was provided by the beaver, bavier or volant-piece (mentonnière).

The salade gave place to the armet in the latter half of the 15th cent. (See page 223.) It was connected to the cuirass by the gorget. At the end of the 16th cent. the burgonet came into use among foot soldiers and light cavalry. A distinguishing feature is the crest or comb.

Lighter forms of the Burgonet are known as the morion and cabasset. (See page 223.)

The Civil Wars of the 17th cent. witnessed the passing of body armour from the field of battle.

The helms seen suspended above monuments in old churches are funeral helms and were usually a mark of gentility used at the funeral of the deceased in conjunction with hatchments and other paraphernalia.

HERALDRY—Heraldry played a prominent part in the life of a knight and figured conspicuously on the battlefield. Originating in the studded shields of Classic and later times, in the early medieval period these structural features were adopted as a basis of design to distinguish the principal knightly families on the field of battle. Primary colours were first used to blazon the shields at the time of the Norman Conquest the type and shape of which are clearly depicted in the Bayeux Tapestry, being kite-shaped—elongated with a curved top. In the 13th cent. the " heater " shaped shield was in favour, becoming broader in the 14th and 15th centuries. As defensive body armour tended to cover the wearer's face completely, it became imperative for a knight to blazon his armorial bearings on shield, jupon and horse coverings (trappings). After the Reformation heraldry became debased by what might be termed illegitimate blazonry— endless quarterings and meaningless charges. Likewise the shape of the shield became grotesque.

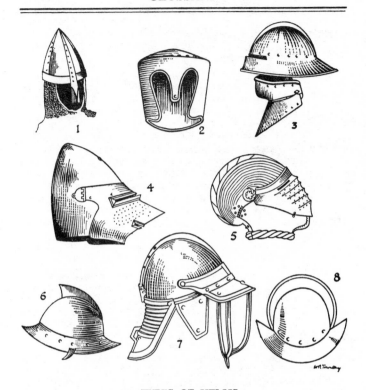

TYPES OF HELMS

1. Casque of the Norman period.
2. 13th-century Heaume.
3. Salade and Bavier (late 15th-cent.).
4. Bascinet with pointed vizor (c. 1400).
5. Fluted close-helmet or armet (early 16th cent.).
6. Cabasset (temp. Elizabeth).
7. Lobster-tailed Burgonet (Civil War period).
8. Morion (temp. Elizabeth).

HOARDING—(See under BRATTICES).

HOT-TRODLAW—(See page 10).

JACK—A sleeveless quilted garment lined with metal plates or
mail which came into use in the 15th cent. and was the
forerunner of the " stiele cote " of the Armada period.

JAMB—The side support of a doorway, window or fireplace
opening.

JAMBART (JAMB : JAMBIERES : DEMI-JAMBES : CANBERIA : or GREAVES)—A plate of iron or steel worn to protect the shins. (See pages 205 and 207.)

JAZERINE (JESSERAUNT)—Small plates of steel attached to some strong flexible material, worn as light armour by archers. Brigandine was used for a similar purpose but the metal plates were worn *inside* the material.

Sometimes known as mascled armour, the best historical example is depicted in the Bayeux Tapestry.

JOGGLE—Where it was impossible to use one large stone for a lintel over a doorway or window opening, the difficulty was overcome by dowelling or " jigsawing " smaller stones in a most ingenious manner so that gravity pulled the voussoirs (q.v.) into position, on the keystone principle. (See under Edlingham and Ferniehirst Castles.)

JUPON—A tight-fitting sleeveless leather jacket worn *over* the cuirass. It was very often blazoned with the knight's armorial bearings to distinguish the wearer on the field of battle.

KEEP (DONJON)—The massive, isolated tower which was often the principal feature of the stone castle under the Norman and early Plantagenet kings. In theory it was designed as an impregnable citadel to which the garrison could retire when the outworks of the castle had fallen. The earliest, and greatest, of the English keeps is the White Tower in the Tower of London; its building was commenced by the Conqueror's orders in 1078. Many keeps, e.g. Middleham, Colchester and London, were spacious buildings on which centred the communal life of the castle; other, and generally later, keeps such as Helmsley, Scarborough and Richmond-in-Swaledale, were more purely defensive with restricted accommodation. At the close of the 12th century Henry II raised a magnificent series of keeps in the north of England. The final development of the keep was away from the original rectangular plan to the circular and quatrefoil forms of Conisborough and York. (See page 2 ; also SHELL-KEEP.)

KIRTLE—A loose gown or outer petticoat.

LAMBOYS (BASES)—Sometimes in place of the taces of Tudor plate armour are found large vertical fluted steel plates buckled to the cuirass. The name is derived from the early medieval pleated skirt. (See also CULETTES.)

LAMBREQUIN—(See under MANTLING).

LAMES—Thin steel plates made to slide one over the other to form a flexible defensive armour. Lamina are seen in sollerets and taces (q.v.).

GLOSSARY

LANCET—In architecture, a narrow, pointed window-opening, especially of the thirteenth century, shaped like a surgeon's lancet.

LELAND, JOHN—Born 1506, died 1552. He was appointed King's Antiquary by Henry VIII in 1533 and his *History and Antiquities of This Nation* and *Itinerary* are of much value to the present day archaeologist.

LETTERS-PATENT—A document conferring a patent, or authorising a person to enjoy some privilege, so called because written on open sheets of parchment.

LICENCE TO CRENELLATE—(See CRENELLATE, LICENCE TO).

LIGHTS—The principal compartments of a window-opening as divided by the mullions (which see).

LINTEL—The headpiece of a door, window or fireplace.

LOOP-HOLES (OILLETS : OYLETS)—(See under ARROW SLITS).

MACHICOLATION—An opening between the corbels of a projecting stone parapet through which liquids and missiles could be discharged on the heads of assailants. They were evolved from BRATTICES, which see. (See page 219.)

MAIL—The name given to the defensive armour of the early medieval period which consisted of inter-linked metal rings on a flexible basis of *cuir bouilli* or thick woven material. Little is known as to the method of manufacturing this ancient type of armour, few good specimens having survived.

MAINEFAIRE (MANEFAIRE)—The name given to the laminated plate armour devised to protect the mane of a war horse.

MALVOISIN (French, " bad neighbour ")—A medieval siege-tower of wood constructed outside the wall of a castle and made higher than the battlements so as to command the ramparts. (See also under BELFRY).

MAMELIERE—An iron boss or roundel (q.v.) afixed to the front of the cuirass. Attached to this was the chain which held the helm in position.

MANGON (MANGONEL)—A military siege engine used in early medieval warfare for hurling heavy stones, arrows or darts (javelins). It consisted of a heavy timber framework which, when mounted on wheels or rollers, was known as a carroballista. The principle was a long arm which, when loaded with some heavy missiles such as stones, blazing material, etc., was suddenly propelled upward by releasing the force of a twisted skein of sinew or hair thus projecting the load into the enemy's ranks.

An early form of this instrument was known as a swepe and appeared as a rebus in the arms of the Magnalls.

MANTLING (Cointise : Contoise : Quintise : Lambrequin)—The scarf of woven material or silk worn over the helm, supposedly for protection from the heat of the sun.

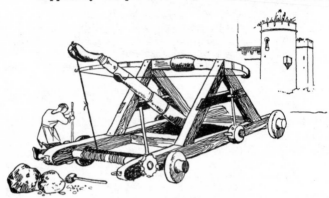

A MANGON (SIEGE ENGINE)

This feature is preserved as an integral part of heraldic design.

MARTEL-DE-FER—A heavy medieval weapon combining a pick and hammer, used by mounted knights for breaking open armour.

MASCLED ARMOUR—(See under Jazerine).

MASON'S MARK—A small design, generally of some geometrical shape, put upon his work by each mason after he dressed a stone. It served to check his output and the quality of his work.

MENTONNIÈRE—(See under Gorget).

MERLON—(See under Battlement).

MERSE—The broad, fertile lowland stretching from Kelso to Duns and Coldingham in the north, and to Berwick in the south.

MEURTRIERES—Square openings occasionally found in the passage roofs of castles (e.g. Chepstow). Their original use is doubtful but they were probably used for dropping missiles on the enemy who had succeeded in gaining this point in the siege.

MINSTRELS' GALLERY—In medieval times, a balcony at one end of the Great Hall for the use of professional minstrels attached to the house.

MISERICORDE—A small thin-bladed dagger introduced in the 14th century, carried at the right hip. (See page 213.) The name is said to be derived from the fact that it was used to deliver the death blow or " mercy " stroke to a fallen foe. The blade was thin to facilitate its insertion under or between the enemy's armour or penetrate the visor-holes (ocularia) of his helm. (See page 223.)

MISSAL—An office book of the Catholic church containing the service for the Mass throughout the year.

MONTHLY TRUCES—(See page 10.)

MORION—(See under HELM).

MOSS-TROOPER—A robber infesting the mosses, or bogs, of the Border; a riever.

MOTE-HILL—The artificial mound used in Anglo-Saxon times for the council meetings of the elders of the community.

MOULDING—An ornamental edging.

MOTTE—(See INTRODUCTION, page 1).

MOULINET—(See under Bows).

MOUNT AND BAILEY (MOTTE AND BAILEY)—The primitive type of earthwork introduced into this country after the Norman Conquest of A.D. 1066. It consisted of a mound of earth (the motte) surrounded by a levelled courtyard of horse-shoe shape (bailey). Access to the motte was gained by a timber bridge which could be easily removed in time of siege. Around the flattened summit of the mound was erected a wooden stockade. Enclosing the whole earthwork was a ditch, the inner slope of which was further fortified by a timber fence. (See page 1.)

" MOUSE " (TEREBRA)—The name given to a large bore fitted with a pointed iron snout of *square* section which was forced in between the ashlar walling of a castle and twisted until some of the stones were loosened, when a breach could easily be effected by picks or *martels-de-fer*.

MUNIMENT CHEST—A strong-box for charters or records.

MULLIONS—The upright bars or divisions of a window-opening.

MURAL—Within a wall, or pertaining to it.

MUSTERS—Gatherings of able-bodied men for Border defence, including all horsemen and footmen between the ages of sixteen and sixty. Many tenants held their land subject to continual service and " to sustain horse and gear for the defence of the realm."

NEWEL (VYSE)—The vertical column around which the circular stairs in an angle—or wall—turret wind in corkscrew fashion, usually anti-clockwise. Sometimes a " trip-stair," one higher or lower than the rest, was introduced. Usually the newel staircase is built in the thickness of a wall in military architecture for protection, but sometimes it is contained in a small tower or turret as in church towers, built on to the surface of the walling. This is sometimes known as a tourelle.

OCULARIA (VIZOR-HOLES)—The small horizontal apertures or " sights," enabling the wearer of a helm to see, when it was closed.

OREILLETTES—In defensive armour, discs of iron at the side of the helm to protect the ears. Sometimes each oreillette carried a strong spike which gave further protection by warding off sword thrusts at the neck and shoulders.

ORLE—In the 15th cent. a circular padding was worn round the bascinet to diminish the pressure of the helm which was worn over it at this period. This is the orle or " wreath " which is always included in the blazon of an heraldic crest. In heraldry, a border within a shield at a short distance from the edge.

OUBLIETTE (French, *oublier*, to forget : DUNGEON)—A secret underground pit or prison in a fortress provided only with a trap-door at the top presumably for the admission of prisoners. Little air could reach these terrible places and no light whatever. They were often probably used as storage places though doubtless many were used as places of incarceration.

PALETTES—The name given to the oval or oblong discs of steel fastened in front of the armpits. (See ROUNDELS.)

PANACHES (PENNACHES)—The plume of feathers borne above the helm of a knight as a crest.

PAULDRONS—Steel protective devices for the shoulders. Often only the left shoulder was thus protected. (See also AILETTE.)

PAVIS—A shield used by medieval bowmen to cover the whole person when carrying out a siege. Sometimes a cross-bowman would employ a pavisor to carry this shield before him.

PEDIMENT—A triangular or curved finish to the tops of doors, windows, etc.

PELE (PEEL : PILE)—A small massive fortified tower or house found in the Border country between England and Scotland. These are reminders of the times when

Border raids were sudden and frequent. The term was sometimes used to denote a stockaded enclosure. (See page 7.)

PENNON—A lance-flag carried by a medieval knight bearing his armorials. It was usually swallow-tailed at the fly.

PHEON—A heavy iron javelin projected from the cross-bow. It features in numerous well-known family armorial bearings as a charge. (See page 213.)

PIKE—The thrusting weapon carried by infantrymen, consisting of a long lance (some 12 to 14 feet in length) surmounted by a sharp steel or wrought-iron head of varying shapes. Sometimes the butt end terminated in a spike for sticking the pike into the ground. The pike was superseded by the bayonet. (See also HALBERD.) (See page 213.)

PISCINA—A basin or sink on the south side of the altar in old churches, into which was emptied water used in rinsing the sacred vessels, after Mass, or in washing the priest's hands.

PLACCATES—Additional steel plates added to the cuirass for further protection to the lower part of the breast. Demi-placcates were the additional plates to the lower edges of the cuirass.

PLASTRON-DE-FER—A small protective plate worn *under* the hauberk or gambeson in the 12th cent.

POLEAXE—A battle-axe, usually with a long handle, having a spike or hook opposite the blade. (See page 213.)

POLEYNS—(See under GENOUILLÈRES).

POMMEL—The knob on the hilt of a sword. During the medieval period and after, this was often of beautiful design executed in enamels and sometimes inlaid with precious metal or stones.

PORTCULLIS (HEARSE)—The iron or timber grating (studded with iron spikes along the bottom edge) which was suspended on chains in front of the main entrance passage to a castle or Gateway. It was raised or lowered by a windlass and counterbalance weights usually accommodated in a special guard-room above. The grooves in which the portcullis worked are still to be seen in the doorway-jambs of many medieval castles and gateways. The portcullis is a very familiar heraldic charge as it was the badge of the powerful Beaufort family and used by the Tudors. (See page 219.)

POSTERN—A small door or gate through which it was possible to enter or leave the fortifications of a castle without using the main entrance. It could be used for the launching of a sortie in time of siege.

POURPOINT—A padded and quilted body garment worn with armour practically throughout the medieval period to provide additional comfort and protection.

QUILLONS—The arms or cross-hilt of a sword. In the late medieval period they become very elaborately ornamented, together sometimes forming an ogee curve. When the hilt was straight it was termed capularis ; when curved, ansa. (See under Swords).

RAMPART—In earthwork and timber fortifications this was a broad baulk of earth bearing a stockade along its outer edge ; the top of the baulk, behind the stockade, formed a fighting platform for the defenders. The term is loosely used for any type of fortification in which the defenders work under the protection of a parapet ; thus the tops of the curtain walls or towers, where the men stood behind the battlements, are called the ramparts.

RECETTING—Receipt of stolen goods, or harbouring of a robber or other offender.

RENAISSANCE—Literally, " New Birth " : the period in the fifteenth century when the revival of arts and letters took place, marking the close of medieval times.

RELIEVING- or DISCHARGING-ARCH—An arch built into a wall above a door or window to take the strain from the lintel.

REREBRACES (Arriere-Bras)—(See under Brassarts).

REVETMENT—An outwork, embankment or bastion that has been faced with a layer of stones or concrete for additional strength.

RIEVER—(See Moss-Trooper).

ROUNDELS—Discs of steel plate affixed to the armpits for protection when using the sword. (See also Palettes.) (See pages 205 and 207.)

RUBBLE (Hourdage)—Structural work consisting of an admixture of plaster and stones without any attempt to lay the latter in courses.

SABBOTONS—The broad-toed laminated steel shoes worn by knights of the late medieval period.

SALADE—(See under Helm).

SALLY PORT—An underground passage connecting the inner with the outer works of a fortification ; or a postern gate used when making a sally or sortie. (See also under Postern.)

SAMBUCA—A medieval scaling-ladder.

SCARP (ESCARPMENT)—In military fortification the steep slopes of a fosse or ditch dug before the rampart (q.v.). The surface facing the enemy was the scarp, the outer surface the counterscarp. The talus was the name given to the wall sometimes found in addition to the fosse. The slope was always at 45 degrees, as giving the maximum resistance to the enemy.

SHAFT—The part of a pillar between capital and base, used at the sides of doors and windows, and to separate lights (which see).

SHELL-KEEP—When a mount-and-bailey castle was 'modernised' by the erection of buildings and defences in stone, a very usual feature of the work was the replacement of the timber stockading round the summit of the mount by a curtain wall. Against the inside of this curtain residential buildings were erected. Such a structure is known as a "shell-keep", though the term is unfortunate as there is little keep-like about it except its function. Alnwick is an example of an elaborated shell-keep. (See page 2.)

SHIELD—(See under HERALDRY).

SHOULDERED—Narrowed in the upper portion—applied to a door, window, portcullis, etc.

SIEGE TOWER—(See under BELFRY).

SOLAR (SOLLAR)—A small apartment built off the main hall of a castle or house for the private use of the Baron or Constable. Sometimes this apartment was apparently reserved for the exclusive use of the Lady of the Castle. The origin of the term is derived from the fact that a solar was designed to receive a maximum of sunshine.

SOLLERET—The articulated foot-covering consisting of lames of steel plates, often tapering to a fine point. (See pages 205 and 207.)

SORTIE (SALLY)—A sudden attack launched by the garrison upon the besiegers. Such attacks, which were usually directed against some siege-work of particular menace or to the relief of pressure on another part of the fortifications, had to be very carefully guarded against since the short internal lines of communication inside the castle made it possible to concentrate an attacking force with great rapidity.

" SOW "—(See under BATTERING RAM : TESTUDO).

SPLAY—The widening inwards of a door or window opening, in the latter case to allow a better diffusion of light into a building.

" SPRINGAL "—A weapon of siege warfare which first came into general use in the 13th cent. It consisted of a springy piece of timber fixed at its lower end. The missile, in the form of a large iron dart or lance, was placed at a point where it would be struck forcibly by the free end of the timber when released and so projected into the enemy's ranks.

SPURS—An important equipment of a mounted knight throughout the medieval period. Affixed to the heels, the earliest form are known as prick spurs, consisting simply of a sharp pointed goad used to irritate the horse into a maximum speed. This type persisted into the middle of the 14th cent. From the late 13th cent. onwards the rowel spur came into use. This was a wheel toothed with sharp points. Spurs were only worn by knights during the medieval period. (See pages 205 and 207.)

SPURS—Sometimes a circular tower or bastion is strengthened by a vertical strip of masonry or spur being added to the most exposed part. Being triangular in section, the spur thus generally takes the form of an elongated cone with base below ground level built as part of the foundations. Chepstow and Goodrich furnish typical examples of this feature.

STANDARD OF MAIL—The name given to the collar worn by a knight during the early medieval period. At first constructed of linked mail, later it was evolved into the gorget (q.v.).

STUCCO—A plaster of lime and fine sand, used as a coating for walls in preparation for decoration.

SUB-INFEUDATION—The practice of letting off portions of a fief to sub-tenants on terms of feudal service.

SURCOAT—A white sleeveless linen garment worn *over* the armour and confined by a girdle. It was fashionable during the 13th and 14th centuries. Falling to the knees both back and front at first, it ultimately reached almost to the ground and became a serious impediment to a knight suddenly dismounting and was therefore slit up and cut away. (See under CYCLAS.) Before the surcoat passed out of date it became the fashion for a knight's lady to embroider it with some design— either religious, heraldic or fanciful.

SWORDS—As a weapon of defence, the sword goes back to remote times; as a symbol it has represented justice, martyrdom, sainthood, peace, and war, while of course the sword has always figured conspicuously in State, civic and public ceremonials and functions.

At the time of the Norman Conquest the sword had usually a wide blade, short pommel and iron hilt, and was used only for cutting, being useless for thrusting. By the 15th cent. it had become much longer, tapering to a fine point and was furnished with a long grip and was thus admirably adapted for a thrusting action. A further development was the two-handed sword, often five feet in length. This was designed purely for cutting with a sweeping action demanding sufficient clearance for use. The 16th cent. saw the introduction of sword-play necessitating elaborately designed guards and counter-guards, to protect the ungauntleted hand, superseding the simple cross hilt of the earlier periods. Later was developed the sword with only one cutting edge, the curved blade, ogee quillon and basket hilt. (See page 213.)

TABARD—The short sleeved white coat worn over the armour by a medieval knight for displaying his armorial bearings. It figures conspicuously in the jousts and was of course of the greatest importance heraldically. It survives in the modern heralds who proclaim the accession of the Sovereign, etc.

TACES (Tassets)—Metal plates worn to protect the hips and thighs. They first appear in the 15th cent. and are depicted in many contemporary monumental brasses. Known as tuilles, they became a very prominent feature of the ornamental armour worn during the Elizabethan period as shewn in many alabaster reclining tomb effigies of this period. Overlapping upwards, the taces were usually buckled on the right and hinged on the left-hand side. (See under Cuirass and page 207.)

TALUS—(See under Scarp).

TAPUL—The name given to the ridge usually seen down the centre of the Elizabethan breastplate. It is sometimes known as the peascod doublet and was very fashionable, appearing in many portraits and tombs of the period.

TENANT-IN-CHIEF—A lord holding his land direct from the king.

TENANT-IN-MESNE—A lord holding his land of another lord as distinct from a tenant-in-chief.

TEREBRA —(See under " Mouse.")

TESTUDO ("Sow")—The *Testudo Arietaria* was a portable shed covered with hides used by the operators of a battering ram when storming a castle wall. The term was also applied to a party of soldiers who joined their shields overhead to form a testudo, while attempting to scale or mine a rampart.

THIEVES' RODES—Well-frequented tracks used by moss-troopers across the Cheviots.

TORMENTA—A term found in innumerable medieval MSS. and used to denote the various forms of siege engines employed from time to time to batter the walls of castles. The term bears reference to the *twisting* of the ropes of fibre or hair to provide the propulsion for the projectile.

TRACERY—Ornamental stone-work in window-openings.

TRÉBUCHET (TRÉBUCKET)—A siege instrument similar to the mangon but somewhat simpler in principle, introduced in the late 12th century. It was actually a huge catapult consisting of a long beam of timber pivoted near one end on to a stout timber framework or trestle; from the end of the beam nearer the pivot was suspended a load of earth or stones. The end of the long arm of the beam was provided with a leather sling which was loaded with the missile (heavy stones, a dead horse or enemy soldier !). When released the arm would be swung upward (by gravity acting on the loaded short arm of the beam) with terrific force, hurling the missile into the enemy ranks. (See opposite page.)

TREFOIL—An ornament or window tracery with three segments.

TROU-DE-LOUP (TRAPHOLES)—A series of conical excavations concealed in the ground, each studded with a sharp spike. These trous-de-loup proved a very effective impediment to the progress of the enemy, both cavalry and infantry.

TUILLES—(See under TACES and CUIRASS and page 207.)

UMBRERE (UMBRIL)—A projecting shield to the eyes found in helmets of the late medieval period.

VAMBRACES (AVANT-BRAS)—Plates of iron or steel fastened to the forearms of a medieval knight for additional protection. (*Vide* also BRASSARTS.) (See pages 205 and 207.)

VIZOR (OCULARIA)—During the Tudor period the helm became a highly artistic product of the armourer's craft and the famous "bellows" type of vizor are master-pieces of ingenuity and design. (See under HELM and page 223.)

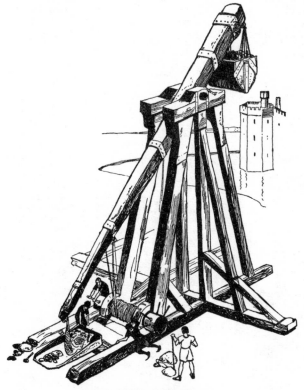

A MEDIEVAL TREBUCHET—
about to be "touched off"

VOUSSOIR—One of the wedge-like stones which form part of an arch.

WAMBAIS—(See under AKETON).

WARD—(Same as BAILEY, q.v.).

WHEEL-STAIR—(Same as NEWEL-STAIR, q.v.).

WREATH—(See under ORLE).

YETT—Scottish word for "gate," often in the form of an iron grille.

GENERAL INDEX

(Principal references to Castles and Peles are shown in bold type)

B

Also Published by Sandhill Press

AMBLE AND DISTRICT by T.L. McAndrews

ANGLO SAXON NORTHUMBRIA by T.H. Rowland

BIGGEST MINING VILLAGE IN THE WORLD by Mike Kirkup

THE BODY IN THE BANK: Famous Northern Murders

THE BORDER REIVERS by Godfrey Watson

CUSTOMS AND TRADITIONS OF NORTHUMBRIA

THE GREAT GUNMAKER : Lord Armstrong by David Dougan

HISTORY OF NORTHUMBERLAND by Cadwallader J. Bates

IN AND AROUND - Alnwick...Morpeth...Rothbury...Warkworth
by Ian Smith

THE LAST YEARS OF A FRONTIER by D.L.W. Tough

**MEDIEVAL CASTLES, TOWERS, PELES AND BASTLES OF
NORTHUMBERLAND** by T.H. Rowland

MYTH AND MAGIC OF NORTHUMBRIA

NORTHUMBERLAND PLACE NAMES by Godfrey Watson

NORTHUMBRIA IN PICTURES by Beryl Sanderson

NORTHUMBRIAN COASTLINE by Ian Smith

NORTHUMBRIAN NATURE DIARY by Wendy Dickson

NORTHUMBRIAN PUB by Lynn F. Pearson

TALES OF THE BORDER REIVERS

UPPER COQUETDALE by David Dippie Dixon

**VICTORIAN & EDWARDIAN NORTHUMBRIA
FROM OLD PHOTOGRAPHS** by J.W. Thompson and D. Bond

WARKWORTH by Ian Smith

WATERS OF TYNE by T.H. Rowland